The Koto

A Traditional Instrument in Contemporary Japan

The Koto

A Traditional Instrument
in Contemporary Japan

Henry Johnson

Hotei Publishing, Amsterdam

Contents

To Lisa

Acknowledgements

This book is the product of research undertaken over many years, during which time numerous people have influenced my research and provided valuable comments and information. I am indebted to many *koto* players – professional and amateur – who have shared their knowledge of the instrument and their culture, in particular members of the following Ikuta-ryū (Ikuta tradition) groups: Tōdō Ongaku-kai, Kyōto Tōdō-kai, Nihon Tōdō Ongaku-kai, Kikui Sōgaku-sha (Kisaragi-kai), and Miyagi-kai. The assistance of several museums and archives is also gratefully acknowledged, especially Osaka College of Music (Museum of Music), Kunitachi College of Music (Collection for Organology), Musashino Academia Musicae (Museum of Musical Instruments), Hikone Castle Museum, the Tokugawa Art Museum, and Ueno Gakuen College (Research Archives for Japanese Music). Many instrument makers have provided a wealth of data about *koto* construction, including Fukuoka Akoya (in Fukuoka Prefecture), Mitsuya Koto Seizō (in Saitama Prefecture), and all the members of Fukuyama Hōgakki Seizōgyō Kyōdō Kumiai (Fukuyama Traditional Japanese Musical Instrument Manufacturing Cooperative) in Fukuyama (in Hiroshima Prefecture): Ogawa Gakki Seizō, Makimoto Gakki, Mishima Gakki, Shinwa Kingaku, Oda Kazuyuki, Fujita Fusahiko, Fujii Yoshiaki, Terada Yoshiko, Watanabe Masayuki, and Eki Akio. In the United Kingdom I would like to extend my thanks to Dartington College of Arts, School of Oriental and African Studies (University of London), Pitt Rivers Museum (University of Oxford), and Horniman Museum.

   I am particularly obliged to the individuals, publishers, libraries, museums, and archives who have made it possible to include several of the illustrations included in this book, in particular Benseisha, Dai Nippon Katei Ongaku-kai, Fukushima Kazuo and the Research Archives for Japanese Music (Ueno Gakuen College), Gemeentemuseum Den Haag, Hakushindō, Hakusuisha, Heibonsha, Hikone Castle Museum, Hōgakusha, Kikuhara Kōji, Kinden-ryū Taishōgoto Zenkoku Fukyū-kai, Kinkōdō, Kunitachi College of Music (Collection for Organology), Kyoto Prefectural Library and Archives, Maekawa Shuppansha, Miyagi Kazue, Miyagi Michio Memorial Museum, Musashino Academia Musicae (Museum of Musical Instruments), Nakanoshima Hiroko, Nakashima Yasuko, National Diet Library, Nihon Gagaku-kai, Osaka College of Music (Museum of Music), Tenri-kyō Dōyūsha, and the Tokugawa Art Museum. Permission to reproduce several photographs taken and used by the author initially in *Journal of the American Musical Instrument Society* and *The Galpin Society Journal* (*see* Johnson 1996b, 1997, 2003) is here also gratefully acknowledged.

   Thanks are also to be extended for the assistance provided by a Japanese government Monbushō (Ministry of Education) Research Scholarship, which provided a base for me at Kyoto City University of Arts; a Japan Society for the Promotion of Science Postdoctoral Fellowship; and a Japan Foundation Research Fellowship. I am particularly indebted to Nakagawa Shin for his help with my studies in Japan. Additional assistance was made possible through the generous support of the John Lobb Memorial Trust, the Oxford-Sasakawa Fund, the Japan Foundation Endowment Committee, Exeter College (University of Oxford), and the University of Otago. I would also like to thank Mark McGuire for his design work in figures 26, 31 and 76, and Lisa for her invaluable comments and support. Lastly, special thanks must be made to the numerous museums, archives, publishers, Japanese musicians, instrument makers, scholars, and enthusiasts not singled out above – there are far too many to mention by name – who have shared with me knowledge of their truly fascinating culture.

Editorial Notes

General

Japanese names and terms have been transliterated in accordance with the modified Hepburn system of Romanization. Japanese words using other transliteration systems, as found in quotations or references, are shown in their original form, and should confusion occur, the modified Hepburn transliteration is included thereafter in square brackets. Literal translations of the names of institutions, societies, etc., are given unless there is an established English name, in which case the latter has been opted for such Japanese institutions whose names appear regularly throughout the text (*see below, Establishful English Names of Japanese Institutions*). Japanese personal names are given in traditional order, with surname preceding first name. A select character list of Japanese terms is given at the end of the book.

Koto Notation

The illustrations that depict Japanese *koto* notation have a transnotation shown immediately underneath them (i.e., the Japanese notation is changed into Western five-line staff notation). The following symbols are included in several of these transnotations and are explained in detail in the subsection on ornamentation in Chapter 5 (the arrow for *kakite* is reversed in fig. 100 because of the tuning used – *kokinjōshi*).

2	right-hand index plectrum
3	right-hand middle plectrum
ヒ	*hikiiro*
⟨	*kakite*
⟨	*warizume*
ス	*sukuizume*
ツ	*tsukiiro*
ユ	*yuriiro*
slurs	pressing/releasing a string

Established English Names of Japanese Institutions

English

Hamamatsu City Musical Instrument Museum
Hikone Castle Museum
Kunitachi College of Music, Collection for Organology
Kyoto City University of Arts
Kyoto Prefectural Library and Archives
Miyagi Michio Memorial Museum
Musashino Academia Musicae, Museum of Musical Instruments
National Diet Library
Osaka College of Music, Museum of Music
Research Archives for Japanese Music, Ueno Gakuen College
The Tokugawa Art Museum
Tokyo Music School
Tokyo National University of Fine Arts and Music

Japanese

Hamamatsu-shi Gakki Hakubutsukan
Hikone-jō Hakubutsukan
Kunitachi Ongaku Daigaku Gakkigaku Shiryōkan
Kyōto Shiritsu Geijutsu Daigaku
Kyōto Furitsu Sōgō Shiryōkan
Miyagi Michio Kinenkan
Musashino Ongaku Daigaku Gakki Hakubutsukan
Kokuritsu Kokkai Toshokan
Ōsaka Ongaku Daigaku Ongaku Hakubutsukan
Nihon Ongaku Shiryō Shitsu, Ueno Gakuen Daigaku
Tokugawa Bijutsukan
Tōkyō Ongaku Gakkō
Tōkyō Geijutsu Daigaku

Introduction

After my first few encounters of live *koto* performance I became increasingly aware of the many differences in instrument design and performance practice. Why were instruments made somewhat differently? Why was the instrument placed on a high stand on some occasions and on detachable legs or a small stand on others? Why were different types of plectra used by different players? Why did some players face the instrument directly while others were at a slight angle? Why were performance traditions, or other groups, always contrasted against one another? Why did some performers play the same pieces differently? Why did some players read music notation from left to right in rows and others right to left in columns? Why was the *koto* so often represented as a traditional Japanese musical instrument? While the chapters that follow answer some of these questions, others continue to fascinate me in my ongoing exploration of the *koto* and its intriguing place in Japanese culture.

My field research with *koto* players has covered numerous levels of comparative and focused inquiry. I began learning the instrument in 1985 in the United Kingdom, first at Dartington College of Arts and then the University of London. Yet, it was not until my first field trip to Japan in 1990 that I was able to look at the place of the instrument in the broader context of Japanese culture. An ethnographic approach has always underpinned my research, and having the opportunity to learn the instrument from Japanese performers also gave me an insider's perspective as a player. Likewise, investigation of instrument manufacture with *koto* makers resulted in a wealth of data about the construction process, instrument form and meaning. Study with *koto* players and makers was carried out on a number of levels, taking the form of interviews, lessons, as well as follow-up and comparative research. Unlike most *koto* players, however, my instruction in the *koto* has been from several teachers, something I soon realized would have been extremely difficult for Japanese players to do. This yielded much data about differences between diverse performance traditions. It also made me aware of the inherent social cohesiveness of Japanese music traditions, where players usually become a member of a group that functions as a social unit, which in turn mirrors many facets of Japanese society.

Short- and long-term instruction in several performance traditions enabled me to study a diverse range of music styles, including *gagaku* (court music), Tsukushigoto (a rare *koto* tradition) and everyday *koto* music, or *zokusō* (common/everyday/popular *koto*).[1] I was especially interested in investigating *koto* music (*sōkyoku*) of *zokusō* traditions, with its many professional, amateur-professional and amateur *koto* players, the latter proving to be some of the most fascinating in terms of learning about the social dynamics and organization of the groups to which they belong. As a non-Japanese researcher I was fortunate to be able to undertake comparative research among a variety of performance traditions. I did not have one main *koto* teacher during my initial period of field research in Japan, nor did I have strong ties to any particular performance tradition. This was an asset in the early stages of field research. While some researchers might embark on extensive work with one performance tradition and one teacher in order to have what Clifford Geertz (1973) labels a "thick description" of that group, my approach was broader so as to gain a comprehensive picture of a mixture of traditions. Such an approach would be almost impossible for a student of one style of *koto* performance, as a comparison between traditions might well be understood or interpreted as disloyalty to one's teacher or group. However, my lack of long-term affiliation proved advantageous and in fact facilitated comparative research. Moreover, it also became apparent during this research that my informants accepted such a comparative approach because I was a non-Japanese researcher and was perhaps not expected to have a strong social affiliation with one specific performance group.

In Japan, the aim of my research was to understand the place of the *koto* in its cultural context. In order to gain an overview of the instrument, its performance traditions and its music, numerous performances were attended, and many hours of interviews were undertaken with instrument makers, academics and with players from a number of performance traditions. Instruments and research materials were studied at all the main Japanese museums, archives and private collections (*see* Johnson 1999). Several Japanese universities have outstanding collections of *koto* in their musical instrument museums, in particular Osaka College of Music and Musashino Academia Musicae (*see* Ōsaka Ongaku Daigaku Fuzoku Gakki Hakubutsukan 1984, 1998; Musashino Ongaku Daigaku Gakki Hakubutsukan 1969, 1974, 1979, 1985, 1989, 1995, 1996). Other significant collections studied were those of Hikone Castle Museum, Hamamatsu City Musical Instrument Museum, the Tokugawa Art Museum, Miyagi Michio Memorial Museum, and Kunitachi College of Music (Collection for Organology). Two archives that house outstanding collections of *koto* notations are the Research Archives for Japanese Music at Ueno Gakuen College, and Miyagi Michio Memorial Museum.

There are many writings on the *koto* in Japanese. These encompass the myriad introductory *koto* tutors and handbooks – far too many to mention here – that tend to be succinct in their text and usually include pieces for beginners. There are also several general texts on the instrument that merit special mention, such as those by Kikkawa (1992), Kishibe (1982a), Kubota (1984), Nakajima and Kubota (1984), Nogawa (1994), Shadan Hōjin Nihon Sankyoku Kyōkai (1976), Tanabe and Hirano (1982), Tanimura (1992), and Tōyō Ongaku Gakukai (1967).[2] More detailed descriptions of specific performance traditions and genres are provided by authors Andō (1986), Chūjō and Hotta (1985), Kishibe (1973), Kishibe and Sasamori (1976), and Tsuda (1983). Hirata and Kaihara (1988) and Hiroshima Kenritsu Kōgei Shikenjō (1987) provide comprehensive overviews on *koto* construction, and Shōsōin (1967) examines the Nara-period instruments preserved in the Shōsōin repository.

Not to be ignored is the literature on the *koto* by Western writers.[3] Accounts of Japanese music and musical instruments were included in works by early European travelers to Japan such as Philipp Franz von Siebold (1796-1866; e.g., Siebold 1852). While Siebold wrote little on the *koto*, he did provide a number of extremely detailed hand-drawn color illustrations of Japanese instruments (one depicts a lavishly decorated *koto*, albeit back to front). Several early non-Japanese scholars of Japanese music should be mentioned, for example Abraham and Hornbostel ([1975] (1902-3), Kraus (1878) and Piggott (1891, 1892, [1909] 1971). The so-called "Berlin School" of comparative musicologists, working mainly with recordings, included Otto Abraham (1872-1926) and Erich M. von Hornbostel (1877-1935) who also observed *koto* performance by visiting Japanese musicians. The Italian Alessandro (Alexandre) Kraus (1853-1931) first published *La musique au Japon* in 1878 to coincide with the Paris Exposition Universelle et Internationale (Paris World Exposition), where he displayed his catalogue of instruments and photographs illustrated in his book (a second edition of his book appeared in 1879; *see* Sestili 2002). *The Music and Musical Instruments of Japan* of 1883, a second edition of which was published in 1909, was written by the Englishman Sir Francis T. Piggott (1852-1925) and was to have an enormous impact on Western scholarship of Japanese music. Much later, several in-depth summaries of the *koto* were written by, for example, Adriaansz (1984, 2001),[4] Harich-Schneider (1973) and Malm ([1959] 2000).

Studies since the second half of the twentieth century – by both Japanese and Western scholars alike – have tended to concentrate on specific music genres or individual performance traditions. For example, extensive musicological studies are presented by Adriaansz (1973) in his examination of *kumiuta* (song cycles with *koto* accompaniment) and *danmono* (instrumental pieces) repertoires (*see also* Adriaansz 1967, 1970); Wade (1976) in her analysis of *tegotomono* (alternating voice and instrumental sections) repertoire; and Burnett (1989), Halliwell (1994b), and Loeb (1976) in their exhaustive study of *koto* music (*see also* Ayer 1997). A slightly different approach is taken by Ackermann (1990) and Tsuge (1983a), who focus specifically on song texts with no musical analysis. Various other writings on the *koto* include, for instance, the ethnographies of the Sawai and Miyagi performance traditions by Falconer (1995) and Prescott (1997), respectively; the study of the Yamada tradition and its repertoire by Ackermann (1986) and Read (1975); and several articles in the now defunct journal *Hogaku* (Traditional Japanese Music) (e.g., Read and Locke 1983; Zomick 1986). Apart from succinct descriptions of the structure and classification of the instrument itself, most of these works offer little more than a cursory description of the physical form of the *koto*. Kikkawa (1997), which was actually published in an earlier form in Japanese in 1961 to accompany a set of LPs produced by Victor Records, provides a brief background to instrument form and a substantial overview of the development of the instrument's repertoire. Also, some of the information in this present study is drawn from my earlier writings (e.g., *see* Johnson 1993, 1996b, 1996-97, 1997, 2002, 2003, 2004).

Each of these sources, as well as many others referred to in this book, has been invaluable in compiling an overview of the instrument, but the study of the *koto* as an object of Japanese music material culture is also indebted to other disciplines and sources. Anthropological studies of Japan have been especially influential in terms of the ethnographic materials and comparisons they have provided (e.g., Befu 1971; Benedict 1946; Hendry 1987, 1993; Hendry and Webber 1986; Nakane 1970). The metaphorical model of unwrapping or wrapping Japanese culture in layers of meaning has been influential in this instance (*see* Ben-Ari, Moeran and Valentine 1990; Hendry 1993; Oka 1967, 1975, 1988). While not applied in practice to every aspect of the instrument in this book, these studies have been useful when looking at such facets as the physical wrapping of brocade, head covers, decoration, and cases. Cultural unwrapping has shown multilayered meaning embodied in the instrument.

This book is not meant as an in-depth anthropological or sociological discussion of the *koto* and its place in Japan. Nevertheless, it does offer an introduction to the instrument that will be of interest to scholars from diverse disciplines. Through first-hand experience as a *koto* player, engagement with *koto* makers and performers, and the use of textual sources, this book builds on and adds to our existing knowledge to provide a compendium of information on the instrument, its performance traditions and performance contexts. At the same time, it also focuses on the most common form of the *koto* today, the *zokusō*.

In order to understand the instrument as a meaningful object of Japanese culture, the *koto* is examined in three distinct and interrelated spheres: its form, its performance traditions and its performance setting. These areas of study reveal a musical instrument that holds a truly unique place in Japan. Contemporary Japan – or at least Japan since the pre-modern Meiji era to the present day – still possesses many objects that are perceived as part of "traditional" Japanese culture. They are often juxtaposed with objects and/or concepts that have a distinct recent source from outside Japan, usually from Europe and America. The resulting dichotomy translates as the "traditional" – those pre-dating the Meiji Restoration of 1868 – and the "modern" – those post-dating the Restoration. Musical instruments too form part of this classification and are divided between traditional Japanese instruments (*wagakki* or *hōgakki*) and Western instruments (*yōgakki*). While the *koto* has accepted Chinese origins (*see* Chapter 1), it is now very much a traditional Japanese musical instrument, firmly rooted in Japanese culture, even though its form, materials and repertoire have undergone a number of recent innovations and its physical structure, its music and its performance contexts have at times been influenced by non-Japanese culture.

As there has been, and continues to be, a diversity of *koto* traditions with the instrument played in numerous contexts, it would be impossible in a book such as this to include detailed information on all aspects of the *koto* and its music. Therefore, the aim of this book is to provide a glimpse into this instrument's extraordinary history, physical structure, performance traditions, and performance contexts. The text concentrates on instrument construction and different *koto* types by looking at performance groups and the *koto* player's contexts of music performance. The book does not analyze music or examine song texts, but it does touch upon the instrument's performance contexts as an aid to our understanding of how and where the instrument is played.

While acknowledging the unique place of many *koto* performance traditions, the focus of this book is on the everyday type of *koto*, in other words the instrument that is used primarily in secular contexts. This *koto* – the *zokusō*, especially the type labeled *Yamadagoto* (Yamada-tradition *koto*) – had the most profound impact on *koto* performance traditions throughout Japan, especially during the twentieth century. In discussing the *koto*, emphasis is placed on its physical form, although a social level of inquiry is found in connection with the instrument's dissemination through its various performance traditions. Also, as the primary function of the *koto* is to play music, the performance context is considered a means by which to introduce the instrument's wider physical context and interconnections with the performer and the music. In order to understand why different types of instruments have been made, one must look closely at the social level of music making, where the interrelationship between the instrument, the player and the music demonstrates how *koto* performance contexts can add further meaning to the instrument.

Chapter One sets the scene, placing the *koto* within a historical context and briefly outlining its cultural significance. This chapter introduces the *koto* by providing a succinct description of its history in Japan and its cultural significance as an emblem of a real and perceived notion of traditional Japan. Many of the ideas introduced here are taken up later in the book.

The *koto* is described on various levels of classification throughout Chapters Two and Three in order to exemplify how its component parts come to form the whole instrument, and is in keeping with an approach influenced by Kartomi's (1990, 271) view that "concepts and classifications of instruments ... are part of a seamless web of cultural knowledge." Associated with this is the metaphor of wrapping culture, whereby in this book the layers of cultural meaning surrounding the *koto* are "unwrapped" through this and other chapters to reveal how meaning is interwoven with the *koto* as a significant object of Japanese traditional culture in contemporary Japan.

Chapter Two explores the range of *koto* types that are differentiated and classified within the diverse spheres of *koto* performance. This chapter looks at the number of ways that the instrument is labeled, especially in connection with the instrument's various names and the *kanji* (Chinese characters used in Japanese writing) employed for writing these names. This chapter also discusses the changes that have occurred in instrument structure and social contexts of performance over time. The establishment of the instrument type referred to as *Yamadagoto* is outlined with regard to its broader historical, social and cultural context. Also included in this chapter is a look at some of the modified, small and large *koto* that have recently become more popular, in particular the numerous instruments devised during the twentieth century under the influences of Western and new Japanese music forms. The purpose of this section is to illustrate some of the ways the structure of the *koto* has been altered as a result of a changing social milieu.

Chapter Three is concerned primarily with the manufacture of the *koto* and its component parts. It includes information gained through ethnographic field research with instrument makers, and the study of instruments in the collections of museums, archives and *koto* performers. Each stage of the production process is examined, together with the manner of classifying and labeling the instrument, as well as a review of the details of instrument form and decoration. This chapter looks specifically at instrument manufacture in the present day, focusing on the instrument of everyday performance, and the discussion outlines the process of construction and the component parts that make up the whole instrument. It ends with an examination of the aesthetic system of grading instruments according to quality and quantity of decoration, and techniques of construction. Here the instrument is further classified variously as a means to illustrate its aesthetic characteristics and monetary value.

Chapter Four reviews *koto* performance traditions as social organizations and how they regulate and influence the transmission of the instrument and its music. From the start of everyday *koto* performance in the seventeenth century to the present day, *koto* players have especially been influenced by social groups of one form or another. Elaborating upon information introduced in Chapter Two, this chapter begins with an overview of the instrument's performance traditions, including an examination of the instrument's performer in a variety of social contexts. This is followed by a review of the ways performance groups are structured and regulated. Performance traditions and lineages are investigated in terms of their group structure and hierarchy. Two sub-sections therein look at permit systems and performing names as key parts of the performance group social system. In this chapter an emphasis is placed on the concept of the group as an illustration of the internal structures of traditions, as well as *uchi* (inside) and *soto* (outside) perspectives that are part of knowing one's place as a *koto* player (student or teacher) in Japan. This part of the discussion does not argue that Japanese groupism is any more well integrated than groups in any other society, or that Japanese society is any more unique than any other, but it does draw attention to the fact that performance groups and membership in those groups is very much part of the transmission of *koto* performance. Of the numerous levels of identity that an individual might have, groupings of *koto* players show social relationships internally within their own traditions, and externally vis-à-vis other traditions. In this light, several other approaches to studying Japanese society and culture have also been useful (e.g., Befu 1980; Mouer and Sugimoto 1986; Sugimoto 1997; Sugimoto and Mouer 1989), as have critiques of ideas linked to the idea of *Nihonjin ron*, or discussion of Japanese uniqueness (*see* Dale 1986).[5]

Chapter Five introduces the *koto* in its performance contexts. This chapter demonstrates how an examination of the interrelationship between music sound, material object, performer, and performance contexts can help open up the plethora of cultural meanings that are embodied in the performance event, and thus connected directly to the *koto* itself as an object of traditional Japanese culture. Although this chapter sets forth neither a history nor an analysis of the instrument's music per se, it does exemplify how an organological study such at this can look to the contexts of performance and the performer as a way of obtaining a further understanding of the form, function and meaning of musical instruments. After introducing performance contexts as meaningful sites of study, the first part of the chapter expands on the discussion of the player found in Chapter Four. The two main topics for study are players' posture and attire. The second part of the chapter looks at performance contexts where there is not a performer per se (i.e., in mediated contexts). The third part of the chapter looks at notations and oral mnemonics. The instrument has passed through several different social spheres, and in each it has often used different forms of notation. A study of these visual forms of music representation evinces how diverse performance traditions have used and devised notation systems that provide an additional conduit by which a performance tradition can identify itself vis-à-vis other traditions – the instrument is seen to exist in a culture of difference. This is followed by a study of the tuning and ornamentation of the *koto*. It is here that the instrument's form helps determine some facets of *koto* music. The instrument has a number of idiomatic ornamental techniques that often have symbolic meaning and further help delineate the instrument's place in Japanese culture. The final sub-section introduces several of the instrument's representative music genres, and attempts to illustrate their place in Japanese culture.

Undertaking field research on and writing about Japanese music raises numerous questions on cultural representation. One question that continuously surfaced during my own research was "Can I truly represent Japanese culture?" As a student of the *koto* I have adopted aspects of Japanese culture and the instrument in my own learning process. I cannot solely represent Japanese culture, but I can introduce my interpretation of it as a way of celebrating its complexity and diversity. I can translate aspects of a fascinating culture that not only has become entwined into my own life, but is increasingly influential the world over. This book has been written because the *koto* and its culture have never ceased to captivate me. Some of the questions I first asked as a student in the mid-1980s, in addition to numerous others raised since, have continued to occupy much of my study of Japanese culture. Some of those questions are answered here, some in other areas of my work, while others must await further research.

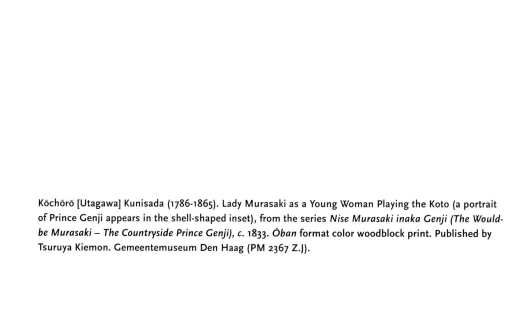

Kōchōrō [Utagawa] Kunisada (1786-1865). Lady Murasaki as a Young Woman Playing the Koto (a portrait of Prince Genji appears in the shell-shaped inset), from the series *Nise Murasaki inaka Genji (The Would-be Murasaki – The Countryside Prince Genji), c.* 1833. Ōban format color woodblock print. Published by Tsuruya Kiemon. Gemeentemuseum Den Haag (PM 2367 Z.J).

1 The Setting

The Instrument

The *koto* – also called *sō*, *sō no koto* and, occasionally, *jūsangen* – is a thirteen-string Japanese zither (figs. 1-2). Traditionally about 182 cm long, the instrument has thirteen movable bridges placed under the strings on the upper surface of its slightly arched soundboard to establish tunings, a fixed bridge toward each end of the soundboard, and strings running lengthwise along the top of the soundboard that are ordinarily plucked by plectra worn on the right-hand thumb, index and middle fingers. The player is positioned facing the long side of the instrument near the end known as the "head" to their right (the other end, the "tail", is to the player's left),[1] and plucks the strings close to the fixed bridge at that end. The strings are of equal length, size and tension. While today *koto* strings are usually produced from the synthetic material tetron, nylon was frequently used in the early twentieth century, and before that silk was the traditional material. The player's left hand often manipulates the strings behind the movable bridges, toward the tail end, in order to change their pitch, especially using ornamental techniques. Bare fingers of either hand can sometimes be used to pluck the strings, as might other striking devices, particularly in Western-influenced and new Japanese music.

Together with numerous other objects and ideas, the instrument was transmitted to Japan from China. It was established as a Japanese musical instrument with the founding of the Gagakuryō (*Gagaku* [court music] Bureau) in 701 at the Chinese-styled imperial court.[2] There are several other East Asian zithers – all still in use – with close physical similarities to the *koto*, suggesting that they might all share common origins (*see* Mitani 1980). Some of these include the Chinese *guzheng* (old *zheng*) or *zheng* (usually sixteen and twenty-one strings); the Korean *kayagŭm* (traditionally twelve strings); and the Vietnamese *dan tranh* (traditionally sixteen strings).[3] However, it is the Chinese *zheng*, which has the same *kanji* (Chinese character) as the *koto*, that is generally accepted by scholars to be the immediate counterpart of the *koto*. The instument was established in Japan in the eighth century in a form that the Japanese maintained, while in China it has undergone significant modification that included increasing the number of strings to sixteen or twenty-one and using metal strings on some instruments.

While slight variation in instrument size, design and decoration is generally linked to the preference of makers, performers, or to regional standardization of measurements, a traditional

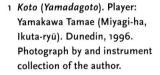

1 *Koto (Yamadagoto).* Player: Yamakawa Tamae (Miyagi-ha, Ikuta-ryū). Dunedin, 1996. Photograph by and instrument collection of the author.

2 **Sankyoku** ensemble. *Left*, *koto* (*Yamadagoto*); *center*, *sangen* (*shamisen*); *right*, *shakuhachi*. Members of Kisaragi-kai, a performance group with wider connections to Kikui Sōgaku-sha, Tsuguyama-ryū and Ikuta-ryū. Osaka, February 1992. Photograph by the author.

form of the instrument has been preserved since the eighth century even though smaller, larger and experimental *koto*-type zithers have been developed since, especially in the twentieth century. Such variations can be seen in aspects like outer decoration, repertoire, techniques of performance, playing position, in addition to shape, size and materials of plectra. Each imparts the instrument and its players their own identity within the performance tradition in which the *koto* is played and to which the players belong.

In a modern-day setting the *koto* is understood as a traditional Japanese musical instrument (*hōgakki* or *wagakki*) and accordingly its music is labeled *hōgaku* (traditional Japanese music).[4] The concept of *hōgaku* usually refers to Japanese music that existed before widespread Western influence from the latter half of the nineteenth century, or to music that has continued a style of Japanese music since that time. The term is used in contradistinction to the word *yōgaku* (Western music), which was adopted in Japan in the latter half of the nineteenth century during the country's period of modernization and Westernization following the Meiji Restoration of 1868 and its transition from a feudal system to a nation state.[5] At this time, dichotomies such as the *hōgaku/yōgaku* division became part of a wider language of Japanese classification as applied, for example, to terminology concerning food (*washoku/yōshoku*, Japanese food/Western food), clothes (*wafuku/yōfuku*, Japanese clothes/Western clothes), and rooms (*washitsu/yōshitsu*, Japanese rooms/Western rooms).

Cultural Significance

The *koto* has been used in numerous cultural contexts, covering many spheres of Japanese society. Over the centuries it has been played in music genres as widespread as folk and court music, by both male and female players, and at times in styles restricted to only blind male professionals, in religious (Shinto and Buddhist) and secular contexts, and in traditional, crossover and contemporary music styles.[6] Not only has *koto* music come to embody the nostalgic image of "traditional Japan" (i.e., antedating Western influence from the Meiji era onward), but the instrument itself is also frequently encountered in visual imagery of historical and present-day Japan as an object that does much to symbolize an idealized past.

In addition to its historical place in Japan, in recent years the instrument has appeared abroad in contexts as diverse as Japanese migrant communities and descendants of those communities (Olsen 1980, 1983), touring performers and academics, and even as an instrument played by non-Japanese professionals, enthusiasts and students studying the music of world cultures (Falconer 1995, 265-82). However, it is specifically the genre of *koto* music (*sōkyoku*) called *zokusō* (common/everyday/popular *sō*) – dating to the early Edo period – that has transmitted the *koto* and its music through numerous performance traditions of everyday *koto* playing, and allowed it to become socially, culturally and geographically widespread in Japan. The *zokusō* style of music underlies the rapid popularity of the instrument, especially in the late nineteenth century with the breakdown of restrictions as to who could play the instrument, and it was from this style of music that most current everyday *koto* performance is derived.

Everyday *koto* performance is conventionally learned in a socially rigid, hierarchical and group-oriented system. As a traditional Japanese musical instrument that is studied predominantly in a private context, the exact number of players is extremely difficult to calculate. Nevertheless, in the early 1990s it was estimated that the number of *koto* players registered with performance traditions was approximately two million, around 1.6% of Japan's then population of some 123 million (Falconer 1990, 471).[7]

Knowledge of the *koto* is also gained in Japan through traditional Japanese literature and arts in which the instrument appears. In Japanese literature, for instance, the numerous references to traditional instruments such as *koto* is evidence that they were considered valuable cultural objects in Japan. An early record of the term *koto* in Japanese literature is found in the ancient Japanese books *Kojiki* (*Records of Ancient Matters*, 712) and *Nihongi* (also called *Nihon shoki*, *Chronicles of Japan*, 720), at a time when the word was used for string instruments in general (*see* Chapter 2).[8] In the *Kojiki*, for instance, an instrument believed to be a zither is mentioned in a religious context linked to the emperor, who was seen as descendant of the cosmogonic deities Izanami and Izanagi:

> The emperor was playing the cither [zither], ... in order to seek the divine will.
> Then the empress became divinely possessed ...
> "This is a dreadful thing. My lord, continue to play the cither!"
> Finally, then, he drew the cither to him and began to play reluctantly.
> After a while, the sound of the cither stopped. When they raised the lights, they
> saw that he was dead. (Philippi 1968, 257-58)

It is the use of the *koto* in this imperial context, which has continued to this day with court and other Shinto music, that helps give the instrument a special association. Not only does the connection in this case illustrate a supernatural situation, but the very place of instruments such as the *koto* in these settings raises its status and meaning as an emblem of traditional Japan.

The *koto* is also mentioned in many other historically significant literary works, such as the noteworthy poetry anthologies *Man'yōshū* (*Collection for Ten Thousand Generations*, c. 750) and *Kokinshū* (also referred to as *Kokin wakashū*, *Anthology of Poems Ancient and Modern*, c. 905). The following example from the *Man'yōshū* is one such poem of several that feature the *koto*:

> When I take the *koto*, sobs break forth;
>   Can it be that in its hollow space
> The spirit of my wife is hiding? (Nippon Gakujutsu Shinkōkai [1940] 1965, 290)

Two of the most historically important and well-known works of Japanese literature of the Heian and Kamakura periods are the novels *Genji monogatari* (*Tale of Genji*, c. 1001-10) and *Heike monogatari* (*Tales of Heike*, c. late twelfth to early thirteenth century).[9] Each is extremely rich in musical references, and one passage from the chapter entitled "Akashi" (place name) in *Genji monogatari* is particularly significant in that it describes Genji playing the *koto* with Murasaki's messenger:

Sending to the house on the hill for a lute [biwa] and a thirteen-stringed koto, the old man [messenger] now seemed to change roles and become one of these priestly mendicants who make their living by the lute. He played a most interesting and affecting strain. Genji played a few notes on the thirteen-stringed koto which the old man pressed on him and was thought an uncommonly impressive performer on both sorts of koto [the other being the seven-string *kin*, Chinese *qin*]. ...

The old man had a delicate style to which the instruments were beautifully suited and which delighted Genji. "One likes to see a gentle lady quite at her ease with a koto," said Genji, as if with nothing specific in mind. (Murasaki 1976, 255)

A twelfth-century picture scroll of *Genji monogatari* includes an illustration depicting the *koto* in the Chapter "Hashihime" ("The Bridge Maiden", fig. 3; *see also* Morris 1971). This chapter recounts the story of Kaoru (Kashiwagi's son) who had decided to visit Genji's half-brother, the Prince Hachi (literally, "Prince Eight"), at his residence in Uji near Kyoto. When Kaoru arrives, the Eighth Prince is not at home, but Kaoru can hear music being played on the *koto* (*sō no koto*) and *biwa* (*biwa no koto*) by his two daughters Oigimi and Nakanokimi. Kaoru is much moved by the setting and the encounter:

3 Illustration of Kaoru watching Prince Hachi's daughters playing music, a scene from the chapter "Hashihime" ("The Bridge Maiden") in *Genji monogatari emaki* (*Tale of Genji Picture Scroll*), early twelfth century. Ink and color on paper. A *sō no koto* and *biwa no koto* appear to the right and left, respectively. The Tokugawa Art Museum, Nagoya.

As he drew near the Uji house, he could hear the plucking of he did not know what instrument, unimaginably still and lonely. He had heard from the abbot that the prince liked to practice with his daughters, but somehow had not found occasion to hear that famous koto. This would be his chance. Making his way into the grounds, he knew that he had been listening to a lute [*biwa*], tuned to the *ōjiki* [*ōshiki*] mode. There was nothing unusual about the melody. Perhaps the strangeness of the setting had made it seem different. The sound was cool and clean, especially when a string was plucked from beneath. The lute fell silent and there were a few quiet strokes on a koto. He would have liked to listen on, but he was challenged by a man with a somewhat threatening manner, one of the guards, it would seem. (Murasaki 1976, 784)

The *Genji monogatari* is set around Murasaki Shikibu's experiences in the imperial court. By contrast, another great work of classical Japanese literature, *Heike monogatari*, is an historical work based on fact. The following extract from *Heike monogatari* concerns Kogō, an attendant and accomplished *koto* player, who was presented to the emperor by the empress. In this passage, a man is sent by the emperor to search for Kogō who had left the palace:

Close to Kameyama, in the direction of a pine grove, he heard the faint strains of a zither [i.e., *koto*]. Was it a gale on the peaks? Was it the wind in the pines? Or might it be the instrument of the lady he sought? He spurred forward and drew near. Someone was indeed playing the zither with a brilliant touch inside a house where there was a single-doored gate.

He pulled up to listen. Beyond a doubt, it was Kogō's style. She was playing, "Yearning for My Husband," a song in which a woman expresses nostalgia for her spouse. Just as he had surmised, she had been thinking of the Emperor; most admirably, she had chosen that composition from among the many she might have played. (McCullough 1988, 203)

While these works are unquestionably some of the finest in classical Japanese literature, and imbue the *koto* and other instruments with an abundance of cultural meaning relating to a perception of traditional Japan, it is only within the last one hundred years that some so-called traditional objects such as the *koto* have been used or rediscovered by writers as iconic of an idealized Japan. Whereas representations of the *koto* in classical literature certainly help reinforce the instrument's special place in Japanese culture, in contemporary Japan the *koto* supplies an interesting paradox as a traditional instrument. Although *hōgaku* is not played by most Japanese, it is nevertheless emblematic of traditional Japanese culture, as a part of a collective cultural ethos rooted firmly in an age before extensive Western influence, and as a style of music with nostalgic connotations of a real or imagined Japan of a bygone era. Such a cultural role is likewise exemplified in works of more recent Japanese authors of pre- and post-World War II Japanese literature. Writers such as Nagai Kafū (1879-1959), Kawabata Yasunari (1899-1971), Mishima Yukio (1925-70), Osabe Hideo (*b.* 1934), Murakami Haruki (*b.* 1949), Shimada Masahiko (*b.* 1961), and Yoshimoto Banana (*b.* 1964) have all referenced traditional music "in the spirit of their times, wherein traditional performing arts ... are experienced by most Japanese as remnants of a past that is their own, yet somehow not their own" (de Ferranti 2000, 39). Such writers might be tagged cultural nationalists in their use of such symbols of the past – or an imagined past – where heritage is seen to embody an ideal that has been obfuscated in the present.[10]

In Japan's visual arts too, there are many images that depict the *koto* and other musical instruments such as the *shamisen* (three-string lute) and *shakuhachi* (end-blown flute). For example, the Ukiyo-e woodblock prints of the Edo period and early-mid Meiji era were especially popular in their portrayal of everyday life. Their significance is such that they have come to embody an idealized past and symbolize the very essence of traditional Japan. A representative collection of woodblock prints that depicts traditional Japanese musical instruments is found in

Kyrova et al. (2000; see also Haags Gemeentemuseum 1975). Of the prints illustrating the koto in this publication – there are of course many other such prints not included – the contexts in which the instrument is depicted are typical of such images and imaginations.¹¹ This is also seen, for example, in such works as the 1891 print by Ogata Gekkō (1859-1920), whose subject appears to be the embodiment of feminine gentility in her representation of manners and customs of women of the time (see page 11). Woodblock prints depicting scenes from *Genji monogatari* (*Tale of Genji*) have always captured the imaginations of woodblock artists and the Japanese public. One such print by Kōchōrō Kunisada (Utagawa Kunisada, 1786-1865) depicts Murasaki playing a highly decorated koto with an insert of Prince Genji above – a *Genjimon* crest symbol is shown in the top right-hand corner, which stands for the chapter "Hana no En" ("Festival of the Cherry Blossoms") (see page 19). The koto illustrated in a work by Yashima Gakutei (1786?-1868) is part of a multisheet print of the *sankyoku* ensemble of koto, shamisen (*sangen*) and *kokyū* (fiddle). The lavishly adorned koto is portrayed in intricate detail, showing the layout of the thirteen movable bridges, decoration at each end and along the sides, as well as several accessories in the foreground (see page 29). A print by Katsukawa Shuntei (1770-1820) from the series *Hanagasaren shichifukujin* (*The Seven Gods of Good Fortune for the Hanagasa Poetry Club*, 1821), limns a similarly decorated koto, but here a young woman plays the instrument in a room overlooking a garden (see page 51). The symbolism in this print is especially strong: the woman has shell patterns on her kimono and there is a view to the island of Enoshima on the screen to the top right. Each of these motifs refers to Benten, one of the *shichifukujin* or Seven Gods of Good Fortune. A very intriguing work by Toyokawa Yoshikuni (act. first half of 19th c.) illustrates the actor Nakamura Fukunosuke playing a koto, with the instrument placed on a table and the player sitting on a chair (see page 89). The position of this stylized koto is unusual; moreover, it has many decorative elements that would have typically adorned the instrument at this time (i.e., marquetry at each end and symbolic images such as birds along the side). A print by Suzuki Harunobu (1725?-70) from the series *Zashiki hakkei* (*The Eight Parlor Views*, c. 1776), depicts two women by a koto. Each is preparing to play the instrument in a traditional Japanese room with screens and *tatami* mat, and a garden view. Of particular interest is the use of a music score entitled *Kinkyoku shū* (*Koto Music Collection*), which is perhaps a collection of song texts that were popular among amateur players. In this print too the beautiful wood grain on the upper surface of the koto is mirrored in a similar pattern visible on the wood at the bottom of the sliding screen behind the players (see page 111). A print of the courtesan Kumoi of the Tsuruya brothel in the Yoshiwara pleasure quarters by Keisai Eisen (1791-1848) and from his series *Keisei dōchū sugoroku – Mitate Yoshiwara gojūsantsui* (*Courtesans as the Board Game Sugoroku Along the Highway – The Yoshiwara as the Fifty-three Stations*, c. 1825-26) includes the "head" end of a koto. Artistic license has surely been taken in the portrayal of the instrument as it does not show its usual thirteen strings (see page 161).

Even a cursory look at the diverse images of the koto in some classical and contemporary literature, as well as in Ukiyo-e prints, is enough to realize the intense historical and present-day significance of the instrument as an object of traditional Japanese culture. It is the emphasis on tradition (*dentō*) in contemporary Japan that is especially significant for understanding the place of the koto in Japan. As Tokumaru (1991, XII) points out, "traditions are always considered in the contextual aggregate of the past, the present and the future rather than exclusively in terms of the past." The koto belongs to a living tradition where its transmission historically and in the present day through various performance groups and music genres not only contributes to and establishes it as an integral part of Japan's cultural heritage, but also part of a wider notion of a "traditional" Japan that is perpetuated in the present, one that is as dependent on the future as it is on the past.

In terms of the current popularity of the koto, as Falconer (1990, 474) has observed, even today in Japan's modern, technological society, many Japanese would probably be able to name several celebrated pieces of traditional koto music – "Rokudan no Shirabe" ("Investigation in

Six Sections"), "Haru no Umi" ("Spring Sea"), or "Sakura" ("Cherry Blossom"), to name just a few.[12] Despite the acknowledged roots of the *koto* in Chinese culture over thirteen hundred years ago, "the general meaning of the *koto* in Japan as a whole (i.e. the shared meanings of most Japanese people) is one that sees the instrument as embodying the characteristics of traditional Japan; the *koto is* a symbol of traditional Japan" (Johnson 1993, 287). Nevertheless as Falconer (1990, 475) concludes, "hōgaku, in short, is generally presented as something that has nothing to do with reality."

As a symbol of traditional Japan the *koto* can act in other ways. *Koto* music might be heard on auspicious occasions, or in locations that seek to recreate an image of traditional Japan or place importance on Japan's history and cultural heritage. To effect such an atmosphere, recordings of *koto* music are used as background soundscapes with the aim of lacing a contemporary place with sonic images of the past – real or imagined (*cf.* B. Anderson 1991). Even a performance context itself conjures up a set image connected with the instrument. That is, traditional performance contexts usually feature players in traditional attire, kneeling on a red carpet with a gold screen behind them. Still, some contemporary performers purposefully attempt to break with the past by performing not only original compositions, but also challenging traditional stereotypical images so often associated with the instrument.

Even though *hōgaku* might be considered a symbol of traditional Japan, it has been transformed as a direct result of more than one hundred years of intensive Western influence. As a continuation of the *Nihonjin ron* (discussion of Japanese uniqueness) phenomenon of the 1970s and 1980s (e.g., Doi 1971; Nakane 1970), the 1990s witnessed a resurgence in nationalist sentiment in many spheres of Japanese life, especially after a period of economic decline and the bursting of the country's bubble economy in 1989/1990 (McCormack 2002; Yoshino 1992, 2002). It was within this economic climate that the Ministry of Education, Culture, Sports, Science and Technology (Monbukagakushō) took the decision to implement a compulsory school unit on traditional Japanese music from April 2002 which requires that all junior-high school students learn a traditional Japanese musical instrument (e.g., *koto, shamisen, taiko* [drums]). Such a requirement has not been witnessed in over one hundred years of state education due to the adoption of Western music and marks a radical change in Japan's music education. That *hōgaku* has been introduced into the educational system seems to be a "rediscovery" or "reinvention" (*cf.* Hobsbawm and Ranger 1983) of a real or imagined Japanese cultural heritage.[13]

To a certain extent the Japanese government is reinventing tradition in an attempt to impose ideas on the Japanese people in what appears to be a policy of cultural nationalism. If *hōgaku* is not played or consumed by most Japanese, why make it a part of compulsory state education? Many questions are easily raised with regard to the introduction of a type of music into the education system that seems on the one hand to represent only a small part of contemporary Japanese culture (i.e., in terms of its consumption), yet on the other hand is a highly symbolic and significant part of Japanese heritage. But if Japanese state education has excluded *hōgaku* from the system for so long, what place can it possibly have in modern society and why introduce it now? An immediate answer might be that in an era of cultural nationalism, *hōgaku* has become extremely significant as a cultural emblem of traditional Japan, that is, the Japanese state. *Hōgaku* is synonymous with traditional Japan – a Japan of the past, especially before late nineteenth-century Western influence and the country's subsequent modernization.

For many Japanese school students, if not most, the sounds of instruments such as the *koto* are still exotic and often out of step with Japan today (*cf.* de Ferranti 2000, 39; Mathews 2000, 30). For the few who actually play traditional instruments, there is a huge cultural difference between their world as traditional musicians and their everyday lives outside traditional society. That is, while learning the *koto*, for example, in its characteristic homogenous performance groups and traditions, it might seem to the student that playing *hōgaku* is a commonplace art to learn in modern Japan. But when compared to the activities of most other school students, it actually turns out to be quite unusual, even though it is meant to be a very Japanese thing to do. As Mathews notes, for one *koto* player he interviewed, "when she first went to school as a child, it came as a surprise to her to learn that for her classmates *koto* was not a natural part of their everyday lives, but something unusual" (2000, 40). The apparent lack of interest in *hōgaku* and the proliferation of Western music in Japan have been emphasized in many writings on Japanese music. The distinguished Japanese musicologist, Kishibe, notes that there are many concerts of Western classical music, and "Japanese TV is dominated by American Jazz and popular songs, or music and dance by Japanese, but in the American style. ... The traditional music seems to have been forgotten" (1982b, iii). This particular writer seems to be lamenting the loss of a perceived traditional Japan, one that has almost vanished in a context of Western cultural hegemony, but the culture that is supposed to have gone astray is, to a certain extent, an imagined one – or at least an invention vis-à-vis the predominance of Western cultural icons – as "the vast majority of Japanese through history have never practiced most traditional Japanese arts" (Mathews 2000, 41). So, the loss is for a culture that perhaps never was for all, but instead has been constructed in the collective imaginations of many Japanese over countless years as a symbol of Japaneseness, and today is especially relevant and prevalent in an age of globalization that is interconnected to an era of cultural nationalism. In contemporary Japan, we can especially witness a fascinating irony where so-called traditional music is a minority art: it is a symbol of Japaneseness and for the first time ever forms part of a national school curriculum, even though most Japanese who learn *hōgaku* do so privately. Yet, while some contemporary musicians are very dismissive of traditional Japan and even reject the so-called traditional arts altogether on the grounds that if no-one needs them then "'let them vanish!'" (Mathews 2000, 50), instruments such as the *koto* not only construct culture for those who play and learn them, but, as distinct symbols that are connected to and associated with many spheres of traditional – real and imagined – Japan, they play an important role in constructions of individual, group and national identity.

Not surprisingly, the 1990s also witnessed the restoration of nationalistic symbols such as the Japanese anthem and flag, as well as the contemporary political climate with the right-wing writer Ishihara Shintarō (*b.* 1932) who was elected governor of Tokyo in 1999. Perhaps in the same way that these emblems of Japaneseness were restored in an era of renewed cultural nationalism, so too were traditional instruments as national objects and emblems that were perceived to represent an idealized past that had been for over one hundred years obfuscated by the compulsory teaching of Western music. The late twentieth century was, according to McCormack (2002, 153-54), a time of "unprecedented crisis – with the phenomena of classroom collapse, bullying, school refusal, violence, and suicide ... the resort to such pressure to enforce standardized, disciplined national symbols and rituals seems strikingly inappropriate." Furthermore, as Starrs (2001, xxv) has put it, "feelings of nostalgic longing for the 'strong Japan' of the past are also characteristic of the present conservative mood."

The *koto* is certainly an instrument of Japan's *past*. With a history of over thirteen hundred years as a Japanese musical instrument, its connection with the imperial household, which has continued since its first introduction to Japan until the present day, is certainly one social association that helps give the instrument cultural significance as an important object of traditional Japan. Along with Buddhism and Shintoism, as well as the blind, male, professional guilds that regulated who could perform and what could be learned, the instrument has certainly had a range of social connections, each of which contributes to a history that gives the instrument special importance in Japan. While in a post-bubble Japan "it is quite natural to turn one's gaze backwards when one can find nothing positive in looking forward" (Nakao 2001, 174), "the Japanese today are searching for answers and directions like never before" (J. Nelson 2000, 2-3). While the *koto* is certainly a symbol of traditional Japan, and has a long and rich association with many Japanese arts and diverse social spheres, its special place in Japanese history is reinforced even further with the state policy of requiring traditional Japanese music to be learned by all school students, even though it is often a cultural "other" as well as an icon of cultural heritage and traditional Japan.

Within the prevailing climate of diverse connections and associations, the *koto* is defined as a unique and distinguished object of Japanese culture. As an instrument possessing layers of historical and contemporary importance, the *koto* is one example of a traditional Japanese object that holds a singular place as an emblem of cultural heritage and living performance traditions in a country which increasingly looks outward in a process of internationalization, while at the same time is closing inward in an attempt at maintaining and reinforcing this heritage and identity. It is within this environment of object and meaning that the instrument's form, transmission and performance contexts will be explored in the following chapters.

Yashima Gakutei (1786?-1868). A Beauty and her *Koto*, center sheet from a triptych "Sankyoku" ("Three Musical Instruments"), 1822. Square *surimono* (privately published de-luxe print), 209/210 x 182/186 mm each. Gemeentemuseum Den Haag (PRM-0000-2376).

2 Instrument Names and Types

The *Koto* and Its Variant Names

琴 *kin, koto, gon*

箏 *sō, koto*

箏のこと *sō no koto*

An understanding of the various names of the *koto* and the characters (*kanji*) used to write them is an integral part of any discussion of the instrument.[1] While the term *koto* is today the one most commonly employed for it, during its long history in Japan the *koto* has also been known as *sō*, *sō no koto* and occasionally *jūsangen* (*see* character insert above). During the Nara and Heian periods, the word *koto* referred to string instruments in general, so that a zither and a lute, for example, were both types of *koto*.[2] This category likewise included the string instruments *sō no koto* (the thirteen-string zither called *sō*, i.e., the *koto*), *kin no koto* (the seven-string zither called *kin*) and *biwa no koto* (the four-string lute called *biwa*), which were among the many objects imported to Japan from China.

Examples of the word *koto* are found in a number of early Japanese literary classics, where it appears independently or as a suffix to other instrument names. This is evident in works such as *Kojiki*, *Nihongi*, *Man'yōshū*, *Utsubo* (or *Utsuho*) *monogatari* (*The Tale of the Cavern*), *Genji monogatari*, and *Heike monogatari*. In the eleventh-century *Genji monogatari*, for instance, the chapter entitled "Hahakigi" ("The Broom Tree") mentions a *sō no koto* in the passage where an officer recounts one of his encounters to Prince Genji:

> "'Excuse me for asking. You must not be parsimonious with your music. You have a by no means indifferent listener.'
> "He was very playful indeed. The woman's voice, when she offered a verse of her own, was suggestive and equally playful.
> > "'No match the leaves for the angry winter winds.
> > Am I to detain the flute that joins those winds?'
> "Naturally unaware of resentment so near at hand, she changed to a Chinese koto [*sō no koto* in original Japanese text] in an elegant *banjiki* [*banshiki*, a *gagaku* mode]. (Murasaki 1976, 31)

When the term *koto* connotes zithers in general – historically and today – it is sometimes written in phonetic script (*hiragana* or *katakana*), which to the scholar of *koto* history and to the etymologist is the source of much uncertainty as to how to decipher the meaning. Around the mid-Heian period, with the waning popularity of the zither called *kin* in Japan,[3] the character to write its name was sometimes read *koto* and was even used on its own to refer to the *sō*.[4] Confusion sometimes results regarding the exact type of instrument under discussion when the character for *kin* is used.[5] The character *kin*, not the reading, can be misleading as one might at first think that the *kanji* refers to the seven-string *kin* when in fact it often denotes the *koto*. After all, the *kin* is a different type of zither to the *koto*: it is slightly shorter, does not have movable bridges placed along the upper surface of its soundboard, and its strings are stopped against the soundboard.[6] Even in the terminology associated with the *koto*, the confusion of terms and the characters used to refer to them is particularly apparent. This is seen in words such as *kindai* (a *koto* stand used to raise the head end) and *kinkyoku* (*koto* music), or in the titles of several collections of *koto* tablature, such as *Kinkyoku shifu* (*Guide on Koto Music Notation*, comp. 1772, pub. 1780) and *Kinkyoku shō* (*Collection of Koto Pieces*, 1695).

When the word *koto* is written with the character for *sō*, it not only refers to the instrument in this study, but also signifies an instrument that has movable bridges. While in the Nara and Heian periods this *kanji* was the "correct" character for the *koto*, its use today is usually restricted to academics and specialists, even though it is learned at school. (This *kanji* is still employed in the instrument's Chinese precursor, the *zheng*.) In describing the parts of the character *sō*, Falconer (1995, 115) comments that "the top ... means bamboo, while the bottom part ... means to dispute, to conflict, to be tense. This is thought to have been chosen to indicate that the strings are struck and pulled in both directions, creating a reverberating tension among them, while the bamboo is a generic representation of wood." Adriaansz provides an interesting aside on the mythical origin of other Asian zithers as relates to the character *sō*:

> Two sisters quarreled for possession of a [Chinese] se [zither] made of bamboo. In a solution worthy of Solomon, if not David, they split the instrument in two, thus obtaining two cheng [*zheng*], one with twelve and the other with thirteen strings. The presence of the twelve-stringed instrument in Korea (the kayakeum [*kayagŭm*]) is explained by adding that one of the two sisters emigrated to Korea, while the other remained in China. (Adriaansz 1973, 23)

Although it is not particularly current, the term *sō* is a Sino-Japanese reading of the character sometimes applied by scholars and specialists when making reference to the *koto*. Because of the historical inconsistencies connected with the spoken and written name for the *koto*, the character *sō* is nowadays also read *koto*. While several of the *koto* tablature collections mentioned earlier included the word *kin* in their title, there were also collections that included the word *sō*, most notably *Sōkyoku taiishō* (*General Selection of Koto Music*, 1779).

The term *sō no koto* (the *sō* type of *koto* [string instrument]) mixes Japanese- and Chinese-derived readings. Like the word *sō*, this term is used mainly by specialists of the instrument who wish either to compare the *koto* with other zithers, or to refer to the instrument during the period soon after it was transmitted to Japan.[7] As seen above in *Genji monogatari*, the term *sō no koto* was sometimes used in Japanese classical literature as a way of distinguishing a specific type of *koto*. In the late tenth-century *Utsubo monogatari*, which is particularly rich in musical references, several kinds of *koto* are clearly indicated. In fact, *Utsubo monogatari* is set around players of the *kin* (Chinese *qin*) and the power the instrument possesses for those who play it. In the chapter "Fukiage" ("Fountain" [Part 2]), for instance, one passage lists a variety of instruments including several so-called "*koto*":

> The ex-Emperor himself took a biwa, and gave a wagon [six string zither] to Nakatada, a sō no koto to Nakayori, and a koto [i.e., *kin*] to Suzushi to play in concert. Suzushi played the koto very skilfully. When the concert was over, the ex-Emperor ordered Suzushi to play a sō no koto. He played it so skilfully that the ex-Emperor was much moved, and exclaimed.

> "It has grown up into a pine grandly shading the earth, though I had been told that it was still a seedling." (Uraki 1984, 170)

The term *jūsangen* (thirteen strings) is not a common name for the *koto*, even though it is sometimes cited to distinguish this thirteen-string instrument from other types of zithers. It is similar to the names of several other traditional Japanese musical instruments, such as the *ichigenkin* (one-string zither), *nigenkin* (two-string zither) and *sangen* (three strings, an alternative name for the *shamisen*). Especially since the development from the 1920s onward of *koto* with more than thirteen strings, the term *jūsangen* has been used increasingly when the *koto* is compared to other *koto*-type instruments that are defined by their number of strings. The latter category includes zithers such as the *jūshichigen* (seventeen strings), *nijūgen* (twenty strings), *sanjūgen* (thirty strings), and *hachijūgen* (eighty strings), each of which occasionally appears with the suffix *sō* or *goto* (*koto*).[8] (*See below* for a discussion of these and others.)

Classifications of the Instrument:
Gakusō, *Chikusō*, *Zokusō*, and Modified, Smaller and Larger *Koto*

4 *Gakusō* in *bugaku* ensemble. From *Jinrinkinmōzui* (*Illustrations of Everyday Life*, 1690), a woodblock-printed illustrated book depicting everyday scenes. Courtesy Heibonsha. Reprinted by permission from *Jinrin-kinmōzui* ([1690] 1990, 77).

The *koto* is classified and named in numerous ways (Johnson 1996a, 1996-97). In addition to being labeled a musical instrument (*gakki*), it is more narrowly grouped as a chordophone (*genmeigakki*) and therein a zither (*chitā* or *tsitā*). As a Japanese musical instrument seen in contradistinction to a Western instrument, the *koto* is defined as a type of *wagakki* (Japanese musical instrument) or *hōgakki* (Japanese musical instrument),[9] and in *gagaku* the instrument is grouped together with *kangen* (wind [pipes]/strings).[10] Two other broad classifications – *gengakki* and *hikimono* – should also be mentioned here. They categorize the *koto* according to instrument structure and the way it is sounded. *Gengakki* (string instrument) is the strings part of the instrument grouping comprising strings, wind and percussion; *hikimono* (plucked object) belongs to part of the grouping of plucked, blown and struck objects into which the *koto* falls. Moreover, the term *koto* also includes several specific instrument types, and those outlined below are part of a more specific level of discourse that differentiates instruments according to their performance tradition. This classification system is significant in that instruments are given names that identify the place of the *koto* in performance within a specific music tradition. The origins of the names are based on several determining factors: music genre, region, social stratification, and performers' names.

Three broad scholarly classifications of *koto* are often used to define the performance tradition in which the instrument is played (*see* Table 1): *gakusō* (*gagaku sō*), *chikusō* (Tsukushi *sō*; sometimes called *Tsukushigoto*),[11] and *zokusō* (common/everyday/popular *sō*).[12] Closely associated with *zokusō* is the term *zokugaku* (common/everyday/popular music), frequently applied to some types of music to distinguish them from, for example, religious music, the court *gagaku*, or the music of *nō* theater:

> The word *gagaku* originally meant 'noble, correct music' as opposed to 'vulgar [secular] music' (*zokugaku*). ... In Japan, any music that had been imported from China tended to be regarded as *gagaku* (even if it was, in fact, 'vulgar music'), while all traditional Japanese music, e.g. *kagura* [Shinto music], *saibara* [a genre of court songs], *rōei* [a vocal genre using Chinese poems], and later also *koto* – and *shamisen* – music, was considered as 'vulgar music' (*zokugaku*), as music of a lower order. (Kikkawa 1984b, 280)

The instrument type called *zokusō* actually divides into two principal categories: *Ikutagoto* (Ikuta *koto*) and *Yamadagoto* (Yamada *koto*).[13] However, while the instruments *gakusō*, *chikusō* and *zokusō* encompass the entire history of the *koto*, only two main types are now found: the court *gakusō*, which is rare, and the everyday *Yamadagoto*, which today is by far the most predominant type. Furthermore, these terms and others, as outlined in Tables 1 and 2 below, are not traditional names for different types of *koto*, but are used mainly by instrument makers and scholars to distinguish specific types of instruments.

A further level of instrument classification – utilized principally by *koto* makers and scholars – is seen in the technical names of the *chikusō* and early forms of *zokusō* (i.e., non-Yamada instruments). (The other type, *gakusō*, is classified separately, even though it shares many of the features of *chikusō* and early forms of *zokusō*.) The *chikusō* and *zokusō* are further

Table 1. Instruments and Traditions

Instrument Classification	Tradition/Genre	Period
Gakusō	*Gagaku*	From at least the late seventh century and firmly established during the eighth century
Chikusō	Tsukushigoto	From Kenjun (1534?-1623?)
Zokusō	*Zokusō/zokugaku*	From Yatsuhashi Kengyō (1614-85)
Ikutagoto	Ikuta-ryū	From Ikuta Kengyō (1656-1715)
Yamadagoto	Yamada-ryū and most other everyday traditions today	From Yamada Kengyō (1757-1817)

Table 2. Classifications According to Outer Surface Decoration

Type of Instrument	Classification
Chikusō and some earlier forms of the *zokusō* other than the *Yamadagoto*	*Nagaisohonjitate(goto)* (long-sided properly made [*koto*])
	Kazarigoto (decorated *koto*)
	Makiegoto (*maki-e koto*)
	Ryūkyūgoto (Ryūkyū *koto*)
	Nagaiso(goto) (long-sided [*koto*])
	Honjitate(goto) (properly made [*koto*])
	Isogoto (side *koto*)
Yamadagoto	*Sugotojitate(goto)* (simply made [*koto*])

divided according to the type of added decoration that can take the form of gold/silver lacquer (in the *maki-e* technique), inlay and marquetry (*yosegizaiku*), veneer (*hakuhan* or *usuita*), edging (*fuchi*, which is usually ivory [*zōge*], or plastic on less expensive instruments), tortoiseshell (*kikkō*), and mother-of-pearl (*raden*).

Table 2 delineates some of the classifications of the non-Yamada and Yamada types of *koto* based on the various characteristics of the instrument such as structure, amount of decoration and performance location. Of the two main types of instruments listed in Table 2 (*chikusō* and *Yamadagoto*), the first classification of *nagaisohonjitate(goto)* indicates the instrument's long sides on which lacquer work and veneer would normally be found. Only early types of *zokusō* were so embellished, with later examples occasionally influenced by the style of the *Yamadagoto*, which were typically more sparsely decorated. The terms *kazarigoto* and *makiegoto* indicate the quantity of lacquer work, marquetry and veneer added to the main body, to distinguish them from later instruments that omitted such lavish features. *Ryūkyūgoto* is the only term that is site related and demonstrates that the Ryūkyū islands are the main context of this type of highly decorated instrument today. The three terms *nagaiso(goto)*, *honjitate(goto)* and *isogoto* are sometimes utilized for the non-Yamada instrument and are linguistic alternatives that are easily understood in comparison to the more technical names mentioned above. *Yamadagoto* are labeled *sugotojitate(goto)* to show that this form of instrument does not have the large amounts of applied decoration typical of *chikusō* and earlier types of *zokusō*.

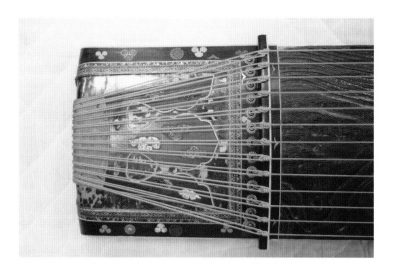

Gakusō

The *koto* used in *gagaku* or court music is nowadays called *gakusō* (*gagaku sō*) to distinguish it from *koto* of other traditions (figs. 4-7). The *gakusō* type of instrument was the first version of the *koto* to be used in Japan. It was imported with *gagaku* from China at a time of immense cultural borrowing nearly thirteen hundred years ago. What is particularly interesting is that while the *gakusō* is acknowledged as the first type of *koto* in Japan, its basic structure has changed very little since its introduction. This contrasts its Chinese counterpart, the *zheng*, which has been modified considerably over the centuries and no longer has thirteen-strings. With the transmission of the *koto* into other social spheres outside the imperial court, its form underwent slight changes, but in terms of size, number of strings and main structural features, most *koto* are very similar. Yet, there are several features of *gakusō* that differ visibly from present-day *Yamadagoto*. Most noticeably, are the often silk strings of *gakusō*, unlike those of *zokusō* which are mainly synthetic. Also, the *gakusō* has fewer ornamental performance techniques (*see* Chapter 5).

   Several examples of early *koto* (i.e., *gakusō*) are housed in the Shōsōin, the eighth-century imperial repository of art treasures from the Nara period at the temple of Tōdaiji in Nara. In shape and size, these *koto* are extremely close to modern *koto* (*see* Hayashi 1964; Kishibe 1984; Shōsōin 1967, 1989).[14] There is also a Heian-period *makiegoto* (*makie koto*) in the Treasure Hall at the Nara shrine of Kasuga taisha, whose entire outer surface (i.e., soundboard) is lacquered and decorated with floral motifs, insects and landscapes scenes.

While the *gakusō* is known from historical records in several genres of *gagaku*, today it is used primarily in the instrumental genre *kangen*, which is found only with larger ensembles. The ancient female Shinto dance, *mikomai*, might also include the *gakusō*, although the more recently developed *Yamadagoto* has more or less replaced it. The *koto* no longer accompanies dance in *gagaku* (i.e., *bugaku*), but that such practices did at one time occur is known to us through Edo-period woodblock-printed books and prints (fig. 4).

There are several large *gagaku* ensembles in Japan, including those affiliated with the Imperial Palace, larger Shinto shrines such as Kasuga, Ise and Meiji, Buddhist temples such as Shitennōji and the headquarters of the religious Tenri sect. There are also groups such as Reigaku-sha that are actively preserving and researching *gagaku*, and reconstructing Nara-period instruments.

An historical comparison of the *gakusō* and the *zokusō*, for example, was made in the late nineteenth/early twentieth centuries in a publication on Japanese music by Sir Francis T. Piggott:

> The Sō-no-koto [i.e., *gakusō*] has low bridges, the strings are coarser and more loosely twisted than those now used, and the *tsumé* [plectra] are of thick paper, gilt or silvered, with a very small piece of bamboo let in, not more than one-fifth of an inch in length. In playing, the paper stall first rubs the string, the bamboo striking it afterwards, but with very little force; the result is a soft woolly tone. In the Japanese Koto [i.e., *zokusō*] these three points are altered; the bridges are raised, the strings are of finer quality, and *tsumé* are of ivory standing clear of the leather stall, enabling the strings to be struck clean. The result is a clear bright tone, tending naturally to the production of lighter and brighter music. (Piggott [1909] 1971, 110)

The most noticeable difference between the *gakusō* and later versions of the *zokusō* is found on the upper surface of the instrument's head and tail. Each part of the *gakusō* is ornamented with considerable marquetry and inlay, details absent from the modern-day *Yamadagoto*. The head of the *gakusō* has a decorative rectangular area in the central frame-shaped section that is sometimes embellished further by such elements as tortoiseshell, gold lacquer, ivory, and mother-of-pearl. The tail end likewise has a similar rectangular section, albeit much larger than that at the head. Some early *zokusō* also had such ornamentation, but this gradually disappeared and at present the degree of decoration is one visual cue to the differences between instruments.

Chikusō

The *chikusō* type of *koto* belongs to the performance tradition known as Tsukushigoto (Tsukushi *koto*; later called Tsukushi-ryū [Tsukushi tradition]). The basic structure of the *chikusō* may be considered identical to the *gakusō*, although the degree of decoration often varies between them (figs. 8-12; *see also* figs. 14-16, which are not classified as *chikusō*, but share the same features). While Tsukushigoto music is today usually played on an *Ikutagoto*, rather than an instrument unique to the tradition, there are several features that have survived: its strings are slightly thicker and tuned an octave lower than those used on a *Yamadagoto*, and it uses slightly smaller movable bridges made of wood, as is usually found on non-Yamadagoto.[15]

By the early seventeenth century the Tsukushigoto tradition of *koto* performance was firmly established in the region of Kyūshū called Tsukushi, an area that roughly corresponds to present-day Fukuoka and Saga Prefectures.[16] It was originally founded at the Buddhist temple of Zendōji in Kurume by the priest Kenjun (1534?-1623?), and is recognized as the oldest non-court *koto* tradition. The music of Tsukushigoto was especially influenced by *gagaku* and music for the seven-string *kin* (Chinese *qin*) (Adriaansz 2001, 827).

It follows that Tsukushigoto players were originally Buddhist priests, Confucian scholars and noblemen (Adriaansz 1973, 6), and, under the leadership of Kenjun's disciple Genjo (*d.* 1662), the performers of this tradition insisted that their music should not be taught to women or blind men, who were often associated with everyday, common forms of entertainment and therefore frowned upon. Under the patronage of the Saga clan, the tradition became associated mainly with the samurai class and was not restricted to the earlier temple tradition. With the Meiji reforms in the late nineteenth century, however, Tsukushigoto lost its patronage and its numbers were reduced considerably (Adriaansz 1973, 6-7). Toward the end of the nineteenth century, the head of the tradition, Noda Chōshō (n.d.), broke with tradition by accepting four female students in an attempt to ensure the survival of the tradition (Adriaansz 1973, 6). Inoue Mina (1895-1995) was one of these students and was active as a public performer. The program notes of a 1974 performance by Inoue include a photograph of her playing a highly decorated *chikusō*. The program also states that Tsukushigoto was designated an Intangible Cultural Property (*mukei bunkazai*) by the Japanese Government in March 1957 due to its special role in the history of Japanese music. Apart from reconstructed performance in the Sei-ha *koto* tradition, performance in the Tsukushigoto style is now only keep alive by Miyahara Chizuko (*b.* 1936), who learned six pieces from her teacher Murai Rei (1887-1958), another of Noda's students. Although Miyahara is actively engaged in promoting and continuing Tsukushigoto music, she uses an *Ikutagoto* with wooden movable bridges, not a *chikusō*.[17]

Zokusō

The *zokusō* type of *koto* dates from the time of Yatsuhashi Kengyō (1614-85), a blind male musician who established a style of everyday *koto* playing outside the court and temple traditions. Yatsuhashi, who was formerly known by other performing names including Jōhide and Yamazumi Kōtō, was taught *koto* by Hossui (also pronounced Hōsui). Hossui was a student of Kenjun in the Tsukushigoto, but he was expelled from the Tsukushigoto tradition because he taught their music to the blind (Adriaansz 1973, 7). Public performance of the everyday tradition that developed with Yatsuhashi was itself restricted to the lower social class of blind, male professional performers, although they would often play for the ruling samurai class and teach the daughters of the wealthy merchant class who wished to acquire skills in the arts.[18] Women, however, were strictly forbidden to perform in public.[19] Adriaansz writes on the general social associations of the *koto*, in particular the *zokusō*:

> With the creation of zokusō, a new shift in [the] social milieu of the music can be noticed. Heian sōkyoku had been the privilege of the aristocracy, Tsukushi-goto that of priests and Confucianists. Zokusō came to be composed and performed mostly by blind professional musicians, while its amateurs were found among the bourgeo[i]sie. To learn Tsukushi-goto was a privilege, granted a student; as for zokusō, its instruction to members of well-to-do families, especially young girls, became a main source of income for the musicians in whose hands it had passed. These blind musicians were organized as the *Shoku-yashiki* [often called Tōdō], a professional organization comparable to a guild, which bestowed ranks[20] upon and protected the professional and material interests of its members. (Adriaansz 1973, 11)

Yatsuhashi Kengyō is recognized today as the first player to introduce the *in* scale to *koto* music.[21] Until this time the *in* scale, which is characterized by half steps above its root and fifth degrees, was associated with *zokugaku* (i.e., non-court, non-religious and non-high-art music). Hence the use of the descriptive term *zoku* for Yatsuhashi's music and its association with everyday music. Until Yatsuhashi's time, this scale – already known in the folk music of commoners – had not been used in *koto* music and as Adriaansz (1973, 9) comments, "it is very

8 *Chikusō*. Head end resting on additional stand. Made by Imamura Masafusa; *c.* 191 cm long, 22.7-24.7 cm wide and 4.5-8.1 cm high. Osaka College of Music, Museum of Music (B03-0484). Photograph by the author.

9 *Chikusō*. Player's side of head of instrument illustrated in figure 8. Osaka College of Music, Museum of Music (B03-0484). Photograph by the author.

10 *Chikusō*. Upper surface of tail of instrument illustrated in figure 8. Osaka College of Music, Museum of Music (B03-0484). Photograph by the author.

11 *Chikusō*. Player's side of tail of instrument illustrated in figure 8. Osaka College of Music, Museum of Music (B03-0484). Photograph by the author.

12 *Chikusō*. Head end. Made by Hata Moritsugu (act. *c.* mid-Meiji) in 1906; *c.* 190 cm long, 24.6 cm wide and 14.4 cm high. Musashino Adademia Musicae, Musical Instrument Museum, Tokyo (A626). Photograph by the author.

Table 3. Frequently Shared Features of *Gakusō*, *Chikusō* and Early Forms of *Zokusō*

Features*

Pointed tongue with near equidistant sides
Key-hole shape sound hole under head
Stylized sound hole under tail
Added decoration such as *maki-e*, marquetry, veneer, mother-of-pearl, and tortoiseshell
Rectangular veneer on upper surface of head
Veneer on long sides
Veneer border around upper surface of tail
Cord nut on fixed bridge at head (*gakusō* strings rest directly on the fixed bridge)
Flatter tail end than the *Yamadagoto*

---

* The *Yamadagoto* differs slightly or does not have these features.

likely, indeed, that Yatsuhashi's introduction of the *in* scale in sōkyoku represents an adaptation of a practice already existing in shamisen music." The fact that this scale was not employed in *sōkyoku* until this period relates to a dichotomy between the elegant (*ga*, as in *gagaku*) and the vulgar (*zoku*, as in *zokusō*) that permeated Japanese arts. Ackermann (1990, 55) believes that the Tsukushigoto "considered itself to be 'elegant' ... and not 'popular/vulgar' ... accordingly it did not make use of half-tone steps, as these were felt to be lewd."

The term sōkyoku[22] describes either solo *koto* music, *koto* and voice (the *koto* player often sings while playing the instrument), or the use of the *koto* in an ensemble with instruments such as the *shamisen*, *shakuhachi* or *kokyū* (three- or four-string fiddle).[23] *Koto* music dating from the time of Yatsuhashi Kengyō falls into several categories. The three best-known styles include *kumiuta* (song cycles with *koto* accompaniment), *danmono* (instrumental pieces) and *jiuta* (alternating voice and instrumental interludes, a form with longer interludes is called *jiuta tegotomono*). Most everyday *koto* traditions trace their lineage to Yatsuhashi, either directly or indirectly, although the term Yatsuhashi-ryū (Yatsuhashi tradition) was not coined until a formal tradition was established by Kagawa Kengyō (1684-1769) and his disciple Kamejima Kengyō (1711-93) in the eighteenth century.[24] As other everyday performance traditions emerged, such as the Ikuta-ryū, Tsuguyama-ryū and Yamada-ryū, names were required to distinguish between them (Adriaansz 1973, 12), even though they all usually trace their lineage back to Yatsuhashi.

Early forms of the *zokusō* share the basic physical features of the *gakusō* and *chikusō* (Table 3). Sometimes instrument makers, or players in a tradition or sub-tradition, might have a personal preference for instrument design or decoration. For example, the *koto* of the Tsuguyama-ryū, which is today usually understood as a branch of the wider Ikuta-ryū, once used a *koto* with front legs that were more curvilinear than other *Ikutagoto*, thus providing a distinct physical feature that helped distinguish this tradition's *koto* from other types (Tanabe and Hirano 1982, 1351).

Zokusō Types: *Ikutagoto*

The *Ikutagoto* originally developed out of the Ikuta-ryū (Ikuta tradition), understood to have been established by Ikuta Kengyō (1656-1715) in Kyoto in 1695. Ikuta Kengyō was a disciple of Kitajima Kengyō (*d*. 1690), who was himself a student of Yatsuhashi Kengyō. The Ikuta tradition was first popular around the Kansai (i.e., Osaka/Kyoto/Nara) area, although today it, like other traditions, are more geographically dispersed. Influenced by the lyrical *shamisen* styles of the region (especially *jiuta*), Ikuta Kengyō changed the design of *koto* plectra to a rectangular shape in order to imitate the sounds of the *shamisen* (i.e., the corner of the plectra used for plucking *koto* strings is similar to the corner of the *shamisen* plectrum). Ikuta Kengyō was also

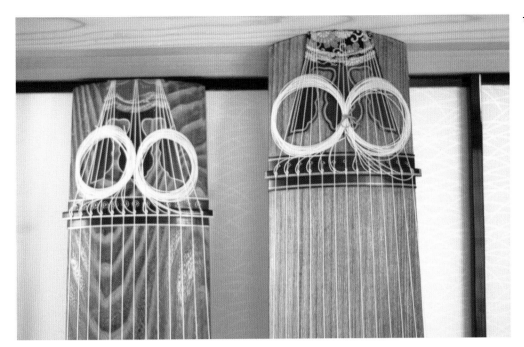

instrumental in combining the *koto* and *shamisen* in *jiuta* ensemble music, and the subsequent use of new *koto* tunings such as *kumoijōshi, hankumoijōshi* and *nakazorajōshi* (*see* Chapter 5) (Kikkawa 1997, 54).

The work that Piggott undertook on Japanese music in the late nineteenth/early twentieth centuries provides a useful description of the various types of *koto* current at that time. With regard to the *Ikutagoto* he notes that:

> The Ikuta-koto is used now almost exclusively in the west of Japan, though occasionally in the east by ladies. Its sides and extremities are covered with elaborate lacquer designs and inlay of tortoise-shell, ivory, and silver; the strings are of different colours, like those of the Western Harp, enabling them to be more easily distinguished and remembered. The *tsumé* are of thick ivory or tortoise-shell set in lacquered stalls, and are cut square at the top. (Piggott [1909] 1971, 110)

While some *Ikutagoto* might have an upper surface that appears identical to that of a *Yamadagoto*, closer inspection reveals that the underneath has Ikuta-ryū sound holes, and the mouth has a pointed tongue (figs 13-15). For example, an *Ikutagoto* housed in the Osaka College of Music (B03-0470) has decoration that is practically identical to that on a *Yamadagoto*, even though the *Ikutagoto* retains such features as the distinctive shape of its sound holes and tongue. Another unique feature of this *Ikutagoto* is on the backboard, where the holes for the removable front legs point toward the length of the backboard rather than across the width as

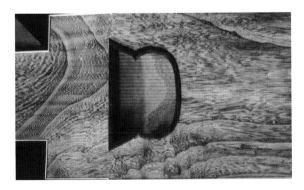

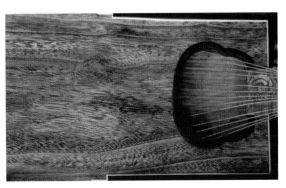

16 Okinawa *koto* (*Ryūkyūgoto*).
Upper surface of tail.
Okinawa, May 2003.
Photograph by the author.

with *Yamadagoto*. Moreover, *Ikutagoto* would usually have a tail end that was not as curved as the one found on *Yamadagoto* (fig. 13). The subsequent popularity of *Yamadagoto* – the first instrument to change significantly the outward appearance of the *koto* – was to influence instrument design considerably in later years. The features of *Yamadagoto* that were sometimes adopted for instruments like *Ikutagoto* included, for example, less lacquer, marquetry and veneer, and the use of a *makurazuno* (ivory or plastic nut) instead of a *makuraito* (cord; also called *itomakura*) on the top of the fixed bridge at the head on which the strings rest.

Ikuta-ryū musicians have now for the most part stopped using *Ikutagoto*, a trend that was especially prevalent in the twentieth century. Instead they prefer *Yamadagoto*, even though there are more *koto* players in the Ikuta-ryū today than in any other tradition.[25] One possible reason for this is that *Yamadagoto* have a stronger sound due to their slightly larger sound chamber, and this is more suitable for larger concert halls (Kishibe 1971, 11). While today the *Yamadagoto* is the predominant type of *zokusō*, even in 1977 the *koto* manufacturer Makimoto Gakki was still advertising seven grades of *Ikutagoto* of various lengths from 5 *shaku*, 5 *sun* (*c.* 167 cm) to 6 *shaku*, 2 *sun* (*c.* 188 cm), and eight grades of *Yamadagoto* all measuring 6 *shaku* (*c.* 182 cm) (*see* Makimoto Gakki 1977).[26] But Makimoto Gakki, like other *koto* makers, does not usually advertise *Ikutagoto*.

However, *koto* makers do still occasionally make *Ikutagoto* or a highly decorated form of this instrument (*see* fig. 16), primarily for use in Okinawa where it is found in several contexts: as an accompanying instrument in folk and classical music and dance, and as a solo instrument (Okinawa Prefectural Board of Education 1998; Thompson 2001, 828). Instrument makers in mainland Japan (i.e., Honshū) generally refer to this instrument as *Ryūkyūgoto* (Ryūkyū *koto*) to delineate its performance location, while players in Okinawa sometimes classify it vis-à-vis other types of *koto* as *nagaiso*. It is normally slightly longer than the standard *Yamadagoto* at about 6 *shaku* 3 *sun* (*c.* 191 cm) (Higa 1992, 792-93).

Zokusō Types: *Yamadagoto*

The type of *koto* known as *Yamadagoto* was derived from the performance tradition established by Yamada Kengyō (1757-1817). This Yamada-ryū (Yamada tradition) was influenced by narrative styles of *shamisen* genres around the Kantō (i.e., Tokyo) region.[27] In addition to the traditional repertoire of *kumiuta*, *danmono* and *jiuta*, the Yamada-ryū has its own genres whose "repertoire includes over 350 pieces. Of these, roughly 40% are still performed with some frequency, and about one quarter of the repertoire, or less than 100 pieces can be considered the current or popular repertoire" (Read 1975, 42-43). Some of these genres include songs with *koto* accompaniment (*utamono*) composed by Yamada Kengyō, adapted compositions from the Ikuta-ryū, and arranged compositions from narrative *shamisen* music (*jōruri*).

Yamada Kengyō modified the structure, performance practice and repertoire of the *koto*. The type of instrument he devised, as well as some other *koto* influenced by its design, does not have the very often copious decoration characteristic of earlier instruments (*see* Chapter Three). Piggott ([1909] 1971, 36-37) notes that in contrast to the *Ikutagoto* and the *gakusō* "in this instrument [the *Yamadagoto*] the eye is gratified only by the beautiful graining of the natural wood, a thing delighted in by the purest Japanese taste." He continues:

In the Yamada-koto, used by all the profession in the east of Japan, superfluous ornament is discarded, the whole art of the maker being devoted to the preparation of the finest wood for the body;[28] only on very costly instruments is a little gold lacquer ornament of the most severe kind introduced. The bridges have again been raised; they are made much stouter, and

Table 4. Comparison of Ikuta-ryū, Yamada-ryū and their *Koto*

Feature	Ikuta-ryū	Yamada-ryū
Region	Kansai (around Osaka/Kyoto/Nara) and toward western Japan	Kantō (around Tokyo) and toward eastern Japan
Sound chamber	Smaller	Larger
Length*	*Honken: c.* 191 cm (6 *shaku* 3 *sun*) *Namiken: c.* 166.8 cm (5 *shaku* 5 *sun*) *Gohachi: c.* 175.7 cm (5 *shaku* 8 *sun*)	*c.* 181.8 cm (6 *shaku*)
Tongue	Pointed with near equidistant sides	Oblique with longer lower side
Shape of tail end	Not as arched	More arched
Pattern formed by strings at tail end	Three groups of strings (4-5-4 or 5-3-5)	Strings usually grouped equidistantly
Sound hole under head	Key-hole shape	Rounder shape
Sound hole under tail	More stylized than *Yamadagoto*	Not as stylized as *Ikutagoto*
Movable bridges**	Smaller than *Yamadagoto*; *c.* 5.1 cm high and 4.7 cm wide at the base	Larger than *Ikutagoto*; *c.* 5.8 cm high and 5.3 cm wide at the base
Front legs	Smaller (usually fixed and with straight sides)	Larger (removable and slightly arched sides)
Kneeling position	At an angle toward tail	Straight on
Top of fixed bridge at head	Originally cord	Ivory or plastic
Plectra (tips)	Rectangular	Pointed or rounded
Music	Influenced by lyrical style of *shamisen* performance	Influenced by narrative style of *shamisen* performance

are either tipped with ivory or made of solid ivory; the strings are of the finest white or yellow silk. The *tsumé* are about an inch long, of ivory in leather stalls, with an elliptical top. On the whole the instrument is more substantial and more workmanlike than the delicately-built Ikuta-koto, and gives a much clearer and more resonant tone. (Piggott [1909] 1971, 110)

* Hirata and Kaihara (1988, 64).
** Tsuda (1983, 167).

The *Yamadagoto* has no veneer, marquetry or *maki-e* decoration on the head, tail or sides, preferring instead to showcase the wood grain pattern of the instrument's main body. Only part of the mouth (i.e., tongue and lips) might have *maki-e*. In contrast to non-*Yamadagoto* that have equidistant pointed tongues, *Yamadagoto* have an oblique tongue with one longer side (the lower one) to enable more surface for decoration to be viewed. Also, the veneer on earlier *koto* that covered some or all of the long sides, head and tail has been replaced in *Yamadagoto* with thin sheets of wood called *shiburoku* (four parts to six) on each side of both fixed bridges on the upper surface that overhang slightly on the long sides.

The *Sōkyoku taiishō*, written in 1779 by Yamada Kengyō's teacher Yamada Shōkoku (act. *c.* 1772-89), illustrated some of the features of modern-day *koto* that demonstrate a break from traditional design. For instance, the instrument depicted in the *Sōkyoku taiishō* named "Akigiri" ("Autumn Mist") has none of the veneer, marquetry and inlay found on previous instruments, even though it retains the same shape sound holes as found on earlier *koto*. However, some smaller-size *koto* mentioned in *Sōkyoku taiishō* actually have the same shape sound holes that are seen today on *Yamadagoto*. An early example of a *Yamadagoto*, in the collection of the Hikone Castle Museum and dated 1808, has identical features to present-day *Yamadagoto* except that it has a small amount of decorative and pictorial inlay on the surface of its head.[29]

Historically, the two main *zokusō* performance traditions – Ikuta-ryū and Yamada-ryū – differed in the type of instrument each group used (*see* Table 4). As noted above, most players from both traditions today prefer to use the *Yamadagoto* (they also share some of the traditional repertoire, but vary considerably in terms of their performance practice – there are also some pieces that are unique to their respective traditions or sub-traditions).[30] While change has occurred in aspects of *koto* construction and performance practice in general, it was only the *Yamadagoto* that initiated significant change since the instrument's introduction to Japan.

Modified, Smaller and Larger Koto

In addition to the types of *koto* outlined above, there are several modified, smaller and larger versions of the instrument that were devised from the Meiji era onward, with new *koto* types still being conceived.[31] When compared to the standard thirteen-string *koto* – or at least a version of it that is perceived as standard – these variants show how the *koto* also represents a family of instrument types. However, these instruments are usually used in very different ways. Modified, smaller and larger *koto* have been, and still are, made in numerous forms, although none has ever achieved the popularity of the standard thirteen-string *koto* (hereafter referred to as "standard *koto*"). The range of variant *koto* types is illustrated in Table 5; some were displayed at a special exhibition in Tokyo in 2001 of such instruments (*see Hōgaku Jānaru* 2001). In the section that follows, several of these *koto* are explored in terms of their connection with the standard *koto*, as well as their impact on and place in traditional Japanese music today.

In the twentieth century some *koto* types were introduced with several component parts that diverged greatly from earlier instruments, but nevertheless attempted to maintain the traditional form as much as possible. Examples of modified *koto* of any size include electric *koto* (*erekutorikkugoto*), which, like some instruments designed for beginners and unlike the standard *koto*, would normally have tuning pins (*nejizuke*) or pegs (*pegu*, i.e., machine heads) placed inside the head end (mouth) and were often visible at the head end (they are sometimes hidden behind a removable plaque). Other more recent modifications to the *koto* are the use of synthetic strings as opposed to silk, folding *koto*,[32] extended string length on some strings,[33] the use of plastics and other synthetic materials for component parts (e.g., *kābongoto jūsangen*,

Table 5. Modified, Smaller and Larger *Koto*

Instrument Name/Term	Instrument Name/Term
Arutogoto (alto *koto*)	*Minichuagoto* (miniature *koto*)
Ayamegoto (iris *koto*; short)	*Minigoto* (mini *koto*)
Bēsugoto (bass *koto*)	*Mijikai koto* (short *koto*)
Bunkagoto (culture *koto*; short)	*Nagaisō* (long *sō*)
Dai-jūshichigen (large seventeen strings)	*Neo-koto* (new *koto*; short)
Erekutorikkugoto (electric *koto*)	*Nijūgen* (twenty strings)
Goshakugoto (5 *shaku koto*)	*Nijūichigensō* (twenty-one string *sō*)
Hachijūgen (eighty strings)	*Poppukōn* (popcorn; seventeen strings)
Hansō (half-size *sō*)	*Sanjūgen* (thirty strings)
Himegoto (small *koto*)	*Sanshakugoto* (3 *shaku koto*)
Imamuragata jūshichigen (Imamura-style seventeen strings)	*Shin-Fukuyamagoto* (new Fukuyama *koto*; short)
Jūgogen (fifteen strings)	*Shō-jūshichigen* (small seventeen strings)
Jūhachigen (eighteen strings)	*Sopuranogoto* (soprano *koto*; short)
Jūrokugen (sixteen strings)	*Tangoto* (short *koto*)
Jūshichigen (seventeen strings; bass)	*Tan-nijūgen* (short twenty-strings)
Kābongoto jūsangen (thirteen-string carbon-fiber *koto*)	*Teion-nijūgen* (or *tei-nijūgen*: bass twenty strings)
Kazune (Japanese sound; short)	*Teion-nijūgogen* (bass twenty-five strings)
Kogatagoto (small-size *koto*)	*Yonshakugoto* (4 *shaku koto*)
Kurumagoto (carriage *koto*)	

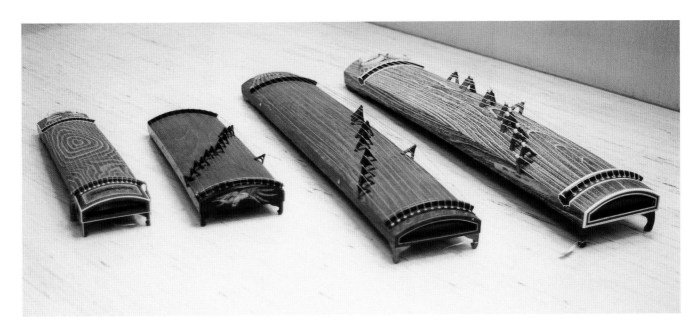

13-string carbon-fiber *koto*), and an extra piece of wood along the side closest to the player on which the movable bridge for the thirteenth string rests in order to keep it steady.[34] Still, these are seen as only slight modifications to extant *koto* form, rather than as new types of instruments in their own right.

As well as such minor modifications to the instrument, several smaller and larger *koto* have been invented over the last century. While these instruments are viewed as versions of the *koto*, they are usually identified by a specific name and hold their own place in *koto* music. Thus, they can be seen as *koto* on one level of discourse, but also as a unique type of instrument on another. These instruments are sometimes classified variously as *tagensō* (many-string *koto*), *atarashii koto* (new *koto*), *niigoto* (new *koto*), or *shinsō* (new *koto*). They are the direct result of a period of modernization from the mid-nineteenth century onward that witnessed immense Westernization, industrialization and modernization. This period of mammoth change affected just about every sphere of Japanese society, and with regard to the development of new types of *koto* shows how modifications in instrument design can reflect changes in society. Many of the new instruments were devised in order to expand or vary the range of the *koto* so as to mimic some of the sounds and instrument ensembles of Western music. In the Meiji era there was widespread adoption of Western art music, which was introduced at schools as the main music of Japanese state education.[35] This policy was espoused by the music educators Izawa Shūji (1851-1917) and the American Luther Whiting Mason (1828-96), who were pivotal in the development of state music education.[36]

Even though most innovations to *koto* design were undertaken after substantial Westernization in the nineteenth century, some smaller types of *koto* were known before this time, especially during the earlier Edo period. For example, the aforementioned collection of *koto* tablature, *Sōkyoku taiishō*, illustrates a smaller-size *koto* measuring 4 *shaku* 1 *sun* 7 *bu* (126.35 cm). This length is considerably shorter than the standard *koto*, as would anything smaller than around 5 *shaku* (151.5 cm). Several terms are used for such smaller *koto*, including *hansō* (half-size *sō*), *ayamegoto* (iris *koto*; fig. 17),[37] *kurumagoto* (carriage *koto*), *himegoto* (small *koto*), *minigoto* (mini *koto*), *mijikai koto* (short *koto*), and *minichuagoto* (miniature *koto*). The larger of these would almost certainly have been played as an alternative to the standard *koto*, while the smaller examples would be used as toys, models or as props in *kabuki* and *bunraku* theater.

A small *koto* of the early twentieth century was the *tangoto* (short *koto*).[38] Devised by the *koto* composer and virtuoso player Miyagi Michio (1894-1956), it had the same pitch as the

17 *Ayamegoto. Left, c.* 75 cm long and made in the middle of the nineteenth century; *second from left, c.* 69 cm long and made by Hata Moritsugu around the end of the nineteenth century; *second from right, c.* 129 cm long and made around the middle of the nineteenth century (also labeled *ryōsō* [enjoyable *sō*]); *right, c.* 135 cm long and made by Torii Masahi. Osaka College of Music, Museum of Music (B03-0404, B03-0403, B03-0402, B03-0886). Photograph by the author.

standard *koto* and was about 4 *shaku* (121.2 cm) long. It was made by the instrument manufacturer Tsurukawa Koto-Shamisen-ten and first sold in early 1932 (Chiba 1989b). Initially tuning pins were positioned on the upper surface of the head (Chiba and Chiba 1993, 57); on later instruments these were hidden inside the mouth. Earlier versions also had folding front legs and smaller movable bridges on the lowest four strings (Prescott 1997, 83-84). Tanabe (1964, 235-36) notes four advantages of the *tangoto*, points which might also be applied to many other types of smaller *koto*: its convenience, as the standard *koto* was too big and too long to carry easily; its smaller size, which meant that it was cheaper; its strings, which were easier to tighten than those of the standard *koto*; and its size, which enabled the player to sit in a chair.

Some instrument makers manufacture other types of smaller *koto* according to the Japanese measurement system using the unit *shaku* (30.3 cm). For instance, Fujita Fusahiko, a *koto* maker in Fukuyama City in Hiroshima Prefecture, produces four main sizes of *koto*: *sanshakugoto* (3 *shaku koto*: 90.9 cm), *yonshakugoto* (4 *shaku koto*: 121.2 cm), *goshakugoto* (5 *shaku koto*: 151.5 cm), and *rokushakugoto* (6 *shaku koto*: 181.8 cm), the latter being the standard size instrument (fig. 18).[39] Other makers, however, might simply design smaller *koto* without adhering to specific measurements.

18 **Small *koto*.**
   Left, sanshakugoto;
   center, yonshakugoto;
   right, goshakugoto.
   Instruments made by Fujita Fusahiko and also referred to by the maker as *mijikai koto* (short *koto*). Fukuyama, June 1997. Photograph by the author.

In 2001, the *koto* manufacturing cooperative Fukuyama Hōgakki Seizōgyō Kyōdō Kumiai (Fukuyama Traditional Japanese Musical Instrument Manufacturing Cooperative) introduced a new type of *koto* called *shin-Fukuyamagoto* (new Fukuyama *koto*). This instrument is 4 *shaku* 5 *sun* (*c*. 136 cm) long and retains the same width as the standard *koto*. The *shin-Fukuyamagoto* has been designed at a time when makers are increasingly looking to the new education market as a result of the legislation passed in 2002 requiring that all school children learn about traditional Japanese music. Smaller *koto* like *shin-Fukuyamagoto* would be easier to store and transport, and maintenance such as tuning and changing strings – often a problem for most *koto* players – could be managed through the use of tuning pins. Another smaller *koto* that keeps the pitch of the standard *koto* is the *neo-koto* (new *koto*),[40] which was first made in 1994 by the company Neo Kikaku (Neo Plan). Measuring about 120 cm long, it has smaller bridges and a shorter vibrating string length (112 cm, a standard *koto* is *c*. 150 cm) than the standard *koto*, as well as tuning pins, and a colored set of strings (a longer version also with tuning pins is made at 183 cm).

The proliferation of small *koto* due to changing educational requirements and cultural needs is evidenced by other more recent additions such as the *kazune* (Japanese sound; *kogatagoto* [small-size *koto*]; *see Hōgaku Jānaru* 2001, 52; Mizuhara 2000). This *koto* is made by Iwate-ken Kōgyō Gijutsu Sentā (Iwate Prefecture Industrial Technological Center) and was first promoted for use in education (especially at primary level) in 2000. It is 90 cm (*c*. 3 *shaku*) long, and has the same width as the standard *koto*, but unusually it does not have a backboard. An even smaller instrument is the *bunkagoto* (culture *koto*). First marketed by the Zen'on company in the mid-1990s, this *koto* is 86 cm long and 20 cm wide. It is normally played on a high stand or table, has string numerals written to the left of the fixed bridge at the head, and its notation uses Arabic numerals on strings 1-10 and *kanji* for strings 11-13. Another type of smaller *koto* that has a higher pitch than the standard *koto* is the *sopuranogoto* (soprano *koto*; fig. 19). Use of this instrument began in the 1960s and 1970s in ensemble music, which required a range of registers beyond the standard *koto*. In comparison with the standard *koto*, its strings are thinner and the movable bridges are about half the size. Usually around 118 cm long, the *sopuranogoto* normally has tuning pins in its mouth.

In the Meiji and Taishō eras there were several attempts at designing larger types of *koto*. One such instrument, the *nijūichigensō* (twenty-one string *sō*), was made in 1881 by Tokyo Music School as the result of the collaboration between Yamada-tradition *koto* player Yamase Shōin (1845-1908) and *koto* maker Shigemoto Iwajirō. The *nijūichigensō* was 185.5 cm long, somewhat longer than the standard *koto* (*see* Chiba 1995, 2; Tōkyō Geijutsu Daigaku Geijutsu Shiryōkan 1994, 24). Another example was the *nagaisō* (long *sō*), devised in 1919 by Yonekawa Kin'ō (1883-1969) together with Nomura Kitarō and Yamanaka Toraichi of the instrument manufacturer

19 Three *koto* types. *Left, sopuranogoto; center, koto; right, jūshichigen.* Collection of Matsuzaki Shūsetsu (Ikuta-ryū). Ogōri, July 1990. Photograph by the author.

20 Head end of *jūshichigen* illustrated in figure 19 on *torii* stand. The removable tongue is shown in front of the instrument. Collection of Matsuzaki Shūsetsu (Ikuta-ryū). Ogōri, July 1990. Photograph by the author.

Nomura Gakki-ten. However, it was only several years later that the idea of larger *koto* was fully realized, inspired by the popularity of Miyagi Michio and his invention of new *koto* types.

Like his pivotal role in the development of the smaller *tangoto*, Miyagi Michio was influential in the conception of new, larger *koto*. He designed several, the most noteworthy the *jūshichigen*[41] (seventeen strings) and the *hachijūgen* (eighty strings). The *jūshichigen* was invented in the early 1920s following the collaboration between Miyagi, musicologist Tanabe Hisao and *koto* maker Tsurukawa Shinbee (Prescott 1997, 76). The earliest *jūshichigen* was 8 *shaku* (242.4 cm) long and had tuning pins on the end of the upper surface of the head. It was first used in public on 30 October 1921 with Miyagi's compositions "Hanamifune" ("Flower Viewing Boat"; score now lost), and "Ochiba no Odori" ("Dance of the Falling Leaves"). According to Prescott (1997, 81), "Miyagi created the *jūshichigen* to fill what he perceived as a gap in traditional Japanese music, the lack of a bass voice." Having a bass register, the *jūshichigen* was originally designed for use in an ensemble, although today it increasingly appears as a solo instrument too (figs. 19-21). While working within music styles known as *Meiji shinkyoku* (new music of the Meiji era) and *shin-nihon ongaku* (new Japanese music, or *shin-nihon ongaku undō* [new Japanese music movement])[42] – the latter reaching an apex in the 1920s – Miyagi and others working in this new style of Japanese music were according to Katsumura (1986, 165-66): "driven to innovation by their quest for lower pitch register and larger sound density in order to create ensembles of larger size than traditional ensembles.

21 Four *koto* types. *Left to right, koto, nijūgen, jūshichigen*, and *sanjūgen*. Workshop of *koto* maker Mitsuya Koto Seizō. Saitama, June 1997. Photograph by the author.

In this respect we could also say that the 1920s, the incipient stage of *Shin nihon ongaku*, is characterized by endeavours to explore Western-oriented orchestrational styles with Japanese traditional instruments." It should be remembered that these musicians were extremely conversant in Western music, and Miyagi's musical style included many ideas directly adopted from Western music, including harmony, triple meter and tremolo effects.

A smaller version of the *jūshichigen* was made by Tsurukawa in 1923. With a length of 7 *shaku* (212.1 cm), this *shō-jūshichigen* (small seventeen strings) was so named to distinguish it from the larger instrument, termed accordingly *dai-jūshichigen* (large seventeen strings). The *shō-jūshichigen* was initially played in 1924 with the piece "Sakura Hensōkyoku" ("Sakura Variations") (Chiba 1995). Today, the length of the *jūshichigen* generally spans 210 to 230 cm, depending on the maker, and has tuning pins either on the upper surface (*uenejizuke*) or inside the mouth (*kuchimae nejizuke*), strings that are progressively thinner from the lower to the upper range, and, in comparison to the standard *koto*, larger movable bridges and thicker plectra.

The *jūshichigen* is still very much part of Japanese music. One contemporary *koto* player, Sawai Kazue (*b.* 1941), for example, comments on "the force of sound you can get from the bass koto [*jūshichigen*]. There are so many kinds of sounds. ... It is an instrument that fits contemporary society well" (in Falconer 1993, 89). Similar to several other new *koto* types devised following Western influence on the Japanese soundscape, the *jūshichigen* began as an experimental instrument, but different from those that are no longer used or have yet to stand the test of time, the *jūshichigen* has an established place in new traditional Japanese music. As Katsumura (1986, 168) notes, Miyagi's "*jūshichigen* offered greater possibilities for the development of various new playing techniques suggested by those of Western string instruments. These features eventually proved to be the means by which Miyagi was able to orient his musical style toward a new phase of traditional music under the strong influence of Western music." The instrument occupies a unique place in Japanese music in that it can provide a lower part to the standard *koto* in ensemble playing, or can be used as a solo instrument in its own right (*see also* Andō 1982; Prescott 1997; Tanabe 1974).

Another type of seventeen-string *koto* was devised by Naitō Masako in 2000. Introducing a clever play on words, Naitō called this instrument *poppukōn* (popcorn), explaining that the origin of the name "*poppukōn*" is a mixture of Western and Japanese terms.[43] The first part of the word – *poppu* – is a Japanization of the English term "popular" and is written in the *katakana* phonetic script, while the second part of the word – *kōn* – is used as a modified reading of the *kanji* for "*kin*" (one of the characters used for the *koto*). Unlike Miyagi's seventeen-string *koto*, this is not a bass instrument. One-hundred twenty centimeters long, it is as wide as a standard *koto*, with a range of around two and a half octaves. It has tuning pins in the head extremity, and like some longer and shorter instruments does not have the oak-leaf decoration (*kashiwaba*) on its tail. One striking feature of this instrument is its bright colors – pink, blue or yellow. This contrasts vividly with the standard *koto*, which is made to emphasize the beauty of the wood grain on the soundboard and long sides.

An eighty-string *koto*, *hachijūgen* (eighty strings; fig. 22), was devised by Miyagi Michio and built by Tsurukawa Shinbee and Tsurukawa Kihee (Chiba 1989a; Kamisangō 1979; Kikkawa 1984a, 817; Prescott 1997, 81-83). Its strings and movable bridges varied in size, and it was built to have a range similar to a piano. Measuring 9 cm high, it was about 213 cm long, 98 cm and 37 cm wide at its widest and narrowest points, respectively. Tuning pins were positioned on top of the head in three rows, and the player would sit in a chair. The *hachijūgen* was used only once in public performance on 26 November 1929 at Japan Youth Hall (Nihon Seinenkan Hōru) in Tokyo by Miyagi with the pieces "Kyō no Yorokobi" ("Today's Joy"), which was originally composed for *koto* and *jūshichigen* (Chiba 1993), and a transcription of a J. S. Bach "Prelude". Sadly, the instrument was destroyed in an air raid in 1945. A reconstruction made in 1978 by Tsurukawa is today housed in the Miyagi Michio Memorial Museum, Tokyo.

22 Head end of *hachijūgen*. Miyagi Michio Memorial Museum, Tokyo. Photograph by the author.

There have been several other larger *koto*, some as bass instruments and others with a range wider than the standard *koto*. Some are named according to their pitch, such as the standard-size *arutogoto* (alto *koto*) or *bēsugoto* (bass *koto*; an electric instrument 106 cm long), and others are named according to the number of strings, sometimes using either the suffix *koto* (*goto*) or *sō*. In addition to the seventeen- and eighty-string *koto*, a number of other instruments with more than the usual thirteen strings were designed in the twentieth century, including the *jūgogen* (fifteen strings),[44] *jūrokugen* (sixteen strings), *jūhachigen* (eighteen strings), *nijūgen* (twenty strings; fig. 21), and *sanjūgen* (thirty strings; fig. 21). Of these, the *nijūgen* has received much attention in recent years and is rapidly growing in popularity. Designed in 1968 and first used by Ikuta-tradition *koto* player Nosaka Keiko in 1969 (*see also* Miki 1996; Nosaka 1996; Wade 1994), the instrument was a collaborative effort between the composer Miki Minoru (*b.* 1930), director of the *gendai hōgaku* (contemporary, traditional Japanese music) group Nihon Ongaku Shūdan (Pro Musica Nipponia or Ensemble Nipponia) that Nosaka joined in 1965, industrial designer Komiya Kiyoshi, and *koto* maker Ogawa Hideo (Wade 1994, 236-37). Ogawa had already made a thirty-string *koto* (*sanjūgen*) for the Yamada-tradition player Miyashita Shūretsu (*b.* 1909) in 1955. Unlike the bass *jūshichigen*, Wade (1994, 234) points out that the *nijūgen* was intended "to be a complete instrument in itself" and "it is entirely possible to play the repertoire of traditional koto compositions ... by using only 13 of the higher-pitched strings." Moreover, a type of *koto* was needed that could meet the range of contemporary compositions (Wade 1994, 240).[45] Of particular interest is that the *nijūgen* continued to be developed by adding further strings, while at the same time retaining the name *nijūgen*. Nosaka first played a twenty-one string version in concert in 1971; a twenty-two string version in 1989; and in 1991 a twenty-three string version. In 1991, a twenty-five string version of the instrument was made. Compared to the first type of *nijūgen*, this latest version added three strings to the lower register and two to the upper. Several other varieties of *nijūgen* also exist: *teion-nijūgen* (or *tei-nijūgen* [bass twenty strings]); *teion-nijūgogen* (bass twenty-five strings); and *tan-nijūgen* (short twenty-string). Nosaka estimated that in the early 1990s around 600 *nijūgen* had been produced (Wade 1994, 259). In her summary of the place of the *nijūgen* generally, Wade (1994, 232) notes that "the development of the 20-stringed koto occurred as a result of modernization, [and] it is not an example of 'Westernization'." The evolution of the *nijūgen* is testimony to the types of changes that were driven by internal forces within Japan, which were very different to the latter nineteenth century when Western trends were the primary catalysts.

As outlined in this chapter, there are several kinds of *koto*. Slight differences in construction and decoration enable us to distinguish between instrument types, thereby contributing to the identity of the performance tradition in which certain *koto* are used. On the one hand, similarities between standard *koto* (e.g., size, number of strings and shape) demonstrate that the fundamental form of the instrument has remained unaltered since its introduction to Japan. On the other, it is the slight variation in outer decoration and modifications to form that create the instrument's identity within a particular performance tradition. From the *gakusō* to the experimental instruments of recent years, the *koto* in its multitude of forms often possesses specific characteristics that contribute to the identity of the group in which it is used. That is, while variation between performance traditions is typically defined by performance practice and repertoire, the actual form of the *koto* utilized in any specific tradition is likely to have features that either associate it directly with a particular tradition, or is made in such a way that identifies the instrument's place in a culture of distinctiveness and difference. It is from this perspective that the following chapter considers the structure of the *koto* and its signifiers of cultural meaning.

Katsukawa Shuntei (1770-1820). A Young Woman Playing a *Koto*, from the series *Hanagasaren shichifukujin* (*The Seven Gods of Good Fortune for the Hanagasa Poetry Club*), 1821. Square *surimono* (privately published de-luxe print), 215 x 189 mm. Gemeentemuseum Den Haag (PRM-0000-2311).

3 Manufacture and Component Parts

Instrument Makers and the Construction Process

The form and function of the *koto* is wrapped in layers of cultural meaning. From the instrument in its entirety to each of its component parts, *koto* are made slightly differently within a hierarchy of instrument types based on aesthetic and material value. Furthermore, while the component parts of the *koto* carry their own meaning, some are an extension of an aesthetic language found throughout Japanese culture. A study of the manufacture and component parts of the *koto* not only explains why instruments have slight differences in form, but also and perhaps most importantly, it assists in a broader understanding of Japanese culture.

The instrument that is the focus of this chapter is the *Yamadagoto* type of *zokusō*. The discussion includes a survey of the construction process from the raw materials to the finished instrument (*cf.* figs. 23-24). As part of this is a description of each of the instrument's component parts and their place and purpose on the *koto*. Considering the relative ubiquity of *Yamadagoto* today among everyday *koto* players, the design of the instrument between different makers is remarkably similar, with only specific techniques of manufacture and intricacies of decoration at times varying. Most differences in the manufacture of the *Yamadagoto* are to do with the assorted grades that are determined by material and monetary value (i.e., quality of instrument).

About seventy percent of all *koto* are produced in Fukuyama City, Hiroshima Prefecture (Hirata 1996, 60). Most *koto* makers in Fukuyama are members of the cooperative Fukuyama Hōgakki Seizōgyō Kyōdō Kumiai (Fukuyama Traditional Japanese Musical Instrument Manufacturing Cooperative; also known as Fukuyamagoto [Fukuyama *koto*], hereafter referred to as the FHSKK). The FHSKK was formed in 1982 from twelve businesses that ranged from one-man workshops to larger companies with around eighty employees. Today, however, FHSKK consists of eight workshops (some businesses have left the cooperative or have closed down),

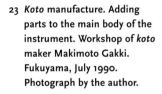

23 *Koto* manufacture. Adding parts to the main body of the instrument. Workshop of *koto* maker Makimoto Gakki. Fukuyama, July 1990. Photograph by the author.

including a *maki-e* (gold/silver lacquer) specialist. Their annual level of *koto* production averages around 13,000-14,000 instruments.[1]

In addition to *koto* production, FHSKK also sponsors concerts and holds a *koto* memorial service (*koto kuyō*) every year on 6 June (*hōgaku no hi*, or Traditional Japanese Music Day) at a Buddhist temple in Tomo no Ura, a town nearby Fukuyama City. Following the service several instruments are often burned as a supplication for future good fortune. The ritual takes place for most of the morning, and in the afternoon a *koto* concert, *koto matsuri* (*koto* festival), is given by local junior high school *koto* groups. The ritual is part of a social sphere of *koto* manufacture in what DeVale, in her study of musical instruments and ritual, would call the receptive mode of musical instrument participation in music where "the instrument is the focus of the ritual; that is, a ceremony or ritual procedure is performed on or for the instrument itself" (1988, 127).

Koto makers in Fukuyama and elsewhere divide the manufacturing process into several clearly defined stages (Hirata and Kaihara 1988, 101):

1. Lumbering
    a. Selection of wood
    b. Measuring
    c. Marking
    d. Sawing
2. Drying
    a. Seasoning
3. Shaping the Body
    a. Scooping out
    b. Shaping
    c. Carving
    d. Scorching
    e. Polishing
4. Attaching Added Parts/Decoration
    a. *Shiburoku*[2]
    b. Fixed bridges
    c. Oak leaf
    d. Lips
    e. Tongue
    f. *Maki-e* (not on all instruments)
    g. Sound holes
    h. Legs
5. Completion
    a. String hole supports
    b. Adjustment
    c. Inspection

24 *Koto* manufacture in Kyoto. From *Jinrinkinmōzui* (*Illustrations of Everyday Life*, 1690), a woodblock-printed illustrated book depicting everyday scenes. Courtesy Heibonsha. Reprinted by permission from *Jinrinkinmōzui* ([1690] 1990, 215).

Smaller businesses generally divide their workshop into several areas to accommodate the various parts of the manufacturing process, while larger businesses might have separate workshops where the stages of the manufacturing process are carried out. For instruments that have *maki-e* applied to the tongue and/or lips and, on some rarer instruments, to other parts of the body, the *maki-e* application is usually undertaken by a specialist at an independent business. Strings are sometimes added later by the retailer. *Koto* makers assume all the costs of the materials for *koto* production, which normally entails sourcing some ready-made component parts from other suppliers, such as metal fittings, strings, brocade, covers, and cases. Wood too is purchased from a supplier, but only as a raw material.

Koto manufacture also occurs outside Japan, but to a much lesser extent. With the introduction of the revised middle school curriculum in 2002, it is thought that about 4.4 million middle school students will now be learning a traditional Japanese musical instrument (*Trends in Japan* 2001). Subsequently, *koto* sales have increased substantially in recent years. Indeed, as one commentator has asked, "will the koto and *shamisen* one day take the place of the piano and violin as the most popular instruments being learned by Japanese children?" (*Trends in Japan* 2001). It should be remembered that since the Meiji era Western music has dominated Japanese music education, with such instruments as the piano and violin being widely learned both within and outside school. The introduction of the new curriculum underlies the recent surge in sales and design innovation, which includes a number of new *koto* types, like the somewhat smaller, lightweight instruments that cater to the educational market (*see* Johnson 2003). In order to meet these new demands and to profit from cheaper labor some manufacturers are now having instruments made in China (*Asahi Shimbun* 2002).[3]

Nomenclature of the Component Parts

The *koto* has many component parts named after the *ryū* (dragon) (figs. 25-26). In everyday discourse, however, many of these parts are often referred to without the term. The physical form of the *koto* with its long soundboard (a dragon's body), one raised end (a dragon's head) and movable bridges along its surface (a dragon's spine), is easily likened to that of a dragon. In fact, some music books and *koto* scores illustrate the *koto* together with its zoomorphic nomenclature alongside a picture of a dragon as a way of reinforcing the connection between the shape of the instrument and the shape of a dragon (e.g., Sakamoto 1945, 8). The association of the dragon in Japan with, for example, good luck, power and the emperor, contributes to the instrument's special significance by providing it with an auspicious reference to other spheres of Japanese culture. Also, some *koto* are made with a rectangular decoration on the upper surface of the head (i.e., on most *koto* other than *Yamadagoto*), in which a dragon

25 *Chikusō*. Outline and nomenclature. "Jūsangen Tsukushigoto no zu" ("Thirteen-string Tsukushigoto Figure"), from the illustrated book of *koto* song texts, *Busōgafu taiseishō* (1805, n.p.). Kyoto Prefectural Library and Archives.

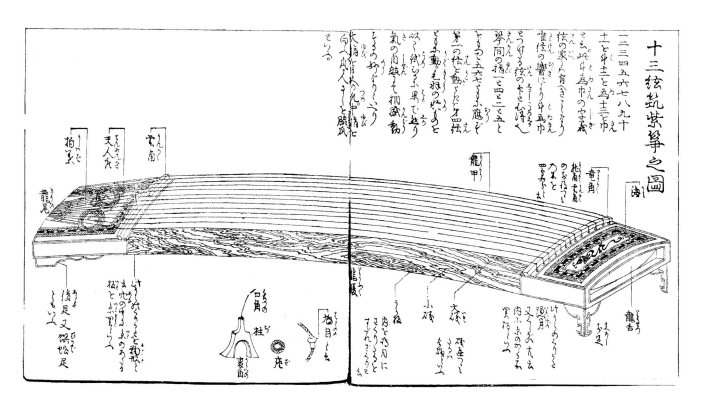

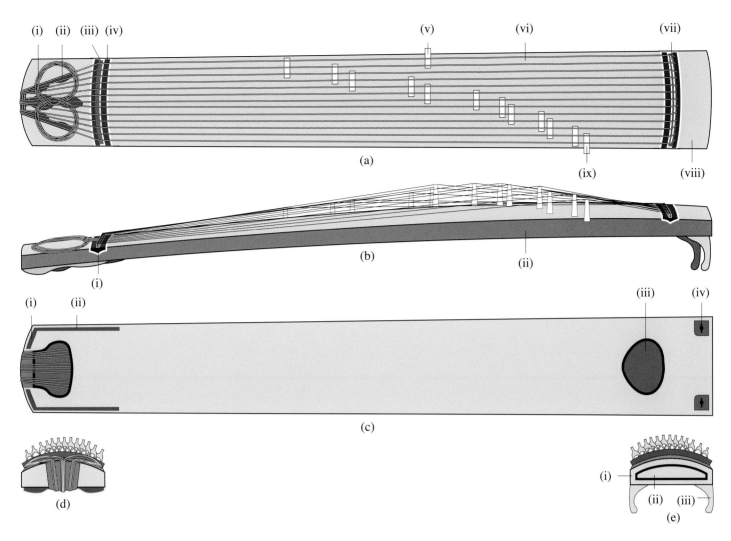

26 *Yamadagoto*. Outline and nomenclature. *(a)* Upper surface of soundboard: (*i*) String coils; (*ii*) Oak leaf (*kashiwaba* or *kashiwagata*); (*iii*) Fixed bridge at tail (*ryūkaku* [dragon's horn]; *unkaku* [cloud horn]). The fixed bridge at the head end is called *ryūkaku*, and the string holes (at head and tail) are called *ryūgan* (dragon's eyes); (*iv*) Strips each side of fixed bridges (*shiburoku* [four parts to six]); (*v*) Movable bridge for the first string (*kotoji* [koto bridge]); (*vi*) Soundboard (*ryūkō* [dragon's back]; *kō* [shell]; *omoteita* [front board]); (*vii*) Raised nut in center of fixed bridge (*makurazuno* [pillor horn]); (*viii*) Head (*ryūtō* [dragon's head]; *ryūzu* [dragon's head]; *tōbu* [head part]; *ryūgaku* [dragon's forehead]). The part of the instrument between the long side and the closest string hole is called *ryūken* (dragon's eyelids). Many non-*Yamadagoto* have a rectangular part called *umi* (sea) or *tamado* (jeweled door; the door to a shrine) on the surface of the head; (*ix*) Movable bridge for the thirteenth string (*kinji* [thirteenth bridge]). *(b)* View of player's side of soundboard: (*i*) Side of the border of the fixed bridge (*sagari* [hanging over]); (*ii*) Side of soundboard (*iso* [beach]). The sides toward the head are called *ryūkyō* (dragon's cheek). *(c)* Backboard. The backboard is called *uraita* (backboard), *ryūfuku* (dragon's belly) or *ryūhai* (dragon's back): (*i-ii*) Legs under tail (*ryūshi* [dragon's legs]; *ryūkyaku* [dragon's legs]; *ryūsoku* [dragon's legs]; *atoashi* [lower legs]; *shimoashi* [lower legs]; *ryūde* [dragon's hands]; *ryūshu* [dragon's legs]; *ushiroashi* [back legs]; *mukadeashi* [centipede legs]; *mukōashi* [opposite legs]; *nagaashi* [long legs]); (*iii*) Sound hole (*inketsu* [sound hole]; *otoana* [sound hole]; *onketsu* [sound hole]; *maruguchi* [round hole]; *ryūku* [dragon's mouth]; *ue no ana* [upper hole], i.e., under head; *shita no ana* [lower hole], i.e., under tail; *uraana* [back hole], i.e., under tail); (*iv*) Hole in which the front legs are attached. *(d)* Tail end (*ryūbi* [dragon's tail]; *bibu* [tail part]; *tenjinza* [celestial seat]). The strings rest on a piece of brocade (*ogire*). *(e)* Head end (*ryūkō* [dragon's mouth]; *kuchimae* [front mouth]): (*i*) *Ryūshin* (dragon's lips); (*ii*) *Ryūzetsu* (dragon's tongue); (*iii*) *Ryūde* (dragon's hands) (also *ryūshu* [dragon's hands], *ryūkyaku* [dragon's feet], *maeashi* [front feet], *kamiashi* [upper feet], *nekoashi* [cat's paws], *ashi* [feet]).

figure is sometimes included, thus adding to the importance of the dragon nomenclature (fig. 12; *cf.* figs. 4, 6-9). The name of the rectangular section (*umi* or sea) adds to the symbolic meaning of the dragon as a mythical creature closely associated with water.

The dragon has immense significance in Japanese culture and is linked to the emperor and Buddhism (*see* de Visser [1913] 1969). Given its powerful symbolism, it is not surprising that there are several Japanese musical instruments with a dragon association. In addition to the *koto*, these include the *wagon* (six-string zither), *ichigenkin* (one-string zither) and *nigenkin* (two-string zither; or *yakumogoto*), each of which has a dragon nomenclature (Tanabe 1964, 50, 66, 72); *gyoban*, a fish-shaped slit drum used in Buddhist temples that depicts two dragons; *bonshō*, a Buddhist temple bell that is surmounted by the head of a dragon; and the *ryūteki* (dragon flute) of *gagaku* (court music), which has sometimes featured a dragon-shaped end. In *gagaku*, the motif of the dragon, together with the phoenix, can also decorate *dadaiko* (the two very large drums that are used in *bugaku*, a *gagaku* dance form), *kakko* (drum) and *gakudaiko* (double sided drum).[4]

Size

The standard *Yamadagoto* is usually 6 *shaku* (*c.* 182 cm) long. Historically, however, *koto* have been made in several sizes depending on the genre and region in which they are produced and used, with instruments ranging from about 5 *shaku* (151.5 cm) to 6 *shaku* 4 *sun* (193.92 cm) (Tanabe and Hirano 1982, 1350).[5] Miyazaki's (1979) comparison of thirty-five *koto* (thirty-one *gakusō* and four *Yamadagoto*) housed at the Hikone Castle Museum and spanning the Kamakura to Edo periods demonstrates clearly the amount of variation in instrument size even in these few specimens. The longest of these instruments is 191.8 cm, the shortest 122.8 cm, although instruments under about 166 cm are discussed as medium- or small-sized *koto* and not generally considered standard instruments. A *koto* in the instrument museum at Osaka College of Music also has unusual measurements. This experimental *Yamadagoto* (B03-0457) is 7 *shaku* (*c.* 210 cm) long, an instrument size that never became popular (Ōsaka Ongaku Daigaku Fuzoku Gakki Hakubutsukan 1984, 91). With *koto* that are considered to be of a standard size, slight differences in length might be explained simply by the size and quality of the wood available, or by the preference of the maker or player.

Historical and regional variation in the unit of measurement called *honken* (main distance) – used for *koto* as well as in Japanese architecture – has also influenced the size of *koto*.

> There is a special value to be placed on the *ken* (the length of the standard architectural module) in certain parts of the Kansai region. ... That is, whereas the official definition of the *ken* makes it 1.82 meters . ..., a common Kansai use of the same unit takes it to be 1.97 meters.[6] ... A possible way of explaining the discrepancy is simply to say that that unit represents the unit of length that Japanese architects – in whatever part of Japan they may be – take as their basic measuring unit. The *ken* is thus the length of a *tatami* [woven rush mat], or twice the width of one, or the distance between two successive vertical supports in a traditional building. It should be understood from this that the modular nature of Japanese architecture makes for uniformity in any locality in the values to be placed on the basic counting units used in constructing buildings. (Webb 1983, 239)

Variation in length is especially apparent within *zokusō* performance traditions that are predominant within a specific region. For example, the standard length of *koto* in Kyoto was 6 *shaku* 3 *sun* (*c.* 191 cm; called *Kyōma* [Kyoto *ma*]),[7] in Edo (later Tokyo) 6 *shaku* (*c.* 182 cm; called *Edoma* [Edo *ma*]) and in Osaka 5 *shaku* 8 *sun* (*c.* 176 cm; called *gohachi* ['five, eight']). The

Table 6. Comparison of Instruments Sizes

Instrument Part	*Gakusō* (cm)	*Ikutagoto* (cm)	*Yamadagoto* (cm)
Length of soundboard between center of head and tail	191.5	176.5	182.5
Length of long sides between side of head and tail	190.15	not listed	not listed
Width at head end	26.3	24.1	24.7
Width at tail end	25.7	22.9	23.5
Height at center of head end	8.3	6.8	8.0
Height with front legs	not listed	11.8	15.9
Height at center of tail end	8.1	6.7	7.0
Height including tail legs	not listed	7.9	8.9

Source: Shōsōin (1967, 77) for the *gakusō*; Tsuda (1983, 166-67) for the *Ikutagoto* and *Yamadagoto*,
in this case part of the Kyō Ikuta-ryū (Kyoto Ikuta tradition), Shimo-ha (Lower Faction).

Table 7. Curvature and Height of a *Yamadagoto*

Position	Tail End (cm)	Fixed Bridge at Tail (cm)	Position 40-70 cm from Head (cm)	Fixed Bridge at Head (cm)	Head End (cm)
Length of widthwise curve across soundboard	24.6	25.1	27	26.5	26.1
Height from ground to top of soundboard with front and back legs	9.5	11.2	18.3	17.7	16.8
Height from ground to bottom of backboard with front and back legs	1.9	3.8	9	9.5	9.2
Thickness of long sides (i.e., soundboard and backboard)*	3.8	3.9	4.8	4.3	4.1

Source: Instrument purchased by the author in 1988 from Kikuya Gakki-ten, Hokkaidō.
* Measured from the lower side of the backboard to the upper side of the soundboard at the point where the curve of the soundboard begins.

measurement 5 *shaku* 5 *sun* (c. 165 cm; called *namiken* [average *ken*]; or *gogo* ['five, five']) and others were also known (Tanabe and Hirano 1982, 1350). The measurements of several *koto* types are shown in Table 6, where basic dimensions are compared in order to illustrate the diversity in size between instruments belonging to a particular performance tradition. The regional variation in instrument dimensions reflects the historical distribution of *koto* performance traditions. The size of *Ikutagoto* in Kyoto was based on the *Kyōma*, in Osaka the *gohachi* and for *Yamadagoto* in the Kantō area the *Edoma*. With the influence of the new capital, Tokyo, from the Meiji era onward, the *Edoma* became the official unit for the *ken*, and hence standardized the measurement throughout the country.

The width of the *koto* is ordinarily around 23 and 25 cm at the tail and head, respectively. The height of the main body of the *koto*, including removable front legs and fixed tail legs, ranges from about 9.5 cm to 18.5 cm along different parts of the instrument. (The movable bridges are about a further 5 cm.) The arch-shaped body gives a greater space between the backboard and the floor toward its center (Table 7).

Materials

The main part of the *koto* body comprises an upper soundboard and a lower backboard. Both are made from *kiri* (paulownia), a fast-growing soft wood. *Kiri* is rare and extremely expensive in Japan today and is now mostly imported from North America, China and Korea. Paulownia wood is used for several other Japanese zithers such as the *ichigenkin*, *nigenkin* and *wagon*, as well as traditional objects such as clogs (*geta*) and chests of drawers (*tansu*).

In Japan, the *kiri* tree has auspicious connotations. Its leaf is used as an imperial family crest associated with the empress, and this connection is seen in the first verse of the *koto kumiuta* (song cycles with *koto* accompaniment) "Kiritsubo" ("The Paulownia Court") by the founder of everyday *zokusō koto* performance, Yatsuhashi Kengyō (1614-85). The piece refers to passages from the eleventh-century literary classic *Genji monogatari*:

Kiritsubo no	The Emperor's vow
kōi no	Of everlasting love
hiyoku-renri no	With the lady of the Paulownia Court –
chigiri mo	To share a wing in the sky and
sadame naki yo no	A branch on earth –
narai tote	How sad to see it
yume no aida zo	An empty dream,
kanashiki	The fate of this transient life.
	(Tsuge 1983a, 16)

Wood harder than the soft *kiri* is usually used for the parts that are added to the body of the *koto*, such as the fixed bridges, *shiburoku*, oak leaf, mouth (including lips and tongue), legs under the head, legs under the tail, and the rims of the sound holes. The wood used for these parts is now by and large imported to Japan from India and comes in various grades depending on the type of wood. From the most to least expensive they are: *kōki* (also called *kōboku* [high-quality red sandalwood]), *tagayasan* (ironwood), *kokutan* (ebony), *shitan* (red sandalwood or rosewood), *karin* (Chinese quince), and *sakura* (cherry). On very expensive instruments such parts might be made of solid ivory. In addition to *kiri* and harder woods, other materials such as polyester, nylon, silk, lacquer (including *maki-e*), brocade, metal, paper, bone, horn, ivory, plastic, and celluloid are frequently employed for some of the smaller component parts that are added to the main body. On some *koto* other than *Yamadagoto*, decoration such as mother-of-pearl, tortoiseshell and marquetry are also sometimes utilized (*see* figs. 5-12, 16).

Soundboard

The wooden soundboard (*omoteita*) of the *koto* comprises the main upper part of the instrument body. It has a lengthwise and widthwise curve with a central apex; the widthwise curve is more acute at the head end than at the tail. *Kiri* planks are cut lengthwise following the measurements of a long ruler known as *isogata* (beach shape), a name in keeping with the instrument's long beach-shaped sides.[8]

Different saws are used at various stages in the construction of the soundboard – for cutting the upper surface, scooping out the inside and for shaping the inner sides (figs. 27-30). At this point the soundboard is also called *sō* (tub), a reference to its scooped out form.[9]

The soundboard is made according to three main designs, each of which reveals a unique pattern of wood grain on the upper, and extremely conspicuous, surface, as well as the long

27 Cutting log to make a soundboard. Workshop of *koto* maker Shinwa Kingaku. Fukuyama, June 1997. Photograph by the author.

28 Cutting underneath of soundboard to form initial shape. Workshop of *koto* maker Shinwa Kingaku. Fukuyama, June 1997. Photograph by the author.

29 Carving out inside of soundboard by hand. Workshop of *koto* maker Eki Akio. Fukuyama, June 1997. Photograph by the author.

30 Carving out inside of soundboard. Workshop of *koto* maker Oda Kazuyuki. Fukuyama, June 1997. Photograph by the author.

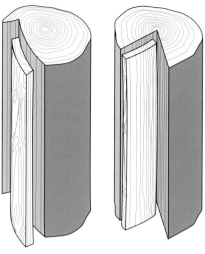

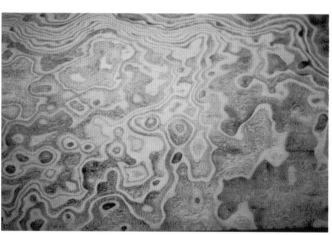

31 Cutting soundboard from log to form different grain patterns. *Left, itame* soundboard; *right, masame* soundboard (after Andō 1986, 15).

32 *Tamamoku* soundboard. Osaka College of Music, Museum of Music (0407). Photograph by the author.

33 *Left, jūshichigen* soundboards; *center, itame* soundboards for *koto; right, masame* soundboards for *koto.* Workshop of *koto* maker Makimoto Gakki. Fukuyama, July 1990. Photograph by the author.

sides (figs. 31-33): *itame* (grain; also called *mokume* [wood grain]), *masame* (straight grain) and *tamamoku* (round grain; also called *uzuramoku* [patched grain]).[10] An *itame* design has swirling patterns on the upper surface and longitudinal lines running along the two long sides. A *masame* soundboard has longitudinal lines running along the upper surface and swirling patterns on the long sides. A *tamamoku* soundboard – extremely rare and considered the most expensive – has an abundance of very fine swirling patterns over the entire length of the upper surface.

The *itame* soundboard is by far the most common design, and it may have several grades depending upon the position in the log from which it is hewn. Progressing from the outside of the log toward the center, and depending on the log's size, these techniques of cutting the wood include *uwakō* (top board), *nibankō* (second board), *sanbankō* (third board), and so on until the central section of the log is reached. This central piece is referred to as *ikakō* (squid board) and is not used for *koto* construction due to its inferior, overly soft composition.[11] *Masame* soundboards can only be cut from larger logs because the width of the board must be within the radius of the log.

Both *itame* and *masame* designs have broader connotations within Japanese culture. For instance, Kikkawa (1986, 6) compares the *itame* design, a major pattern in Japanese carpentry, with the complexities of a Japanese vocal style: "the Japanese tend to prefer a voice with *sabi* (a type of patina that develops with age) or a *shibui* (astringent and refined) voice rather than a voice that is clear and pure. This probably parallels the Japanese aesthetic preference for complicated and knotty woodgrains over smooth fine-grained wood." While examining wooden containers and the metaphor of wrapping in Japanese culture, Hendry (1993, 45-46) notes that "*masame* is the term given to a highly prized method involving wood cut across the grain from the centre of the trunk and split by hand to reveal a very fine straight grain. Boxes created from this wood will not bend or shrink, and gifts presented in such a container are apparently a sign of great respect."

There are two methods of scooping out the inside of the soundboard: *namikō* (plain soundboards) and *kurikō* (scooped-out soundboards). The *namikō* type of soundboard has a backboard attached to it that is visible along the two long sides (i.e., the thickness of the backboard shows on the sides). It also has a piece of wood called *atozuke* (end attachment) added to the tail to fill in the gap where it has been scooped out (fig. 34). The *kurikō* type of soundboard has a backboard attached that would not be visible along the two long sides. The tail end of this soundboard, unlike that of the *namikō* tail, is left intact. Only the head end of this type of soundboard is scooped out. In comparison to the *namikō* type of soundboard, the *kurikō* type is slightly longer at this initial stage of production, as well as being slightly thicker. This permits the long sides to be slightly higher than on the *namikō* soundboard, which will not have their depth increased by an additional backboard. On both the *namikō* and *kurikō* types of soundboard the head end is not filled until a later stage. Once the basic shape of the soundboard of both types and backboard has been made, the body is seasoned in the open air (fig. 35). Seasoning may last from six months to five years depending on the materials, the weather and the maker's preference. Once the wood has dried thoroughly, it can be further shaped.

34 Tail end of several *Yamadagoto* showing *namikō* soundboards and *betazuke* backboards. The overhanging part of the backboards and remainder of the *atozuke* are still to be cut off. Workshop of *koto* maker Makimoto Gakki. Fukuyama, June 1997. Photograph by the author.

The underneath of the soundboard is scooped out even more to form what will become a sound chamber when the backboard is placed beneath it. While a saw would have been used in the initial stages to cut the basic shape of the upper and lower surfaces, this part of the

35 *Namikō* soundboards during seasoning. Workshop of *koto* maker Makimoto Gakki. Fukuyama, June 1997. Photograph by the author.

manufacturing process involves the inside being scooped out with hand tools. After the underneath of the soundboard has been scooped out, its width (i.e., the curved part between the long sides) is ideally about 1.8 cm toward the edges (near the sides), gradually becoming thicker toward the center where it is about 3.6 cm. Inferior boards usually have to be patched or plugged with separate pieces of *kiri*. If, for example, the long sides are not deep enough to form a suitably sized sound chamber, extra pieces of *kiri* are tipped in order to make the instrument thicker. Modifications like this may be made anywhere on the soundboard, inside or out. During my own field research, the *koto* maker Shinwa Kingaku noted that such "patched" instruments are frequently used as *keikogoto* (training *koto*) or *renshūgoto* (practice *koto*), the implication being that they are considered to be of inferior quality.[12] In an effort to prevent the instrument from warping, the inside of the soundboard has several crosspieces (*hariita* or *dōbari*; usually four or five) that are situated between the two long sides.[13] Sometimes a small block of wood is placed between these crosspieces and the underneath of the soundboard to provide more support. The scooped-out head end then has a piece of wood called *sekiita* (barrier board) positioned inside the body to which the tongue is fixed.

Carvings

Some *koto* have carved out areas (*hori*) on the under surface of the soundboard immediately beneath the area visible through the sound holes (figs. 14-15, 36-41).[14] Common carving designs are *sudaremebori* (straight line carvings), *ayasugibori* (herringbone-shape carvings) and *komochi ayasugibori* (herringbone-shape carvings in pairs).[15] *Hori* are thought to improve the sound of the instrument (Chūjō and Hotta 1985, 214), although this has not been established conclusively and in any case can only be determined by acoustic experimentation. However, when this writer questioned *koto* makers about the purpose of such carvings, all were of the opinion that they contributed to the improvement of the instrument's sound and that they were added only to instruments of higher quality.

These carved out areas can perhaps be understood as "hidden signifiers" of the material and monetary value of the instrument, by which is meant that they are only visible when the instrument is not in its normal playing position (e.g., when an instrument is being moved or when a string needs repairing). Also, once the backboard is fixed to the soundboard, the carvings give the impression that they stretch across the entire length of the instrument, when in actual fact they rarely do.

Sudaremebori run longitudinally along the underneath of the soundboard and appear on instruments of slightly better quality than those without carvings.[16] More expensive instruments have *ayasugibori*, herringbone lines that run widthwise across the soundboard. An unusual design for carvings is depicted on a *koto* housed in the musical instrument museum of Musashino Academia Musicae (A609), which has *ayasugibori* running along the length, not

36 Underneath of head of a *Yamadagoto*. Dartington College of Arts, Totnes, England, 1988. Photograph by the author.

37 Sound hole under tail of a *Yamadagoto* showing *asagatabori* carvings, brocade and string grouping. Collection of Kikuhara Hatsuko (1899-2002) of the Ko-Ikuta-ryū (Ikuta-ryū). Osaka, April 1991. Photograph by the author.

38 Sound hole under head end of a Taishō-era *Ikutagoto* showing rhombus-shaped carvings. Osaka College of Music, Museum of Music (B03-1198). Photograph by the author.

39 Carving *ayasugibori* on *kurikō* soundboard. A small space has been left for the *itokaeshi*. Workshop of *koto* maker Makimoto Gakki. Fukuyama, June 1997. Photograph by the author.

width, of the instrument. While not a *Yamadagoto*, the precise details of this instrument are not known, including its date and maker (Musashino Ongaku Daigaku Gakki Hakubutsukan 1969, 11-12).

The *komochi ayasugibori* design, which has a small space between each pair of lines, is reserved for high-quality instruments and, like *ayasugibori*, its lines run widthwise. Other designs are occasionally found on very expensive instruments, such as the six-pointed floral-shaped *asagatabori* (hemp-flower carvings; sometimes referred to as *ajiro* [wickerwork]).[17] A Taishō-era *Ikutagoto* in the collection at Osaka College of Music (B03-1198) is singular with carved out areas in rhombus (*hishi*) shapes (Ōsaka Ongaku Daigaku Fuzoku Gakki Hakubutsukan 1984, 91). This pattern represents the diamond-shaped leaves of the water chestnut.

 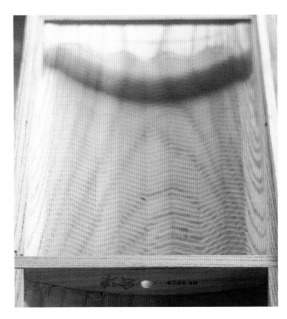

40 *Kurikō* soundboard. Underneath of tail end showing *komochi ayasugibori*, space for *itokaeshi*, and *dōbari*. Workshop of *koto* maker Makimoto Gakki. Fukuyama, July 1990. Photograph by the author.

41 Underneath of head end of *namikō* soundboard showing *sekiita*, *ayasugibori* and *dōbari*. Workshop of *koto* maker Mitsuya Koto Seizō. Saitama, June 1997. Photograph by the author.

Straight lines are used on cheaper instruments because they are made very quickly using a ruler and chisel, whereas all other designs are more complex and might take several days to complete. Once the grooves have been cut for any of the designs, the next stage is to affix a thin strip of wood called *itokaeshi* (string return) to the underneath of the soundboard next to the string holes at the tail. The purpose of this piece of wood is to stop the strings from digging into the soft soundboard (*see* figs. 39-40) for the area where this piece of wood is stuck. The crosspieces are then secured in place, and the backboard and soundboard are bound together with glue.

Backboard

The backboard (*uraita*) of the *koto* is approximately 1 cm thick and constitutes the lower part of the main body. It has a lengthwise curve that follows the lower part of the two long sides of the soundboard. But different to the soundboard, it has no widthwise curve. A cheaper backboard might be made of several pieces of wood glued together (usually lengthwise strips).

There are two ways of attaching the backboard to the soundboard (fig. 42): *betazuke* (plain attachment) and *tomezuke* (scooped-out attachment).[18] The *betazuke* method allows the width of the backboard to be seen from the long sides: the wooden *atozuke* is added at the tail and the backboard is glued to the *atozuke* and to the two long sides of the soundboard. *Betazuke* is utilized for cheaper instruments. In the *tomezuke* method the backboard and soundboard meet so that the sides of the backboard are not visible from the long sides. A backboard is attached to a *kurikō* soundboard, which requires the tail end to be left intact (i.e., it is not scooped out). The *tomezuke* method requires angled edges of 45 degrees all around the lower sides of the soundboard and backboard where the two boards meet so that the join cannot be seen. *Tomezuke* is reserved for more expensive instruments.

Once the soundboard and backboard are glued together the *koto* body is checked for damage or blemishes, such as knots in the wood. If necessary, repairs are made by either plugging a hole with another piece of wood or by adding a wood filler. Some makers might also test the acoustics of the instrument at this stage.[19] The FHSKK company Ogawa Gakki Seizō, for example, carries out checks using computer analysis to ensure its *koto* have the desired acoustic qualities. In this instance, a mechanical device is used to add, temporarily, fixed bridges and strings, the latter of which have movable bridges placed beneath (fig. 43).[20]

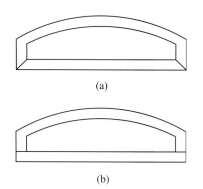

(a)

(b)

42 The two ways of attaching the backboard and the soundboard. (a) *Tomezuke*; (b) *betazuke*.

43 Checking the acoustics of a *koto* during manufacture. All the added parts are placed temporarily on the instrument. Workshop of *koto* maker Ogawa Gakki Seizō. Fukuyama, June 1997. Photograph by the author.

44 Scorching the surface of a *koto*. Workshop of *koto* maker Ogawa Gakki Seizō. Fukuyama, June 1997. Photograph by the author.

45 Brushing the *koto* surface with a wire brush and *aku* after scorching. Workshop of *koto* maker Oda Kazuyuki. Fukuyama, June 1997. Photograph by the author.

Scorching the Surface

The entire outer surface of the *koto* body is scorched with extremely hot irons in order to help bring out the grain pattern of the wood (fig. 44). While some makers apply an ash (*aku*) wash to the surface before it is scorched as a way of darkening it, others obtain a similar finish by scorching it longer. Once scorched, the surface is then rubbed with a wire brush (fig. 45) – sometimes with lime (*sekkai*) – to remove excess burnt wood, then rubbed with a wet cloth, polished with insect wax (*ibota* or *ibotarō*), and finally burnished with an extremely stiff wire brush (*uzukuri*). Unlike some of the added parts, the body of modern

Yamadagoto is not lacquered. (Most historical non-*Yamadagoto* had lacquered and other types of decoration on the sides, the head and the tail.[21])

Interestingly, the use of scorched wood for zithers is recorded in the *Kojiki* and *Nihongi*. These works note, with a similar passage in each, that during the reign of Emperor Nintoku (313-99) a zither was made from an old ship named "Karano" after the wood was burnt (Philippi 1968, 322):[22]

> This tree was cut down and made into a ship, a ship which moved with great speed. At the time the ship was named Karano.
> This ship was used morning and evening to bring water drawn from the cold springs of the island of Apadi for the imperial table.
> When this boat became dilapidated, it was burnt for salt.
> The parts left over from the burning were taken and made into a cither [zither], the sound of which reverberated for seven leagues. At the time [there was] a song [which] said:

Karano was
Burnt for salt,
And the remaining wood
Made into a cither.
When its strings were plucked—
It was like the brine-soaked plants
Growing on the underwater rocks
In the Yura Channel
Which sway slowly—
—Saya saya—
(Philippi 1968, 322-23)

Sound Holes

Every *koto* has two sound holes. They are cut in the backboard toward each end of the instrument, around which a decorative rim made from a harder wood is usually secured to create smoother edges (figs. 46-48).

Sound holes have several functions. Their primary role is to enable the sound pass out of the sound chamber, especially at the head end which is slightly raised from the ground when playing in the traditional way (i.e., not using a high stand). They also provide access at the head end when repairing a broken string, and allow the strings to pass over the tail extremity so that they can be secured at the fixed bridge at that end. Furthermore, the sound holes are also the only areas through which the carved out areas (*hori*) on the under side of the soundboard can be viewed, thus acting as windows for these symbols of instrument quality.

The shape of the sound holes is dictated by the main type of *koto* and even on the same instrument the two sound holes have a slightly different shape. On *Yamadagoto*, the shape of the sound hole under the tail has a straight side toward the tail extremity; this provides

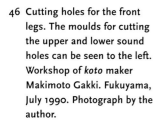

46 Cutting holes for the front legs. The moulds for cutting the upper and lower sound holes can be seen to the left. Workshop of *koto* maker Makimoto Gakki. Fukuyama, July 1990. Photograph by the author.

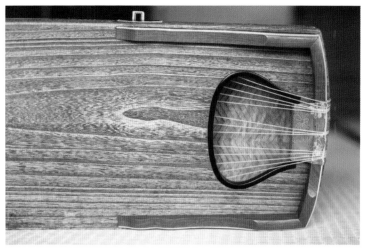

enough space for the strings passing through (this sound hole is sometimes slightly stylized on other *koto*). The variation in the shape of the sound holes between *Yamadagoto* and other *koto* is one way to distinguish instruments. The main difference in shape is seen with the sound hole under the head, which on *Yamadagoto* is rounded but on other *koto* is straight edged toward the head end.

Oak Leaf

The upper surface of the *koto* tail always has a piece of wood shaped like an oak leaf affixed to it (figs. 49-51).[23] The oak leaf (*kashiwaba*) acts to support the extremely high tension of the strings as they pass over the tail area, preventing them from digging into and damaging the soft *kiri* wood of the soundboard. (Brocade is also added to the tail extremity in order to lend support to the strings.) The *kashiwaba* is usually around 3 mm thick and consists of a whole leaf in the center with two half leaves on either side. It is normally prepared by removing several millimeters of wood from the surface of the soundboard on the exact place where the oak leaf is to be adhered. A more expensive design has only an outline design of an oak leaf, whereas other instruments have a solid design. The area on the upper surface of the tail of most *koto* other than *Yamadagoto* would usually have a rectangular border in which the oak leaf is placed.

Most *koto* makers agree that the *kashiwaba* is an important decorative motif that should be included on all standard *koto*, yet they offer no further explanation as to its origin or cultural

47 Underneath of the head end of a *Yamadagoto*. Collection of Matsuzaki Shūsetsu (Ikuta-ryū). Ogōri, July 1990. Photograph by the author.

48 Underneath of tail of *Yamadagoto* illustrated in figure 47. Instrument in the collection of Matsuzaki Shūsetsu (Ikuta-ryū). Ogōri, July 1990. Photograph by the author.

49 Tail of a *Yamadagoto* during manufacture showing *kashiwaba* and space for fixed bridge between *shiburoku*. Workshop of *koto* maker Makimoto Gakki. Fukuyama, July 1990. Photograph by the author.

50 Making *kashiwagata* (outline of oak leaf). Workshop of *koto* maker Makimoto Gakki. Fukuyama, July 1990. Photograph by the author.

67

meaning. However, Davis ([1913] 1992, 348) connects the use and function of an oak leaf with samurai, when it "was hung over the door, in the belief that it would guard him on his journey" (*see also* Joly 1908, 526). Still, no link between this description and the symbolism of the oak leaf motif on the *koto* has been documented in historical sources, although its significance as a design is reflected in its use on some twentieth-century *koto*-related instruments. For example, larger and smaller *koto*-type instruments usually have an oak leaf, unless the instrument is so small that space does not permit its inclusion.[24]

51 Top of tail of a *Yamadagoto*. Collection of Matsuzaki Shūsetsu (Ikuta-ryū). Ogōri, July 1990. Photograph by the author.

52 Tail end of *Yamadagoto* illustrated in figure 51. Instrument in the collection of Matsuzaki Shūsetsu (Ikuta-ryū). Ogōri, July 1990. Photograph by the author.

Brocade

Brocade (*ogire* or *oginu*) is placed at the tail end of the soundboard (figs. 51-52). It partially covers the oak leaf and passes over the tail into the tail side of the sound hole at that end. The brocade protects the wood from the extremely high tension of the strings and is often found on *koto* with three or five slightly overlapping layers. It is usually ornamented with decorative motifs that match those of the head cover (if the instrument has one). The convention of having three or five layers for the brocade perhaps reflects the auspicious nature of these numbers. For example, the number three is echoed in the third day of the third month with Hinamatsuri (Doll's/Girl's Festival), and the number five in the fifth day of the fifth month with Tango no Sekku (Children's/Boy's Day). The physical layering of the brocade might also be compared to the metaphor of wrapping or unwrapping aspects of Japanese culture, one which has been employed by such writers as Ben-Ari, Moeran and Valentine (1990) and Hendry (1993):[25]

> Wrapping in Japan is a veritable 'cultural template', or perhaps we could add another metaphor and call it a 'cultural design'. It makes possible the marking of the whole range of life-stages and statuses, thus representing, and recreating, the hierarchical order which, in turn, gives rise to the locus of power relationships. Different manifestations of this organizing principle reflect and reinforce one another, ... and they thus also offer almost unlimited possibilities for communication, verbal and non-verbal, and for the exercise of power. (Hendry 1993, 172)

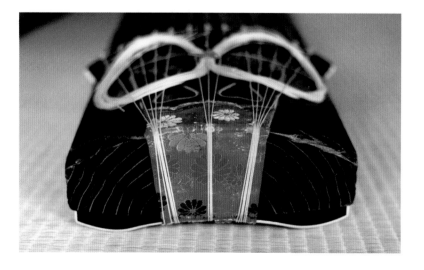

A further level of physically wrapping the *koto* is found with several types of covers or cases, which are sometimes used to protect the instrument when it is not being played or during transit. The various types include a cover that fits over the head, concealing the upper surface of the soundboard and tied at the tail; a slightly more elaborate cover that extends over the entire body; or a case padded or made of wood, fiberglass, plastic, or metal. Other examples of physically wrapping the *koto* in layers of meaning, as explored at other places in this book, are found with the amount of decoration or edging added, the different types of stand used, the type of carvings on the underneath of the soundboard, the position of the performer on stage, and even the type of dress they wear.

Mouth, Lips and Tongue

The head end of the *koto* or *kuchimae* (mouth front) includes the mouth, lips and a tongue. Each is inspired by the instrument's dragon nomenclature (figs. 53-54). The sharp corners of the head end and its decoration are usually protected with a head cover (*kuchimae sakku* [mouth front sack], *kuchimae kabā* [mouth front cover] or *kuchimae bukuro* [mouth front bag]). The head cover usually has an outer layer of brocade, the decoration of which matches that of the tail brocade. This cover is mainly used when the instrument is not in a performance context, although it is frequently found on an instrument being played in a teaching context or at other times that are not exclusively public. In other words, the cover is removed to display the head end and its decoration during important public performances.

The tongue is secured by attaching it to the piece of wood called *sekiita* (barrier board). On instruments that have tuning pins or pegs inside the mouth, a removable tongue is used. Sometimes there is no tongue at all. A removable tongue fits tightly inside the mouth, or utilizes another type of attachment such as a magnet to allow easy

53 Fixing lips to the mouth of a *Yamadagoto*. Workshop of *koto* maker Mitsuya Koto Seizō. Saitama, July 1997. Photograph by the author.

54 Fixing tongue to a *Yamadagoto*. Workshop of *koto* maker Makimoto Gakki. Fukuyama, July 1990. Photograph by the author.

access. Makers generally add a small hole, or holes, in the *sekiita* to help the instrument's acoustics. Instruments other than *Yamadagoto* have a tongue with sides that are equidistant. However, the *Yamadagoto* tongue permits more space for decoration (*maki-e*) and for easier viewing with its short upper side pointing outward and longer lower side pointing inward. The tongue and lips on *Yamadagoto* might also have decoration in the form of edging that assists in determining instrument quality. As with many of the other added parts, those at the head end are made from a wood harder than *kiri*.

Fixed Bridges, *Shiburoku* and String Holes

The *koto* has two fixed bridges that are secured into holes in the upper surface of the soundboard, one toward each end (figs. 55-58).[26] The strings are spaced equidistantly atop each. A thin strip called *makurazuno*, made of ivory, bone or plastic, is placed on the top of the fixed bridge at the head end in order to stop the strings from vibrating against the wood and to help transmit the sound into the soundboard. Historical *koto* other than *Yamadagoto* usually used a cord (*makuraito*), or especially on *gakusō* the strings rested directly onto the fixed bridge. These instruments sometimes additionally had decorative tassels that were attached to each end of the cord.

Thin strips of wood called *shiburoku* (literally, "four parts to six") are added to the upper surface of the soundboard on each side of the fixed bridges. The ratio expressed in the name "four parts to six" refers to the strip that faces the center of the soundboard and the end

55 Top of head of a *Yamadagoto*. Collection of Matsuzaki Shūsetsu (Ikuta-ryū). Ogōri, July 1990. Photograph by the author.

56 Side of tail of a *Yamadagoto*. Collection of Matsuzaki Shūsetsu (Ikuta-ryū). Ogōri, July 1990. Photograph by the author.

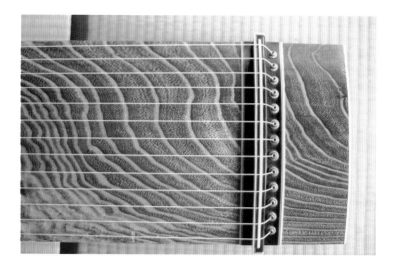

57 Fixing *sagari* to side of the *shiburoku*. Workshop of *koto* maker Makimoto Gakki. Fukuyama, July 1990. Photograph by the author.

58 Side of tail of a *Yamadagoto* showing *sagari* with *tamabuchi* edging. *Koto* shop Uemura Gakki. Osaka, July 1990. Photograph by the author.

extremities, respectively. The strip toward each end of the instrument requires a larger space for the string holes to fit in. The string holes have metal supports (*shinza*) that are generally in the shape of the chrysanthemum flower (*kiku*), the imperial family crest associated with the emperor. The chrysanthemum motif can also be seen in lacquered decoration on the *koto*, as well as on other parts such as covers or the brocade on the head cover or tail. The *sagari* (hanging over) or *i no me* (wild boar's eye)[27] design is usually applied directly below the *shiburoku* on the long sides of the instrument (figs. 56-58).

Movable Bridges

The thirteen movable bridges (*ji* or *kotoji*) of the *koto* are positioned on the upper surface of the soundboard and rest under the strings; the tension of the strings helps to keep them in place. One movable bridge is placed beneath each string to allow the player to establish the tuning of a piece, with the bridge sometimes adjusted during performance (figs. 59-63).[28] Tuning pins or pegs are occasionally employed today, especially on beginners' and electric instruments, and replace the tongue inside the instrument mouth. The movable bridges were historically made of wood, or wood with ivory tips, but today this is only found on older style instruments such as the *gakusō*, the *nagaiso* and the *koto* used in Okinawa *sōkyoku*. Today, on the *Yamadagoto*, ivory and its less expensive substitute, plastic, are the most commonly used materials. Ivory and plastic bridges are white or off-white. In recent years, plastic movable bridges have also been produced in brighter colors, such as red, blue, orange, and silver. But these are very rare.

A connection between the patterns formed on the soundboard by all the movable bridges and that of flying geese in formation has been drawn by some writers (Ackermann 1990, 346-47; Tsuge 1983a, 5).[29] Some historical and rather unique movable bridges were actually made in the

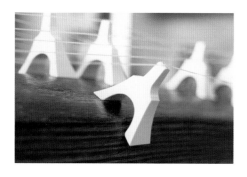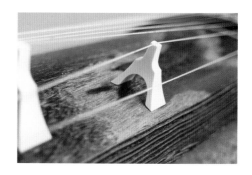

59 Movable bridge for first string of a *Yamadagoto*. Dartington College of Arts, Totnes, England, 1988. Photograph by the author.

60 Movable bridge for thirteenth string of *Yamadagoto* illustrated in figure 59. Dartington College of Arts, Totnes, England, 1988. Photograph by the author.

61 Small movable bridge for second string of *Yamadagoto* illustrated in figure 59. Dartington College of Arts, Totnes, England, 1988. Photograph by the author.

shape of birds (Musashino Ongaku Daigaku Gakki Hakubutsukan 1969, 78). In an intriguing twist of image reciprocity, Adachi ([1913] 1972, 148) shows that several Japanese design motifs in family crests are actually derived from the shape of the movable bridges of the *koto*. In the piece "Okayasu-Ginuta",[30] ascribed to Okayasu Kosaburō (act. *c*. 1710), the text of the first verse clearly references the image of geese:

Tsuki no mae no	In the moonlight
kinuta wa	The fulling block
yosamu wo tsuguru	Sounds out the evening chill.
kumoi no kari wa	Against the clouds
kotoji ni utsushite	Wild geese trace
omoshiro ya	Bridges of the *koto*.
	(Tsuge 1983a, 141)

The third song in the celebrated piece "Fuki" ("Rhubarb") by Yatsuhashi Kengyō relates directly to the resemblance of the movable bridges to geese. In this particular instance the association is with the sound of the *koto* and these birds, one which is undoubtedly linked to the shape of the thirteen bridges on the surface of the *koto* and its comparison to geese in flight:

Tsuki no mae no	Strains of the *koto*
shirabe wa	Before the moon at night
yosamu wo tsuguru	Announce the arrival
akikaze	Of the chilly autumn wind.[31]
kumoi no	Wild geese
karigane wa	In the distant sky -
kotoji ni otsuru	Their song echoes
koegoe	On my *koto*.
	(Tsuge 1983a, 4)

While pre-*Yamadagoto* (i.e., *gakusō*, *chikusō* and *Ikutagoto*) instruments had diverse types of wooden movable bridges, today there are three main designs of ivory or plastic bridges: the standard type (*hyōjuntekiji*), which is normally used on strings 1-12; a bridge for the thirteenth and highest pitch string (*kinji*), which has an extra support to allow the bridge to push against the long side of the instrument near the player, thus stopping it from falling off when the string is plucked; and a smaller bridge (*koji* or *shōji*), which is usually for the second string and allows a lower pitch. The *koji* or *shōji* type of bridge is sometimes made in different sizes with a choice of two, three or even four grooves at a different height through which the string passes. This type is unlike other bridges that have a single central groove. The width of the legs (supports) of the movable bridges of all types appear in several sizes. Those with wider legs are often used by beginners as these bridges are more stable on the soundboard and not liable to fall over, something that is more common with bridges with narrower legs.

62 Wooden movable bridge with ivory on top and bird decoration for instrument illustrated in figure 5. Photograph by the author.

63 Wooden movable bridge with ivory on top for *gakusō* (dated 1437). Hikone Castle Museum (3). Photograph by the author.

Movable bridges can be used in slightly unusual ways. For example, if a smaller bridge is not available, a larger bridge might be placed upside down on the soundboard. Or, if the bridge on the first string is prone to falling off, a bridge for the thirteenth string, which has an extra support, might be used. Perhaps a more complicated scenario is when a string loses some of its tension and its bridge cannot be placed in the appropriate position on the soundboard without it touching another movable bridge. In this case, two movable bridges might be inserted under one string in order to help adjust the pitch.

Strings

The *koto* has thirteen strings (*ito*) of equal length, weight and tension.[32] They are normally numbered 1 through 13 from the string furthest away from the player to the string closest the player, with string 13 usually having the highest pitch (Table 8). Strings 1-10 have standard terms for counting them, while strings 11-13 are identified by terms not normally used in counting. For the latter, a single *kanji* is employed in *koto* notation (*see* Chapter 5), rather than the pair of characters used in everyday Japanese, thus maintaining a systematic form of representation of a single character corresponding to each *koto* string.[33]

Table 8. String Names and Symbols

Number	Kanji*	Name
1	壱 or 一	*ichi*
2	弐 or 二	*ni*
3	参 or 三	*san*
4	四	*shi/yon*
5	五	*go*
6	六	*roku*
7	七	*shichi/nana*
8	八	*hachi*
9	九	*kyū*
10	十	*jū*
11	斗	*to*
12	為	*i*
13	巾	*kin*

* When two symbols are given, the one on the left is usually used in the Yamada-ryū.

As listed in Table 9, an ancient system of nomenclature for every string is noted by Tanabe and Hirano (1982, 1351), although details of its application are vague (*see also* Adriaansz 1973, 28; Andō 1986, 24).[34] This ancient nomenclature has still been retained for strings 11-13. Even though each main symbol in all traditional *koto* notation represents a string, there are also names for the pitches of the notes, which are usually used by *koto* players to refer to the first string so as to establish the pitch of the tuning (Table 10).

Table 9. Ancient String Nomenclature

Number	*Kanji*	Name
1	仁	*jin*
2	智	*chi*
3	礼	*rei*
4	義	*gi*
5	信	*shin*
6	文	*bun*
7	武	*bu*
8	翡	*hi*
9	闌	*ran*
10	商	*shō*
11	斗	*to*
12	為	*i*
13	巾	*kin*

Table 10. Note Names

Japanese Name	Western Name
ichikotsu	D
tangin	D#/Eb
hyōjō	E
shōzetsu	F
shimomu	F#/Gb
sōjō	G
fushō	G#/Ab
ōshiki	A
rankei	A#/Bb
banshiki	B
shinsen	C
kamimu	C#/Db

Hirata and Kaihara (1988, 25) observe that strings 1-5 on historical forms of *gakusō* were the thickest, strings 6-10 medium-sized and strings 11-13 the thinnest. Today, however, *gakusō* and *zokusō* strings are the same size (i.e., the same weight of string is used for all the strings). *Koto* strings were traditionally made of silk, although with the stability of synthetic materials and their reduced cost in the early twentieth century, nylon became an early substitute. The polyester material, tetron, has been the principal material since the 1950s. Synthetic strings are sometimes dyed yellow to make them look like silk.[35] Silk strings are still frequently found on *gakusō*, but their use on the everyday *koto* is extremely rare. The significance of silk in historical Japan has been noted by Tsuge:

> In ancient China, the word "silk and bamboo" (*szŭ-chu*) meant "music." To be more precise, it meant stringed and wind instruments which were made of silk and bamboo. In Chinese, *szŭ* ("string" or "thread") primarily means "silk." In fact, most Chinese stringed instruments (and East Asian stringed instruments of Chinese origin) use silk strings even today. To give but a few examples, *ch'in* (the seven-stringed long zither) and *p'i-p'a* (the four-stringed short lute) of China; *komun'go* (the six-stringed long zither) and *haegŭm* (the two-stringed fiddle) of Korea; *koto* (the thirteen-stringed long zither) and *shamisen* (the three-stringed long lute) of Japan.
>
> Although recently wire and nylon have replaced silk strings of some instruments, we can still see a close connection between the string instruments of East Asia and silk. One may wonder why silk was preferred to gut, horse-tail, or wire for the strings of musical instruments. It is hardly necessary to mention the significance of silk in the ancient world, in both the East and West. The existence of the "silk road" will suffice to remind us of its immeasurable value at that time. (Tsuge 1978, 16-17)

Metal strings are not normally used for the *koto*, unlike its historical Chinese relative the *zheng* or *guzheng*. However, some smaller *koto* (e.g., *yonshakugoto*) or bass *koto* are occasionally fitted with metal strings.

The ends of the strings are secured by fastening them to a tightly rolled piece of paper under the string holes at the head end (fig. 64). They then pass over the fixed bridge at the head, along the length of the soundboard – normally touching the arched surface of the soundboard when the movable bridges are not in place – over the fixed bridge at the tail and through the string holes at the tail. From here, they pass through the tail sound hole, over the tail extremity, and are affixed with a knot above the tail bridge. A pattern is formed by the grouping of the strings at the tail end and over the *kashiwaba* and brocade. It is common in the Yamada-ryū to have strings grouped equidistantly, while in the Ikuta-ryū groupings such as 5-3-5 or 4-5-4 are standard (figs. 51-52). At the tail the surplus length of the strings is usually wrapped into two circular bundles that are positioned on top of the tail. (In Okinawa a single bundle is the norm; *see* fig. 16; *cf.* fig. 5, which is novel in that it has no string bundles.) When a string breaks – more often than not close to the bridge at the head end where the plectra strike the strings – the bundles are unwrapped, the knots undone and the string pulled through a few centimeters to the appropriate position.

64 Sound hole under head of a *Yamadagoto* showing tightly rolled pieces of paper that secure the strings under the head. Dartington College of Arts, Totnes, England, 1988. Photograph by the author.

Plectra

Koto strings are plucked primarily by three plectra (*tsume*). Plectra are worn on the player's right hand thumb, index and middle fingers (figs. 65-68), with the thumb playing the most by far. Like some other parts of the instrument, the plectra, in particular their shape, size and materials, identify a particular tradition of performance. Several types of plectra can be categorized according to the performance tradition in which they are used, and sub-traditions and individual players often have a preference for the exact shape, material, size, or weight. Rings often vary in color, ranging from white, black, red to silver.

The tips of the *gakusō* and *chikusō* plectra are made of thin strips of bamboo; ivory is sometimes employed for the *chikusō*. *Gakusō* plectra are the shorter of the two. In modern *zokusō* the two main types are the rectangular plectra of the Ikuta-ryū and the oval plectra of the Yamada-ryū. Oval-shaped plectra similar to those of the Yamada-ryū are also used in Okinawa *sōkyoku*. Both types might be made of ivory or plastic. The Kikuike-ha and Tsuguyama-ryū, which are branches of the Ikuta tradition, often perform with plectra that are similar to the rectangular-shaped examples of the Ikuta-ryū, albeit slightly wider at the tip than at the base. The tips of all plectra are glued into rings (*tsumekawa* [plectra skin]; *tsumeobi* [plectra belt]; *wa* [ring]; or *fukuro* [sack]) that fit over the player's fingers. The rings for *gakusō* and *chikusō* plectra are made of tightly rolled paper covered with a thin sheet of leather, whereas *zokusō* rings are today primarily made of tightly rolled paper. *Zokusō* rings fit over the tips of the fingers just below the base of the nail; by contrast *gakusō* rings fit over more of the finger tip than in other traditions. The outer surface of the rings are usually painted or lacquered, the latter being very common in *zokusō* traditions.

The differently shaped plectra at times necessitate somewhat dissimilar ornamental techniques (*see* Chapter 5). For example, in the Ikuta-ryū the technique called *chirashizume* is sometimes played by scraping the flat tips of the index and middle finger plectra along the

(a)

(b)

(c)

(d)

(e)

65 Outline shape of plectra. *(a) Gagaku; (b)* Tsukushigoto and Yatsuhashi-ryū; *(c)* Ikuta-ryū; *(d)* Yamada-ryū; *(e)* Okinawa *sōkyoku*.

66 Yamada-ryū plectra. Musashino Academia Musicae, Museum of Musical Instruments, Tokyo. Photograph by the author.

67 Ikuta-ryū plectra. *From right,* Miyagi-ha; Kikuike-ryū; Kyō-ryū; plectra rings. Musashino Academia Musicae, Museum of Musical Instruments, Tokyo. Photograph by the author.

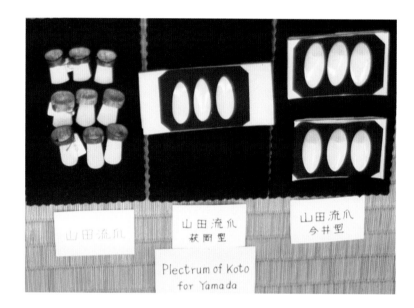

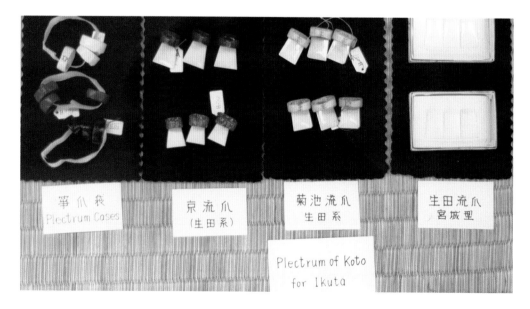

68 Ikuta-ryū plectra. Player: Yamakawa Tamae (Miyagi-ha, Ikuta-ryū,). Dunedin, 1996. Photograph by the author.

strings, whereas in the Yamada-ryū the technique is played by scraping the sides of the plectra along the strings. In contemporary music the plectra are sometimes used to produce sound effects without plucking the strings. For example, the plectra rings might be employed to sound the strings in a percussive way by tapping on them. Other objects too are sometimes employed to pluck or strike the strings in order to produce other sound effects. Bare fingers are also used, especially in more recent music.

Legs and Stands

The *koto* has several styles of legs and stands that are utilized in different performance contexts (figs. 69-75). The legs under the tail of the *koto* are fixed permanently to the instrument and found on three sides of the backboard. Due to their shape, these legs are sometimes referred to by the humorous sobriquet *mukadeashi* (centipede legs). The tail legs raise the instrument slightly to allow sound to emit from the tail sound hole and to help protect the backboard from damage.

69 Head of a *Yamadagoto* with head cover and *torii* stand. Collection of Matsuzaki Shūsetsu (Ikuta-ryū). Ogōri, July 1990. Photograph by the author.

During practice, or for convenience during performance, the player might not remove the head cover that protects the sharp corners and head decoration. In this instance the player might use a *torii* stand – so-named after the post and lintel gates of Shinto shrines – which is easily placed under the head. The player might also use a bridge box (*jibako*), which, as its name indicates, doubles as a box for the movable bridges when they are not in use. This stand too is placed at the head extremity and is made in several sizes. When a *torii* stand or bridge box are not available, the player might even use the head cover itself by taking it off and placing it vertically under the instrument's head. During concerts or other special performances, the removable front legs are normally attached. They are secured in holes at the head end of the backboard.

70 *Koto* on a high metal stand with player sitting on a chair. Collection of Matsuzaki Shūsetsu (Ikuta-ryū). A *shakuhachi* player is shown to the right of the picture. Ogōri, July 1990. Photograph by the author.

Historically, the shape of the front legs has varied between divergent performance traditions. Tanabe (1964, 57) identifies three types: those of the *Yamadagoto*; those of the Tsuguyama-ryū, which are more inwardly arched than any from other traditions; and those of the *gakusō*, *chikusō* and *Ikutagoto*, which have one straight side and are slightly shorter than those of the *Yamadagoto*. The main differentiation today, however, is between *gakusō* and *Yamadagoto*.

The front of the *koto* is raised higher to suit the performer's playing position by placing, for example, the front legs on either a small cushion or a solid stand. Usually, it is only *koto* with shorter front legs than *Yamadagoto* that might require such a stand (in Okinawa *sōkyoku*, however, a small wooden stand is a common feature). By contrast, high stands (*rissōdai*) that

71 Mouth of a *koto* on an additional stand. Collection of Matsuzaki Shūsetsu (Ikuta-ryū). Ogōri, July 1990. Photograph by the author.

72 Mouth of a *Yamadagoto* with *maki-e* on tongue for instrument illustrated in figure 59. Dartington College of Arts, Totnes, England, 1988. Photograph by the author.

73 Mouth of a *koto*. Collection of Matsuzaki Shūsetsu (Ikuta-ryū). Ogōri, July 1990. Photograph by the author.

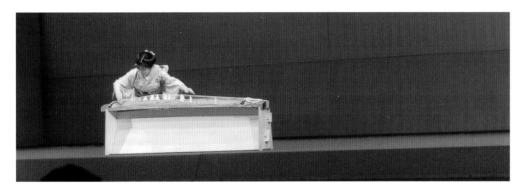

require the player to sit in a chair are often utilized for performances of modern or crossover music. These stands come in several shapes and sizes, and are made from diverse materials including wood, metal and plastic. A simple shape of this type of stand consists of a support at each end that elevates the instrument to an appropriate height. A more complex stand might include a crosspiece, and one is made that actually helps transmit the sound of the instrument with the use of a projection board.[36] During practice a player may even have two chairs act as a rest under either end of the *koto*.

Decoration and Imagery

The *koto* is frequently ornamented with designs rendered in *maki-e* or on brocade. The wooden parts that are added to the *koto* can either be burnished or lacquered, the latter being reserved for instruments of better quality. More expensive instruments might have further lacquer work in the *maki-e* technique applied to the tongue and lips. Many instruments other than *Yamadagoto*, such as the *gakusō*, *chikusō* or *Ikutagoto*, often have *maki-e*, veneer and marquetry on their head, tail and long sides as well. Not only does the addition of *maki-e* increase the value of the *koto*, but the traditional subject-matter of the *maki-e* designs also imbues the instrument with visual and symbolic meaning.

There are a plethora of auspicious motifs in Japanese design.[37] Some are pictorial, others abstract. Many are illustrations of the natural world that symbolize good luck, happiness or longevity, such as the chrysanthemum (*kiku*), which has sixteen petals and symbolic of the emperor; the pine (*matsu*), often found on joyous occasions such as weddings and New Year and a symbol of long life and good fortune; the *shōchikubai* (pine, bamboo, plum) and *matsutake* (pine, bamboo), which are New Year's congratulatory and auspicious symbols; the

79

hexagonal, stylized tortoiseshell (*kikkō*) – the tortoise, like evergreens and bamboo, is thought to live for ten thousand years – and butterflies, a connotation of rebirth.

The *gakusō* in figures 5-7 has pictorial designs that include chrysanthemums, geese (*kari*) and sand bars or trifoils (*suhama*). The *chikusō* in figures 8-11 depicts typical auspicious designs for the historical *koto*, which include stylized plum blossom (*ume*), scroll-like vines (*karakusa*), chrysanthemums, and cranes (*tsuru*). The *chikusō* in figure 12 includes a dragon (*ryū* or *tatsu*), surrounded by a rectangular frame in layers of figurative decoration, and *Genjimon*, or crests used to illustrate chapters of the novel *Genji monogatari*, which are shown around the lips (*see* Koop and Inada [1923] 1960).

Images of cranes – believed to live for one thousand years – are illustrated in *maki-e* on the tongue and brocade head cover of the *Yamadagoto* in figures 69, 71-73. Also visible around the lips of the *koto* in figure 71 is the celebratory design motif of bamboo. Chrysanthemums are depicted on the tail brocade of figure 52 – this pattern would be found on the head cover too. Just like other areas of Japanese design where such motifs are plentiful and today aim to create a Japan of the past, when depicted on the *koto* they help reinforce the instrument's place as an object of traditional Japanese culture. A further level of significance associated with the *koto* and Japanese design is found when images of the instrument or parts thereof are reproduced in general design motifs This is evinced in, for example, several heraldic crests, as reproduced in Adachi ([1913] 1972, 148) and Lee (1981, 157, 187), that illustrate the plectra and movable bridges of the *koto*, as well as some design patterns that show the *koto* itself.

It is interesting to note that many pieces in the traditional *koto kumiuta* repertoire contain song texts with similar images. An image that is particularly evocative of nature and music in Japan is that of the concept of *matsukaze* (wind in the pines). For example, verse 5 of the *koto kumiuta* "Yuki no Ashita" ("Morning of Snow") by Yatsuhashi Kengyō includes this sonic reference:

mine no arashi no kayō ka	the storm-wind in the heights is it?
tani no mizu no nagare ka	or flowing water in the valley?
nezame ni kikishi matsukaze wa	as I wake up they sound alike
koto no ne ni tagawaji	the wind in the pines and strains of *koto* music
	(Ackermann 1990, 415)

Symbolic images can also be found in the piece "Hagoromo no Kyoku" ("Celestial Robes Music"), which, as Tsuge (1983a, 6) notes, is attributed to either Kitajima Kengyō (*d.* 1690) or Makino Kengyō (act. *c.* 1716). Two symbols of longevity (pine and bamboo) are mentioned in the last verse:

Yorozuyo kakete	For ten thousand years
aioi no	The pine and bamboo
matsu to take to no	Have grown together,
fukamidori	Their deep green
kawaranu iro wa	Never changing,
morotomo ni	As if they had promised
oisenu chigiri	One another
narubeshi	Never to grow old.
	(Tsuge 1983a, 7)

Moreover, the first verse in the piece "Tenga Taihei" ("Peace in the Emperor's Realm") by Yatsuhashi Kengyō conveys the sense of "longevity" with its reference to the crane, tortoise and evergreens:

Tenga taihei	Peace in the Emperor's realm,
chōkyū ni	Eternal is his reign.
osamaru miyo no	The wind blesses as it passes
matsukaze	Through the evergreens.
hinazuru wa	Baby cranes enjoy
chitose furu	One thousand years of life.
tani no nagare ni	Tortoises of ten thousand years
kame asobu	Play in the mountain stream.
	(Tsuge 1983a, 47)

Tsuge (1986a, 254) writes that the words "*kaze* (wind) or *arashi* (storm) are often accompanied by a pattern called *hikiren* (a single sweeping stroke across all the strings from the lowest to the highest, with the middle finger-pick) which is visually quite impressive and kinesthetically suggestive." In connection with the instrument's ornamental techniques he comments that "the *kakite* (or *kaki*, 'plucking' two adjacent strings simultaneously with the middle fingerpick) is worth special mention. This technique was at one time considered the most typical koto technique. Consequently it was actually used to describe the poetic image of someone playing the koto" (Tsuge 1981, 120).

In addition to figurative and pictorial decoration, *koto* are sometimes given an individual name that might be painted on the instrument's tongue. According to *Sōkyoku taiishō*, Yatsuhashi Kengyō is understood to have given two instruments the names "Akigiri" ("Autumn Mist") and "Matsunami" ("Murmuring of the Pines"). A further example, where the name is actually rendered in lacquer on the instrument's tongue, is with the well-known twentieth-century figure of *koto* music, Miyagi Michio, who gave his favorite *koto* the name "Etenraku" ("Beyond Heaven Music") after a well-known piece of *gagaku* music. Falconer (1995, 63) notes that with the contemporary performance group Sawai Sōkyoku-in (Sawai *Koto* School) "the kotos the Sawais use regularly have names. Some are named after the people who made them; 'Yano' and 'Yoshimoto.' Some are named after pieces; 'Sakura' ["Cherry Blossom"] and 'Taka' [Hawk]."

Quality and Grades

The *koto* is made in a variety of grades within a hierarchical language of instrument design. Different categories of *koto* are made according to an aesthetic classification system based on the method of instrument construction, the quality of materials used, and even the quantity of certain types of materials. At many stages during manufacture the *koto* is given a unique label that indicates its type of construction and value. Each component part is used according to its compatibility with other parts. For example, a *namikō* soundboard cut toward the center of the log would have cheaper materials for the added parts (e.g., *karin*) and probably would not have any decorative edging or *maki-e*. Conversely, better quality soundboards always have added parts of a higher value and are therefore graded according to the amount and type of edging and *maki-e*. Generally, the more edging there is, the more expensive the *koto*. Moreover, the appearance of double lines or more intricate designs would normally increase the value of the instrument. Edging may be made from ivory, horn, bone, or plastic, which are used on very expensive to cheaper instruments. As well as *maki-e* and edging, other types of decoration on *gakusō*, *chikusō* and earlier forms of *zokusō* other than *Yamadagoto*, might include veneer, marquetry, tortoiseshell, and mother-of-pearl. Such decoration is generally placed on the tongue, lips, long sides, and atop the head and tail.

A representative example of a grading system of *koto* that is categorized hierarchically is presented in Table 11, together with sub-categories, description of features, and price (*cf.* Tables 12-15).[38] Table 11 has thirteen main ranks, together with a preliminary level and several sub-divisions, although the numbers of grades vary between makers, as do prices and some intricacies of *koto* construction. Some makers and retailers might use slightly shorter terms or abbreviations for their grades of *koto* in comparison to those given in Table 11. For example, the second instrument listed in Table 11, *Yamada ichigō beta karinmaki* (Yamada No. 1, plain, Chinese quince wrap), might also be called *ichigō beta* (no. 1, plain), *karin betamaki* (Chinese quince, plain wrap) or simply *beta* (plain). Not all *koto* makers use numbers to indicate the different ranks, preferring instead names that signify the type of decoration. Ogawa Gakki Seizō includes the prefix *Yamada*, which indicates that each instrument is in the form of a *Yamadagoto*. They do not list any *Ikutagoto*. The first instrument named in Table 11 is not allocated a number like the other instruments due to its basic form of construction and recommendation for use in teaching (i.e., for absolute beginners).

Table 11. Grades of *Koto* (Ogawa Gakki Seizō)

Name/Grade	Features (Materials for Added Parts and Decoration)	Price (*yen*) 1990-93	Price (*yen*) 1997-2004
Satsuki beta karinmaki (Fifth month, plain, Chinese quince wrap)[a]	Chinese quince; *betazuke*; *makurazuno*; edging on inside and outside rims of lips; *itame* soundboard; no front legs (must use stand) or *maki-e* on lips or tongue; high-quality red sandalwood or other better woods are used for instruments of a higher quality	55,000	65,000
Yamada ichigō beta karinmaki (Yamada No. 1, plain, Chinese quince wrap)	As above, but with removable front legs	65,000	75,000
Yamada nigō kuchizuno karinmaki (YamadaNo. 2, mouth and horns, Chinese quince wrap)	As above, but with edging on inward-facing edge of fixed bridges and upper and two side edges of the four ends of the fixed bridges; *maki-e* on tongue	70,000	80,000
Yamada nigō kuchizuno shitanmaki (Yamada No. 2, mouth and horns, red sandalwood or rosewood wrap)			
Yamada nigō shitanmaki (Yamada No. 2, red sandalwood or rosewood wrap)[b]	Red sandalwood or rosewood; as above; no front legs (must use stand)	60,000	70,000
Yamada nigō shitanmaki (Yamada No. 2, red sandalwood or rosewood wrap)[c]	As above but with removable front legs	70,000	not listed
Yamada nigō shitanmaki (Yamada No. 2, red sandalwood or rosewood wrap)	As above; average quality	85,000	85,000
Yamada nigō shitanmaki (Yamada No. 2, red sandalwood or rosewood wrap)	As above; better quality than above	115,000	100,000

Name/Grade	Features (Materials for Added Parts and Decoration)	Price (*yen*) 1990-93	Price (*yen*) 1997-2004
Yamada sangō han'uwazuno shitanmaki/kōkimaki (Yamada No. 3, half on the horns, red sandalwood or rosewood wrap/or high-quality red sandalwood wrap)			
Yamada sangō shitanmaki (Yamada No. 3, red sandalwood or rosewood wrap])[d]	As above, but with edging around all of the *shiburoku*, *sagari* and long arched corner of the front legs	100,000 and above	120,000 and above
Yamada sangō shitanmaki kotobuki satsuki (Yamada No. 3, red sandalwood or rosewood wrap, Celebratory Fifth month)	As above	130,000	150,000
Yamada sangō shitanmaki (Yamada No. 3, red sandalwood or rosewood wrap)	As above; average quality	150,000	160,000
Yamada sangō kōkimaki (Yamada No. 3, high-quality red sandalwood wrap)	As above; better quality than above; high-quality red sandalwood	170,000	200,000
Yamada sangō kōkimaki (Yamada No. 3, high-quality red sandalwood wrap)	As above; better quality than above	190,000	220,000
Yamada yongō uwazuno kōkimaki (Yamada No. 4, on the horns, high-quality red sandalwood wrap)			
Yamada yongō kōkimaki (Yamada No. 4, high-quality red sandalwood wrap)[e]	As above, but with edging around oak leaf; red sandalwood or rosewood on cheaper instruments	220,000	250,000
Yamada yongō kōkimaki (Yamada No. 4, high-quality red sandalwood wrap)	As above; average quality	260,000	290,000
Yamada yongō kōkimaki (Yamada No. 4, high-quality red sandalwood wrap)	As above; better quality than above	300,000	330,000
Yamada gogō kinkuchi kōkimaki (Yamada No. 5, gold mouth, high-quality red sandalwood wrap)			
Yamada gogō kōkimaki (Yamada No. 5, high-quality red sandalwood wrap)	As above, but with *maki-e* around lips; average quality	320,000	350,000
Yamada gogō kōkimaki (Yamada No. 5, high-quality red sandalwood wrap)	As above; better quality than above	360,000	390,000
Yamada rokugō nijūmaki honemaki kinkuchi kōkimaki (Yamada No. 6, bone wrap, gold mouth, high-quality red sandalwood wrap)	As above, but using bone for the edging (double lines)	420,000	480,000

Name/Grade	Features (Materials for Added Parts and Decoration)	Price (*yen*) 1990-93	Price (*yen*) 1997-2004
Yamada nanagō kurikō tamabuchi kōkimaki (Yamada No. 7, scooped-out shell, astragal, high-quality red sandalwood wrap)			
Yamada nanagō kurikō tamabuchi (Yamada No. 7, scooped-out shell, astragal)	*Kurikō* soundboard (backboard not showing on long sides); slightly raised edging (*tamabuchi*: astragal), which is made of hard wood, on *shiburoku* and inside and outside rims of lips (not on front legs, fixed bridges or oak leaf); outline of oak leaf (*kashiwagata*); *maki-e* on tongue and lips; the *makurazuno* is the only white part	400,000 and above	500,000 and above
Yamada nanagō kurikō tamabuchi (Yamada No. 7, scooped-out shell, astragal)	Better quality than above	550,000 and above	550,000 and above
Yamada hachigō kurikō tamabuchi kōkimaki (Yamada No. 8, scooped-out shell, astragal, high-quality red sandalwood wrap)	As above, but with ivory tongue	700,000 and above	800,000 and above
Yamada kyūgō kurikō tamabuchi kōkimaki (Yamada No. 9, scooped-out shell, astragal, high-quality red sandalwood wrap)	As above, but with ivory on inside and outside rims of lips	800,000 and above	1,000,000 and above
Yamada jūgō kurikō fukutamabuchi kōkimaki (Yamada No. 10, scooped-out shell, double astragal, high-quality red sandalwood wrap)	As above, but with complex astragal edging	1,000,000 and above	1,200,000 and above
Yamada jūichigō kurikō tamabuchi zōgeiri kōkimaki (Yamada No. 11, scooped-out shell, astragal with ivory, high-quality red sandalwood wrap)	As above, but with an added line of ivory edging on all added parts (including front feet – all outer edges – and tail legs); ivory *kuchimae*	1,400,000 and above	1,600,000 and above
Yamada jūichigō masagoto zōge tamabuchimaki (Yamada No. 11, *masame* soundboard, ivory astragal wrap); also listed with the word *kurikō* before *masagoto*	As above; *masame* (straight lines) soundboard; ivory lines (edging) on front and back legs; double ivory astragal edging on all added parts	2,200,000 and above	2,500,000 and above
Yamada jūnigō kurikō zōge tamabuchimaki (Yamada No. 12, scooped-out shell, ivory astragal wrap)	As above; *itame* soundboard	2,200,000 and above	2,500,000 and above
Yamada jūsangō kurikō sōzōge tamabuchimaki (Yamada No. 13, scooped-out shell, all ivory astragal wrap)	As above, but all added parts are made of ivory	5,000,000 and above	5,000,000 and above

Source: Ogawa Gakki Seizō (1990-93, 2-5; 1997-2004, 2-5).
a-e Recommended as a teaching instrument.

One characteristic of the ranking system is that instruments with increased edging are of a higher quality. Within this hierarchy, there are several terms that often feature in the labels given to the instruments. Labels that are especially prevalent are those that delineate which of the added parts have edging. For example, the terms *beta* (plain), *kuchizuno* (mouth and horns) or *kakumaki* (wrapped horns), *han'uwazuno* (half on the horns), and *uwazuno* (on the horns) indicate, respectively, that the instrument has no edging, edging on part of the fixed bridges, edging around the *shiburoku*, and edging around the oak leaf. As the instruments increase in quality, they generally maintain and build on the decorative features of the previous instrument in the grading system.

Edging can be applied in several ways. One basic way consists of a thin white strip that is placed on the edge of the added parts. Slightly more complex edging might comprise double strips, with a narrow space between them, or diverse types that might include an additional thin strip, sometimes made of another material. A more complex and expensive type of edging is *tamabuchi* (astragal), which is typified by slightly raised edging rather than alignment with the part it is decorating. *Tamabuchi* might be of the same wood as the added parts, or a different (i.e., more expensive) type; it might also have slightly different designs. As noted earlier, the materials for the added parts are graded according to their quality. While several types of hard wood are used, those listed in Table 11 indicate three main kinds: *karin* (Chinese quince), *shitan* (red sandalwood or rosewood), and *kōki* (high-quality red sandalwood). The most expensive instruments have these added parts in ivory. The term *kinkuchi* (gold mouth) means that a decorative rim is placed around the lips. This strip is made in the outline shape of the lips and is often decorated with gold or silver. But it might also be a rim of tortoiseshell or lacquered wood. Moreover, the way of constructing the soundboard is sometimes indicated by the terms *kurikō* and *masagoto*. These types of construction are always limited to more expensive *koto*, hence their placement in the ranking system.

The *koto* is the result of a complex process of instrument construction. From the raw materials to the finished product, the instrument is manufactured in such a way that it is inculcated with cultural meaning. In other words, not only do the instrument and its component parts serve a musical function, but they also possess cultural meaning that nowadays reinforces the instrument's place as a traditional object of Japanese culture. The instrument is wrapped with significance – physically and metaphorically – and made in a variety of forms which adds value to it in a way that offers the viewer a means by which to understand the monetary and aesthetic importance of the *koto*, as well as contextualize the instrument in a broader Japanese cultural milieu. Much of the knowledge about the meaning of the instrument and its component parts is in the domain of *koto* makers and players, and it is from this perspective that the following chapter focuses on the performers themselves and examines the structure of their performance traditions – as social units that are pivotal in the transmission of the instrument and its music.

Table 12. Grades of *Koto* (Mishima Gakki)

Name/Grade*	Features (Decoration and Materials for Added Parts)	Price (yen)**
Karin betamaki (Chinese quince, plain wrap)	Edging on inner side of fixed bridges and upper and two side edges of the four ends of the fixed bridges; no front legs (must use stand) or *maki-e* on lips or tongue	20,000 and above
Shitan kuchizunomaki (red sandalwood, mouth and horns wrap)	As above, but with edging around lips; with removable front legs	35,000 and above
Shitan han'uwamaki (red sandalwood, half on [the horns] wrap)	As above, but with edging around *shiburoku*, *sagari* and long arched side of the corners of front legs	55,000 and above
Kōki uwazunomaki (good quality red sandalwood, on the horns wrap)	As above, but with edging around *kashiwaba*	92,000 and above
Kōki kinkuchimaki (good quality red sandalwood, gold mouth wrap)	As above, but with *maki-e* on tongue and *kinkuchi* lips	120,000 and above
Kōki nijūmaki (good quality red sandalwood, double lines wrap)	As above, but with double edging (none on front legs) and outline *kashiwagata*	300,000 and above
Kōki tamabuchimaki (good quality red sandalwood, astragal wrap)	As above, but with astragal edging	
Zōgemaki (ivory wrap)	As above, but with ivory edging on all added parts; ivory front legs and *kashiwagata*	

Source: Mishima Gakki n.d.; letter to author, 1994; conversation with author, 17 June 1997.
* In 1994 Mishima Gakki added the prefix 1-5 for the first five classifications.
** The price was given during personal communication.

Table 13. Grades of *Koto* (Shinwa Kingaku)

Name/Grade	Features (Decoration and Materials for Added Parts)
Ichigō beta (No. 1, plain)*	No added edging
Nigō shitan kuchizunomaki (No. 2, red sandalwood, mouth and horns wrap)	Edging on inner side of fixed bridges
Nigō-jō shitan kuchizunomaki (No. 2, good quality, red sandalwood, mouth and horns wrap)	As above, but with edging around lips and decorated tongue
Sangō shitan han'uwazunomaki (No. 3, red sandalwood, half on the horns wrap)	As above, but with edging around *shiburoku* and *sagari*
Yongō kōki uwazunomaki (No. 4, high-quality red sandalwood, on the horns wrap)	As above, but with edging around *kashiwaba*

Name/Grade	Features (Decoration and Materials for Added Parts)
Gogō kōki kinkuchi uwazunomaki (No. 5, high-quality red sandalwood, gold mouth, on the horns wrap)	As above, but with edging on straight side of front legs, and gold decoration on lips
Rokugō nijūmaki (*kinkuchi*) (No. 6, double wrap, gold mouth)	As above, but edging has double lines
Nanagō tomekō kōki tamabuchimaki (No. 7, *tomekō* high-quality red sandalwood astragal wrap)	As above, but edging is raised single lines made of wood (none on front legs); outline of *kashiwaba*
Nanagō kurikō kōki tamabuchimaki, kuchimae zōge (No. 7, *kurikō* high-quality red sandalwood astragal wrap, ivory tongue and lips)	As above, but tongue and lips are ivory; outline of *kashiwaba*
Nanagō kurikō tamabuchi zōgemaki (No. 7, *kurikō* astragal ivory wrap)	As above, but all added materials and edging are made of ivory; solid *kashiwaba*

Source: Shinwa Kingaku, conversation with author, Fukuyama, 17 June 1997.
* Added during personal communication. The maker referred to this category as *renshūgoto* (practice *koto*) and *keikogoto* (training *koto*).

Table 14. Grades of *Koto* (Oda Koto Seisaku-sho)

Name	Grade
Ichigō semikiri	(No. 1, see all the back, or No. 1, cheap back)
Nigō kuchizuno	(No. 2, mouth and horns)
Sangō han'uwazuno	(No. 3, half on the horns)
Yongō uwazuno	(No. 4, on the horns)
Gogō kinkuchi	(No. 5, gold mouth)
Rokugō nijū	(No. 6, double)
Nanagō han-tamabuchi	(No. 7, half astragal)
Hachigō tamabuchi	(No. 8, astragal)

Source: Oda Koto Seisaku-sho, letter to author, 1994.

Table 15. Grades of *Koto* (Makimoto Gakki)

Name	Grade
Betamaki	(plainly wrapped)
Kuchizunomaki	(wrapped mouth and horns)
Han'uwazunomaki	(half-wrapped on the horns)
Uwazunomaki	(wrapped on the horns)
Kōki tamabuchimaki	(high-quality red sandalwood, astragal wrap)
Zōge-iri kōki tamabuchimaki	(ivory and high-quality red sandalwood, astragal wrap)
Zōge-sukashi tamabuchimaki	(ivory astragal wrap)
Zōgan-iri zōge tamabuchimaki	(ivory inlay and astragal wrap)

Source: Makimoto Gakki (n.d.).

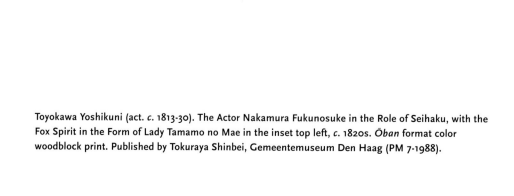

Toyokawa Yoshikuni (act. *c.* 1813-30). The Actor Nakamura Fukunosuke in the Role of Seihaku, with the Fox Spirit in the Form of Lady Tamamo no Mae in the inset top left, *c.* 1820s. *Ōban* format color woodblock print. Published by Tokuraya Shinbei, Gemeentemuseum Den Haag (PM 7-1988).

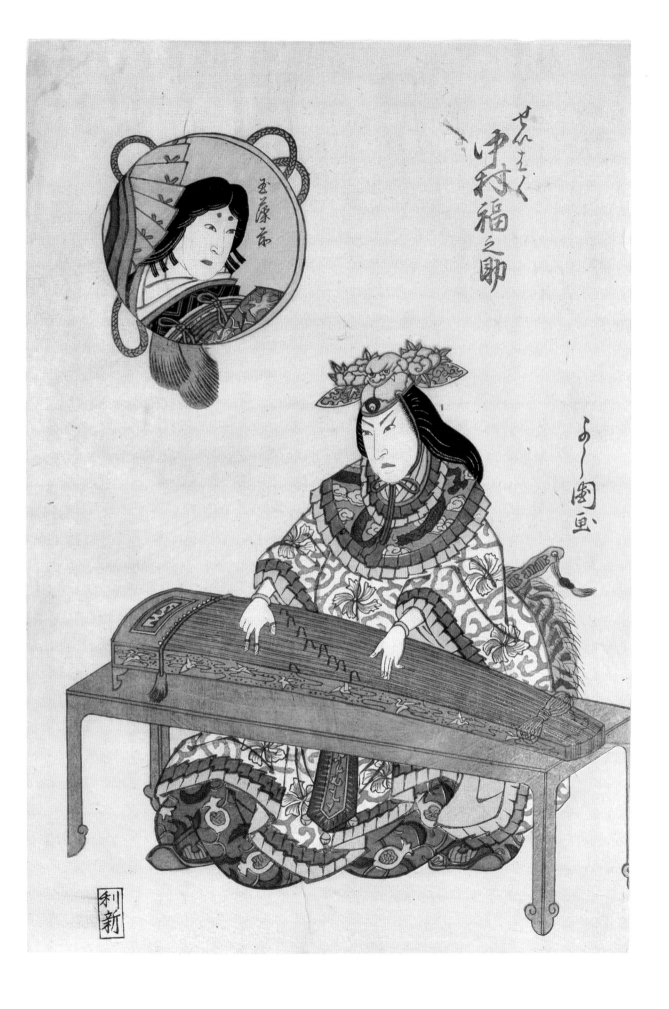

4 Performance Traditions

The multifaceted nature of the *koto* has led to its adaptation in numerous social and cultural contexts, associated with distinct social groups such as aristocracy, blind male professionals and female amateurs.[1] In terms of influencing the popularity of the *koto*, it was the everyday performance traditions[2] that flourished in the Edo period that made an enormous impact. Indeed, it is to the founder of this style, Yatsuhashi Kengyō (1614-85), that most performance traditions today still trace their lineage and musical style, even though they might have developed their own unique place and performance identity within the world of *koto* music. Since the Edo period, and more particularly since late nineteenth-century political reforms, these *koto* performance traditions have been instrumental in the transmission of the *koto* and its music, and have consequently helped shape its place in contemporary Japan.[3]

This chapter explores aspects of the social, cultural and geographic distribution of the *koto* in Japan, and the social systems that are characteristic of the internal structure of everyday performance traditions. After outlining some of the social groups – court and aristocracy, blind male professional and female amateur – that have been connected with the instrument, the discussion turns to the different levels of social groupings that are typical in everyday performance. The chapter ends with a look at group structure and hierarchy, as well as examining permit systems and the use of performing names in contemporary *koto* traditions.

Court and Aristocracy

The Chinese origins of the *koto* embroiders the instrument with rich historical meaning and provides a distinct context that was responsible for its introduction to Japan. As mentioned earlier, the imperial court was the first main context of *koto* performance in the eighth century after the instrument's introduction to Japan; its players were either palace musicians or upper-class members of the imperial household.

Gagaku or court music has had a major influence on many styles of *koto* performance. This is seen in both the music itself (*see* Kubota 1980) and in the social institutions (performance groups and/or family lineages) that underlie the transmission of the music. Throughout the history of the *koto* in Japan, these social institutions have played a pivotal role in the instrument's transmission. Even from the first appearance of the *koto* in *gagaku*, family transmission of music within a hierarchical model has been evident (O'Neill 1984, 631-32). Harich-Schneider (1953, 52) comments that *gagaku* musicians "are recruited from a small number of families with imposing pedigrees claiming more than a thousand years of uninterrupted tradition. Their origin is traced in three lineages: from the aboriginal court clowns and dancers of the first Yamato [Japanese] chieftains, and from Korean and Chinese music teachers, who emigrated to Japan." Garfias (1975, 24) maintains that the function of the guilds of *gagaku* musicians was "not only to perform [at annual festivals] but also to teach younger musicians." In such a manner, a continuing line of performers was guaranteed for important religious and ceremonial events. For example, within the three recognized groups at the shrine Iwashimizu Hachimangū in Kyoto, the temples Kōfukuji in Nara and Shitennōji in Osaka – collectively known as the Sanbō Gakunin or Sanpō Gakujin (three groups of [*gagaku*] musicians) – two ranks of musicians were categorized according to ancestry. (A label was added to the player's name that helped in self-identity.) Later players, who could trace their family line to the Yamato or "Japanese" performers, became the higher-ranking musicians (using the name "ason"), and those of non-Japanese descent were of lower rank (called "sukune"). The sukune were restricted in the repertoire they could perform (Garfias 1975, 24).[4]

Gagaku is still performed in various contexts. Larger ensembles are located at the Imperial Palace, and at several larger shrines and temples such as the shrine of Kasuga taisha in Nara, the Buddhist temple Shitennōji in Osaka, and the Tenri-kyō religious sect in Tenri, Nara. Numerous smaller ensembles, which do not normally include the koto, are found at many smaller shrines, temples and even in secular contexts.[5] Male performers seem to have dominated gakusō performance, although there were and still are a few female players.

Within this historical context the koto has served as a valuable instrument in the imperial household in other ways. Lieberman (1971) has summarized music in the eleventh-century novel Genji monogatari and notes the significance of the koto and other instruments played by the noblewoman Lady Murasaki and the fictional Prince Genji. There are many instances throughout the novel where the koto is mentioned and some passages, as noted by de Ferranti (2000, 31), exhibit a link "with personalized playing styles and with the importance of performance traditions that were either secret or had become little known." The following passage from the chapter "Akashi" (a place name) in Genji monogatari, which depicts Genji and Murasaki's messenger, clearly depicts such images. The messenger comments that:

> On the koto [sō] I am in the third generation from the emperor Daigo. I have left the great world for the rustic surroundings in which you have found me, and sometimes when I have been more gloomy than usual I have taken out a koto and picked away at it.
>
> ...
>
> He did indeed play beautifully, adding decorations that have gone out of fashion. There was a Chinese elegance in his touch, and he was able to induce a particularly solemn tremolo from the instrument. Though it might have been argued that the setting was wrong, an adept among his retainers was persuaded to sing for them about the clean shore of Ise. Tapping out the rhythm, Genji would join in from time to time, and the old man would pause to offer a word of praise. (Murasaki 1976, 255-56)

In everyday koto music there are several striking references to gagaku or the imperial court, be they techniques in performance practice following those of gagaku or references in koto music song texts. The koto kumiuta entitled "Fuki" ("Rhubarb"), for example, which was composed by Yatsuhashi Kengyō in the seventeenth century – or at least adapted by him from an earlier kumiuta of the Tsukushigoto – is actually based on the melody of the celebrated gagaku piece "Etenraku" ("Beyond Heaven Music"). Verse 2 is as follows:

haru no hana no kingyoku	to the spring blossoms ch'in [qin] music
Kafūraku ni Ryūka'en	Kafūraku and Ryūka'en[6]
Ryūka'en no uguisu wa	a warbler in the Willow-Blossom-Gardens
onaji kyoku o saezuru	the same two pieces does it twitter
	(Ackermann 1990, 334)

Many of the sources for kumiuta are classical works that later conveyed imagery of a perceived traditional Japan. A further level of historical and social reference is found in verse 2 of "Fuki" with the reference to the qin (Chinese seven-string zither; see Chapter 2). In Japan, the qin was known as another type of koto (kin no koto), and in both Japan and China it was associated with literati. One of the tools koto composers of the Tsukushigoto and later everyday traditions used was to index an idealized Heian court in their song texts. As such they referenced the qin and the koto in the court context as a way of adding immense cultural importance to the music. As Ackermann (1990, 344) notes, "presumably the koto kumiuta merely wishes to evoke the image of the Heian court and ancient China." Holvik (1992, 448) mentions that this koto kumiuta, as the one normally learned first, helps establish its place in the repertoire: "This is done by connecting it to the venerable history of the instruments of the koto family and their music in China and Japan, particularly to the high position of koto music in the court life of the Heian period ... and to ancient Chinese beliefs in its moral effects and magical powers." Also, it should be noted that Kenjun, the Tsukushigoto player whose *kumiuta* inspired Yatsuhashi Kengyō, actually learned the *qin*.[7] In verse 5 there is a specific reference to life at the Imperial Palace in Heian-Kyō (Kyoto):

Kōkiden no hosodono ni	standing in the *hosodono*[8] chamber
tatazumu wa taredare	of the *Kōkiden*,[9] who are they?
Oborozukiyo-no-naishi no kami	Oborozukiyo, the lady of the Inner Palace
Hikaru Genji no taishō	Prince Genji the shining Lord
	(Ackermann 1990, 335)

Verse 5 is based on the short text in the chapter "Hana no En" ("Festival of the Cherry Blossoms") in *Genji monogatari*. Even this chapter contains a reference to the *koto*:

> He [Genji] played the thirteen-stringed koto, his performance if anything subtler and richer than that of the day before. Fujitsubo [a wife of Genji's father] went to the emperor's apartments at dawn.
> Genji was on tenterhooks, wondering whether the lady he had seen in the dawn moonlight would be leaving the palace. (Murasaki 1976, 153-54)

In addition to the inherent cultural symbolism in its song text, "Fuki" is also connected with other music and dramatic art forms. For example, part of its text can also be found in the *nō* play "Kan'yōkyū" (Japanese reading of "Hsien Yang Palace" in China), which itself references the chapter "Kan'yōkyū" in *Heike monogatari* (*Tales of Heike*):

> The reference of the *koto kumiuta Fuki* to *Kanyōkyū* – a *nō* play of unknown authorship, possibly dating from the early 15th century – is almost certainly to be understood as a powerful allusion to the harmonizing quality of the music of the cithern [*qin*], an instrument capable of restoring a state of balance in the world and the universe. (Ackermann 1990, 345)

Many other *koto kumiuta* have similar references (*see* Ackermann 1990). In addition to "Fuki", several other pieces from Yatsuhashi Kengyō's thirteen *koto kumiuta* repertoire refer to aspects of *Genji monogatari*, or indeed are actually sourced from textual elements of the work: "Umegae" ("On a Plumb Branch", verses 2, 4), "Kokoro Zukushi" ("Exhausting One's Heart", verse 4), "Tenga Taihei" ("Peace in the Emperor's Realm", verses 4-5), "Usuyuki" ("Light Snow", verses 1-4), "Yuki no Ashita" ("Morning of Fresh-Fallen Snow", verses 2, 6), "Usugoromo" ("Thin Garments", verses 5-6), "Kiritsubo" ("The Paulownia Court", verses 4, 6), "Suma" (place name, verses 1, 4-6), "Shiki no Kyoku" ("Piece of the Four Seasons"), and "Ōgi no Kyoku" ("Piece of the Fan", verse 1).[10]

Other genres of *koto* music such as *jiuta sōkyoku* also have pieces that reference *Genji monogatari* (e.g., "Yūgao" ["Evening Faces"] by Kikuoka Kengyō, 1792-1847; "Aoi no Ue" ["Lady Aoi"] and "Kogō" ["Lady Kogō"] by Yamada Kengyō). However, the more formal genre of *kumiuta* abounds with such citations or allusions (*see* further Ackermann 1990; Tsuge 1983a).

The Tōdō and Blind Male Professionals

Since the time of Yatsuhashi Kengyō and the introduction of the *koto* to blind male professional musicians in the seventeenth century, everyday traditions of secular *koto* performance have transmitted the instrument and its music to the present day through diverse social affiliations and cultural contexts. These groups have helped to reinforce the instrument's place as a traditional instrument. While some employed a slightly different form of the instrument, manner of playing and music interpretation, each of which has aided a particular group (small scale) or tradition (large scale) in creating its own identity vis-à-vis others, it is the instrument's everyday social connections and conventions that have had a major impact on the way it has been transmitted in Japanese culture. That is, the use of the *koto* within special social groups dedicated to *koto* performance, ones that are based around hierarchy and solidarity, has been pivotal in the transmission of the instrument and its music in Japanese culture. As a result, dedicating oneself to the tradition of one's teacher is essentially the norm when learning the instrument.

The social institution of blind male professional musicians, or Tōdō,[11] had the greatest bearing on everyday *koto* transmission. Translated as "this way" or "our way", the Tōdō is sometimes referred to as the Tōdō-za (or Tōdō no za), Tōdō Shokuyashiki, or Shokuyashiki (the Shokuyashiki was the administrative office of the Tōdō in Kyoto). At the end of the seventeenth century the Tōdō established an additional central organization in Edo (Tokyo) called Sōrokuyashiki (Fritsch 1996, 76). Further administration houses were set up as the organization disseminated to other parts of Japan, and these were operated by regional groups (Fritsch 1996, 77).

The exact origins of the Tōdō are rather vague, yet one theory states that it was founded by Prince Saneyasu, (Fritsch 1991, 147), the fourth son of Emperor Ninmyō (*r.* 833-50), who became a priest after losing his eyesight due to illness. The word Tōdō was already known in the Kamakura period and was soon associated with blind *biwa* (lute) players (Fritsch 1996, 70). The Tōdō's main historical connection was with *heikyoku* (narrations of the twelfth-century *Heike monogatari* to *biwa* accompaniment), which signified a move from the itinerant *biwa hōshi* traditions (blind itinerant musicians who recited to *biwa* accompaniment) to the formal entertaining art of *Heikebiwa*.

The consequence of Prince Saneyasu being blind is that the musicians of the Tōdō had to be blind. Their profession was perceived as inferior to the so-called "high" arts of *nō* and *gagaku* that were openly patronized by the military rulers and aristocracy. Nevertheless, the blind were once believed to have magical powers – in some parts of Japan they still are – but by the Edo period were deemed a lower class and occasionally linked to the *hinin* or "non-human" caste (Fritsch 1996, 10). However, as Fritsch (1996, 62) has pointed out, while the connection between the Tōdō and *hinin* is not clear, the Tōdō did gain official separation from the *hinin* in the sixteenth century.[12]

During the Edo period, blind musicians, like the increasingly wealthy merchant class, were at the bottom of social ladder. Together they were essentially responsible for the flourishing of everyday *koto* performance – the blind as professional players and the merchant class as amateur practitioners.[13] The Tōdō monopolized everyday *koto* music at this time; women and sighted men were excluded from its ranks. However, in a somewhat ironic twist, *koto* music was often considered appropriate for the daughters of the samurai class, who were taught by their blind teachers (Adriaansz 1971, 64). It was here that the instrument became associated with social refinement outside the court and temple traditions, but in an influential, albeit still essentially private, social sphere. The Tōdō was at first dependent on the patronage of such high-ranking families and religious institutions, but in the early seventeenth century it was officially acknowledged by the ruling Tokugawa shogunate who supported their activities (Tsuge

1983b, 60). From the shogunate the Tōdō received privileges including recognition as a self-administrating organization, of their economic status, as a money lending business, and complete exemption of taxes (Fritsch 1996, 76). In connection with money lending, Seigle (1993, 160-61) comments that as well as making a living through music or massage, some blind men in the Yoshiwara pleasure quarters of Edo might simply have purchased the Kengyō rank and begun money lending: "These blind moneylenders were feared and hated for their ruthlessness in the collection of their debts" (Seigle 1993, 161).[14]

The head of the Tōdō (with the title Sō-Kengyō or Shoku-Kengyō) supervised an inner group that oversaw all members through local branches around the country. The head position would have been held by one of the oldest members of the group, and it was comparable with that of a feudal lord. The blind musicians who belonged to the Tōdō entered at a young age and were addressed by special names that indicated their rank within the group. It was inherently a strict, hierarchical institution, and the tonsured members (in imitation of *biwa hōshi*) consisted of over seventy levels of social rank, which were divided in four main titles somewhat similar to rankings found in Buddhism: Zatō (levels 4-18), Kōtō (levels 19-53), Bettō (levels 54-63),[15] and Kengyō (levels 64-72) (Fritsch 1996, 73-75):

> The combination of these factors resulted in an authoritarian system, characterized by strong reciprocal obligations, that discouraged the development of individual initiative in younger musicians. This suppression of initiative, combined with the exclusion of a good deal of available talent by the practical limitation of professional koto musicians to blind men, is undoubtedly largely responsible for the striking homogeneity of the repertory of the various schools; to a lesser degree aesthetic considerations have also been responsible. Homogeneity eventually led to stagnation, which could be broken only by the emergence of a musician of exceptional talent who might initiate a new style of composition and thereby a new school. (Adriaansz 1984, 467)

The Tōdō was abolished by the Meiji government in 1871, as was the use of ranked titles. Only the term Kengyō is very rarely used today. Since the social changes in the Meiji era, *koto* musicians have still formed performance and organizational groups in a way analogous to those regulated by the Tōdō, which have been a fundamental part of playing the instrument and influencing its dissemination. Moreover, there are several Ikuta-ryū traditions today that still use the term Tōdō in their name, such as Tōdō Ongaku-kai, Kyōto Tōdō-kai,[16] Nihon Tōdō Ongaku-kai, Nihon Tōdō-kai, and Tōdō Yūraku-kai. Some of these groups still award licenses similar to the Tōdō, although much of their former authority has been lost. The very existence of new groups of *koto* performance such as these was in part a response to the abolition of the Tōdō (Galliano 2002, 17).

Women and Amateur *Koto* Playing

Social control in one way or another regarding the transmission of the *koto* has occurred throughout its history. For example, women and blind men were excluded from the Tsukushigoto, which led to the establishment of a tradition specifically for blind men (regulated by the Tōdō), and during the Edo period women and sighted men were excluded from performing *zokusō* professionally, but not from learning as amateurs. While the transmission of *koto* music has been connected with distinct social spheres such as at the imperial court, in the Tsukushigoto and in the traditions of the Tōdō, its survival today depends mainly on its popularity among amateur women players. Indeed, as mentioned earlier, ever since the introduction of the instrument to the Tōdō, blind male professionals would often teach the daughters of the samurai class. Nevertheless, while the instrument has historically had distinct gender associations, *koto* performance traditions and their structures have helped influence the continuity of *koto* performance to the present day where there are no restrictions on who can play the instrument.

Even though blind men dominated professional *koto* performance during the Edo period, there is substantial pictorial evidence, especially in woodblock prints, of women playing the instrument. Moreover, it is through such imagery that the instrument gained an association of social refinement and connection with amateur female arts. There are many woodblock prints that show the *koto* being played by female amateurs and not professional performers.[17] Many different contexts are depicted, including the imperial household, everyday life and courtesans of the Yoshiwara pleasure quarters in Edo.[18] Of course, one has to take artistic license into account as women were often depicted in situations that in real life were dominated by men. However, the fact that women playing the *koto* were depicted at all helped reinforce the place of the instrument among women, something that was taken much further after the abolition of the Tōdō in 1871 when the instrument became predominantly associated as an amateur artistic pursuit for women. From this time onward women had the opportunity to play the *koto* in more social contexts than previously (i.e., they could now perform publicly, teach and lead the performance groups). Nevertheless, while there have been no social restrictions to impede men or women from playing since the mid-Meiji era, and women now dominate *koto* performance, the leading figures in *koto* composition and performance in the twentieth-century were still men like Miyagi Michio (1894-1956), Nakanoshima Kin'ichi (1904-84) and Sawai Tadao (1937-97). Falconer (1995, 77) comments that Sawai Tadao was "the first in his family line to play koto." But in a slight twist to the social context of *koto* transmission, "Sawai's father played shakuhachi, but Sawai was attracted to the koto as an instrument from the time of his youth. He says that he taught himself the basics behind his father's back – because it was seen by his father as an instrument better suited to women. He should play shakuhachi – an exclusively male instrument – rather than koto."

Traditions, Lineages and Groups

"Groupism" is integral to most everyday *koto* performers. A player would normally belong to a performance tradition, which itself might have several hierarchical levels of group affiliation from a teacher's immediate students to larger social units. This belonging might take several forms, but *not* to belong is *not* the norm and would usually only occur when the instrument is used in extreme ways. To know one's place in a tradition, whatever the level, vis-à-vis other performance traditions, as well as one's social position in that group, is not only essential in this area of Japanese culture, but also important in understanding classification and organization in other spheres of Japanese society (*cf.* Ohnuki-Tierney 1993, 99-113). The Japanese sociologist Nakane Chie, for example, has written much on Japanese groupism and notes the term *ba* (frame) as an underlying concept in connection with points of reference (Nakane 1970, 1-8).[19] It is the social frame that is given priority in self-identification, rather than one's personal attributes (*see also* Lebra 1976, 22-25), and the reference group could be, for example, birthplace, house, school or company, and might signify the present or past. Social introductions are replete with questions that first establish the identity of the other party according to their places of reference. Name cards too, which are exchanged ritually in such contexts, usually have the name of one's affiliation(s), together with an indication of one's social position. Such status symbols are further illustrated by the behavior and language that is used during such exchanges, which helps Japanese know their social place.

In *koto* performance, this manner of self-identification is similarly made regarding the tradition to which one belongs. While oral and visual symbols can often identify a player according to performance practice (e.g., type of instrument and component parts, shape of plectra and style of ornamentation), further levels of identity are sometimes necessary in order to place oneself within a social web of belonging and difference. *Koto* players primarily belong to performance groups rather than learn as soloists,[20] and these groups more often than not act as the main means by which the instrument and its music are transmitted through teaching and performance. A player might learn in a one-on-one context and even give solo performances, but underlying this is usually an affiliation or association of one type or another to a performance tradition that is essential to knowing one's place in the world of *koto* performance. While there are other ways of analyzing Japanese society – the place of the individual, conflict, competition, social exchange, and psychological models – the notion of groupism should be seen as one significant structuring device that is useful in the study of *koto* performance, its social transmission and the way in which *koto* players negotiate a performance identity among the instrument's various traditions.

The complex arrangement of hierarchies and structures connected with performance groups aids players in establishing their place and identity in *koto* performance. Similar practices have been evident to scholars for many years in Japanese art:

> Since the medieval period [twelfth to early seventeenth century], merchants, artisans and performers of various arts [especially the theatrical genres *sarugaku*, *nō* and *kyōgen*] had formed protective groups called *za* under the patronage of politically influential institutions or individual courtiers to whom they had to provide certain services. This type of subordinate relationship … granted guild-members special status privileges, e.g. exemption from business taxes, and asserted their rights to monopolistic control over specific professional or mercantile activities. (Fritsch 1991, 150)[21]

An interesting point today concerning the performance of, for example, *nō* (an aristocratic genre) and *kabuki* theater (a more populist form) is that musicians and actors usually have their own separate traditions, and it is only during the performance that they come together. A similar situation is occasionally encountered in *koto* performance, where *koto* players of different traditions very rarely perform together.[22] However, when other types of instruments such as the *shakuhachi* or *kokyū* are included with the *koto* in ensemble (i.e., *sankyoku*), it follows that the players of these instruments generally hail from a performance tradition specific to that instrument, thereby bringing different groups together for the performance.

While the world of *koto* music includes solo and ensemble music, soloists are greatly outweighed by the performing group to which he or she would normally belong. Naturally solo performances do occur, but only in connection with the group as a whole. For the player of traditional Japanese *koto* music, group affiliation is usually expected as part of the learning process and is seen to be embedded deeply in the Japanese socio-cultural system. Success as a soloist would normally come through some sort of performance group affiliation, and only then would separation or extension of that affiliation occur. The soloist might subsequently gain the admiration required for the formation of a new group, which itself may gradually become a tradition of *koto* performance, as with, for example, the Miyagi-ha (Miyagi faction). For a *koto* player, as well as for many others engaged in traditional Japanese arts, the need to belong to an artistic group is a fundamental part of one's identity. A player usually belongs to their group for life, and it is rare that a member would leave his or her group to join another.[23] Malm (2000, 202) writes that "the fact that one is not allowed to study with other teachers reinforces this sense of belonging." Even if one moves to another region, one would more often than not seek out a branch of one's tradition rather than join a new group. The uniformity, or harmony (*wa*), of a group is such that a player not only retains a life-long fidelity to their group, but also participates in activities relating to the group like the organization of everyday and special

Hokkaidō

Yamada-ryū

Ikuta-ryū

Tsuguyama-ryū

Tsukushi-ryū

Honshū

Tōkyō

Osaka

Shikoku

Kyūshū

76 *Koto* performance traditions
(after Tanabe 1919, 762).

events. A player's performance group is the *uchi* (inside), those groups with a different identity are perceived as *soto* (outside).

The importance of tradition in terms of one's genealogy – as in most traditions in Japan – is evident even in many Japanese writings on the *koto*, which sometimes include a chart depicting performance lineage or a detailed description that traces the origins of everyday *koto* performance to Yatsuhashi Kengyō.[24] Some *koto* groups can trace their history to the ninth century, although their exact origins should be questioned because sometimes it is seen to be more important for them to have a favorable genealogy than genuinely verified origins (*see* Fritsch 1991).

Tanabe (1919, 762) includes a map from the early twentieth century that outlines the geographical distribution of *koto* traditions at the time. Four distinct traditions can be discerned (fig. 76). If we disregard the pre-*zokusō* temple tradition called Tsukushi-ryū (an alternative term for the Tsukushigoto)[25] and the Tsuguyama-ryū (usually considered today as part of the Ikuta-ryū), there is in fact only two main traditions which are clearly divided geographically – the Yamada-ryū to the east and the Ikuta-ryū to the west (*see* Chapter 2). The repertoire, performance practice, instruments, and geographic distribution of these two traditions are still often compared historically and/or synchronically to each other (and sometimes to other *koto* groups) in order to show their exact historical position and identity.

Within the Ikuta-ryū and the Yamada-ryū there are other levels of affiliation to which players identify. The Ikuta-ryū, in particular, has many sub-traditions, and the Yamada-ryū, which functions more as an homogenous tradition, has a number of groups centering around leading players (*see* Kishibe 1973). Diagrams such as that in figure 77 showing twelve main traditions often include several recurring terms or classifications that point to group affiliation or lineage.[26] For instance, as discussed below, one finds traditions (*ryū*), factions (*ha*) and lines of players (e.g., *suji* or *kei*). These classifications, some of which are often used for scholarly purposes and not always by the players themselves, are instructive in illustrating the broad groupings of musicians as well as the historical and geographical distribution of everyday *koto* performance in Japan. A characteristic of a genealogical chart such as this, which spans nearly

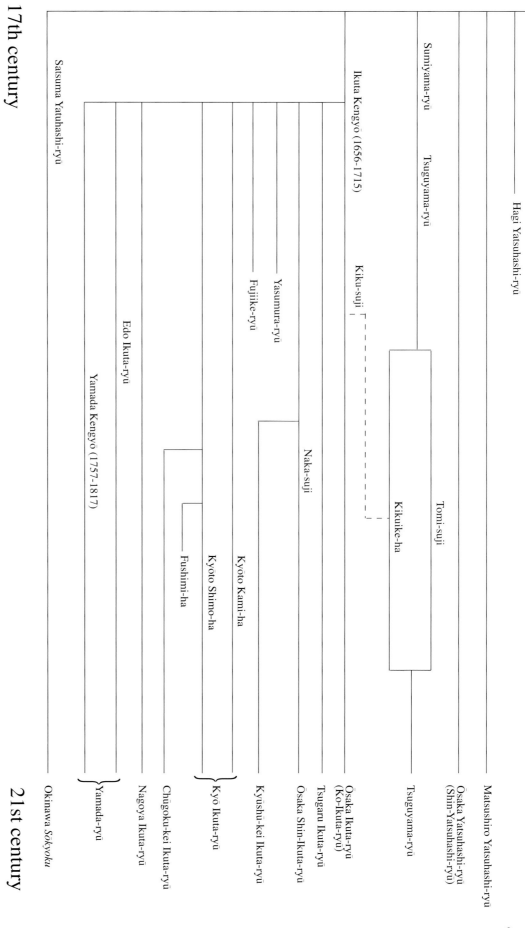

77 Lineage of *zokusō* traditions (after Hirano 1989b, 44-45).

17th century

Yatsuhashi Kengyō (1614-85)

Sumiyama-ryū

Ikuta Kengyō (1656-1715)

Satsuma Yatuhashi-ryū

Hagi Yatsuhashi-ryū

Tsuguyama-ryū

Kiku-suji

Yasumura-ryū

Fujiike-ryū

Edo Ikuta-ryū

Yamada Kengyō (1757-1817)

Naka-suji

Kikuike-ha

Tomi-suji

Kyōto Kami-ha

Kyōto Shimo-ha

Fushimi-ha

21st century

Okinawa *Sōkyoku*

Yamada-ryū

Nagoya Ikuta-ryū

Chūgoku-kei Ikuta-ryū

Kyō Ikuta-ryū

Kyūshū-kei Ikuta-ryū

Ōsaka Shin-Ikuta-ryū

Tsugaru Ikuta-ryū

Ōsaka Ikuta-ryū (Ko-Ikuta-ryū)

Tsuguyama-ryū

Ōsaka Yatsuhashi-ryū (Shin-Yatsuhashi-ryū)

Matsushiro Yatsuhashi-ryū

98

four hundred years, is the increased division splintering into further groups over time. *Keifu* (genealogy), therefore, is an important concept in the understanding of how ideas of place and identity are formulated, and this is reflected repeatedly in other traditional Japanese arts, such as tea ceremony, flower arranging, martial arts, calligraphy, painting, arts and crafts, and other music genres (*see* Hsu 1975, 62).

Several terms listed in figure 77 require explanation. Some place names and family names are used: Matsushiro (in Niigata Prefecture), Hagi (in Yamaguchi Prefecture); Kyoto (Kyō is an abbreviation), Fushimi (in Kyoto), Edo (an historical name for Tokyo), Satsuma (an historical name for Kagoshima Prefecture), Okinawa (a southern island chain),[27] Tsugaru (the north-western part of Aomori Prefecture),[28] Nagoya (a city in Aichi Prefecture), and Chūgoku (a region comprising the southern part of Honshū). Each is the name of the main geographic area in which a tradition is, or was, situated. The terms Kiku, Tomi and Naka denote the performers Kikunaga Kengyō (1742-1824), Tomizawa Kōtō (*d.* 1876) and Nakamura Kengyō (act. *c.* 1828), respectively. Ikuta, Yamada, Yatsuhashi, Sumiyama, Kitajima, Tsuguyama, Kikuike, Fujiike, and Yasumura are drawn from the names of people who have pioneered a specific performance tradition: Ikuta Kengyō, Yamada Kengyō, Yatsuhashi Kengyō, Sumiyama Kengyō (act. *c.* 1664), Kitajima Kengyō, Tsuguyama Kengyō, Kikuike Kengyō (act. *c.* 1830), Fujiike Kengyō (act. latter half of the eighteenth century), and Yasumura Kengyō (*d.* 1779). The terms *kami* and *shimo* refer to the upper and lower parts of Kyoto, respectively; and the terms *ko* and *shin* mean old and new.

Ryū

The term *ryū* generally appears as a suffix in the name of a *koto* tradition. While describing a general level of affiliation, *ryū* also has the meaning of "flowing" and is used to denote a tradition or school of performance. It is usually used as a macro concept in that the tradition is more often than not a large number of performers who share, or imagine sharing, an affiliation through lineage rather than personal acquaintance. The concept of "flowing" is embraced in the structure and function of the tradition with its need for continuity and survival, where ideas are passed from teacher to pupil, and from private to public contexts. It is also encountered in other traditional arts – in swordsmanship, for example, there are as many as seven hundred such traditions (O'Neill 1984, 634).

As shown in figure 77, the main everyday *koto* traditions can be traced to Yatsuhashi Kengyō. Yatsuhashi lived most of his life in Edo, but he traveled frequently to Kyoto. As the founder of everyday performance, one might expect Yatsuhashi to have had his own *ryū*. However, the term Yatsuhashi-ryū was not used during his lifetime, and the formal tradition of Yatsuhashi-ryū was established by Kagawa Kengyō (1684-1769) and his pupil Kamejima Kengyō (1711-93) in order to distinguish the tradition from others that emerged around the same time (Adriaansz 1973, 12). Today, the term Yatsuhashi-ryū has several layers of meaning, each of which refers to a more specific tradition of performance:

1 Yatsuhashi Kengyō or the line of performers until Kitajima Kengyō, which is sometimes referred to as the Ko-Yatsuhashi-ryū (Old Yatsuhashi tradition);

2 The Hagi Yatsuhashi-ryū (Hagi Yatsuhashi tradition);

3 The Matsushiro Yatsuhashi-ryū (Matsushiro Yatsuhashi tradition), discovered in Matsushiro (Nagano Perfecture) in the 1950s (*see* Adriaansz 1971, 63);[29]

4 The Satsuma Yatsuhashi-ryū (Satsuma Yatsuhashi tradition);

5 The Ōsaka Yatsuhashi-ryū (Osaka Yatsuhashi tradition), also called Shin-Yatsuhashi-ryū (New Yatsuhashi tradition); and,

6 The Yatsuhashi style of *shamisen* performance.

Even though Yatsuhashi Kengyō is understood as the father of everyday *koto* music, most *koto* players will identify themselves initially with either the Ikuta-ryū or the Yamada-ryū. The term Ikuta-ryū is used as a general classification or grouping of players who trace their lineage back to Ikuta Kengyō. Up until the time of Yamada Kengyō, Tsukushigoto was also practiced in Tokyo. An Ikuta-ryū sub-tradition of Mitsuhashi Kengyō moved to Edo from Kyoto in the mid-eighteenth century, but was not established in any strength until Yasumura Kengyō of Kyoto sent his student Hasetomi Kengyō (*d*. 1793) to Edo. Hasetomi taught Yamada Shōkoku, a doctor, who in turn taught Mita Toyoichi. Mita later became Yamada Kengyō, the founder of the Yamada-ryū.

The formation of *ryū* is sometimes accompanied by such things as adjustments in instrument construction, modification of playing techniques or a change in performance procedures. With the Yamada-ryū, several such changes were made, especially as the tradition developed a more narrative style compared to the Ikuta-ryū. The rectangular plectra of the Ikuta-ryū became oval shaped, a kneeling position was opted for that directly faced the instrument (rather than the angled kneeling position in the Ikuta-ryū), ornamentation techniques were adapted to suit the new plectra, the instrument itself had most of its lacquer work removed – together with several other changes in instrument design – and unique genres and original interpretation of the traditional repertoire were developed.

While the Ikuta-ryū is the larger of the two main everyday traditions, each exists today vis-à-vis one another, albeit in a kind of symbiotic relationship. It is a division that fits conveniently into the way of dichotomizing culture into concepts of "us" and "them" (*uchi/soto*) that is often foregrounded in Japanese society. The importance of the geographic division between these two traditions is also understood in the broader context of Japan as a whole, for it encompasses a geographic division in the physical sense as well. The two main low-lying areas of the main island of Honshū that are ideally suited for inhabitation are the areas around Tokyo in the east (i.e., Kantō) and Osaka/Kyoto/Nara to the west (i.e., Kansai). As Fairbank, Reischauer and Craig (1973, 324) observe, Japan "is made up of narrow river valleys and alluvial coastal plains separated from one another by stretches of rugged hills. Land communication therefore is not easy." The divisions of Kantō and Kansai are part of a geographic partition that has also influenced such aspects as language and culture. Kantō and Kansai are often contrasted in everyday discourse where aspects of the sub-culture of one side of Japan are compared to those of the other in order to reinforce a binary division of Japanese culture on a macro level. Even today, the Kantō and Kansai dialects are the two that are most frequently compared and differentiated, even though there are many throughout Japan.

The two main everyday *koto* performance traditions today mirror this geographic and cultural division. This dichotomy too might be viewed as a type of *uchi/soto* division, which is seen to underlie many aspects of Japanese society. To belong to a tradition or group is to be on the inside (us), while members of other groups are essentially on the outside (them). But the *uchi/soto* dichotomy is more complex than simply an "us/them" division. There are various types of *uchi/soto*, and the zone lying between the various *koto* traditions is perhaps more often than not an intermediate one where restraint (*enryo*) is shown. There might certainly be rivalry between some *koto* groups that are closer to one another than between *koto* groups that are distantly related. This might be seen as a relationship not based on the idea of an anonymous other, but on an identifiable other where *koto* traditions have many things in common on a general level, albeit where *enryo* is the norm with ritualized and conventionalized behavior that acknowledges similarity on the one hand, but difference on the other.

As concerns the organization of the two main everyday performance traditions, the name Ikuta-ryū signifies a general identity where the tradition does not function as a self-organizing group,[30] while the Yamada-ryū actually has a main organizing body, the Yamada-ryū Sōkyoku Kyōkai (The Yamada-tradition *Koto* Association), which actively controls and influences the direction of most Yamada-ryū performers.[31] This differs from the Ikuta-ryū. While most players identify on a general level with either the Ikuta-ryū or the Yamada-ryū, it can happen, although very rarely, that some are affiliated with both traditions, or belong to collective organizations that include players from both traditions in the form of mixed *ryū* groups. Fujita (1973) lists five such players who include *ryū* affiliation to both the Ikuta-ryū and the Yamada-ryū. Such players are often connected with smaller groups who, through geographic proximity, personal choice of repertoire or by social connections, find themselves not identifying with one specific tradition. Fujita (1973) also lists twenty-one smaller groups (out of nearly 200) as mixed *ryū* with a membership of over 12,000 players. Most of the mixed *ryū* groups are associations rather than traditions or lines of performers in the general sense.

In contrast to the general levels of association with the Ikuta-ryū, a further level connected with the term *ryū* is occasionally found with players whose immediate group operates on several levels at any one time. For instance, the Chikushi-ryū, founded by Chikushi Katsuko (1904-84) in 1949 and centered around Fukuoka and the north of Kyūshū, classifies itself as an independent *ryū*, but on a general level identifies itself with the Ikuta-ryū.[32] A similar yet more specific use of the term *ryū* is with the Kyōgoku-ryū, which was established by Suzuki Koson (1875-1931) in the early twentieth century in reaction to Western influence.[33] As Adriaansz (1973, 20) avouches, "around 1900 a personal response to his confrontation with Western music was given by Suzuki Koson ... in a number of works that have been characterized as a combination of romantic feeling with classic form. ... Nowadays its works are rarely performed." Members of the Kyōgoku-ryū sit crossed-legged to play the *koto* and wear traditional attire that includes a *kanmuri* (head gear) (Kikkawa 1997, 133).

Today there are numerous modern *koto* performance traditions. Many have direct, albeit loose, ties with the Ikuta-ryū, and some have established their own unique identity. The Sawai Sōkyoku-in (Sawai *Koto* School), for example, was founded in Tokyo by Sawai Tadao and his wife Sawai Kazue in 1979; in the mid-1990s it had around 2,500 students (*see* Falconer 1995). Sawai Tadao, a composer and *koto* player, studied at Tokyo National University of Fine Arts and Music. One of his teachers was Miyagi Michio. The Sawai Sōkyoku-in is seen as modern and innovative, even though its players would be conversant with the traditional repertoire. Not only has this school developed its own novel repertoire centered around the compositions of Sawai Tadao, but it is also avant-garde in its performance of music. For example, rather than wearing traditional kimono during a *koto* recital, which is the norm for most *koto* players, Sawai Kazue appeared in black leather pants and boots for a concert in 1986 (Falconer 1995, 47).

Ha

The term *ha* is used in connection with *koto* traditions to signify a group that is on the one hand a branch or faction of a larger group, and on the other hand large enough to be considered a tradition in its own right. In the authoritative and comprehensive dictionary of traditional Japanese music, *Nihon ongaku daijiten* (*see* Hirano, Kamisangō and Gamō 1989), Hirano (1989b; *see* fig. 77) lists four examples of *ha*: Kikuike-ha (also called the Kikuike-ryū), Kyōto Shimo-ha, Kyōto Kami-ha and Fushimi-ha (a branch of the Kyōto Shimo-ha). The first of these is a line within the Tsuguyama-ryū, the others fall within the Kyō Ikuta-ryū. All are part of the broader Ikuta-ryū. Even in the city of Osaka, the prominence of lines of musicians in northern and southern parts of the city have spawned the two classifications of Kita-ha (North branch) and Minami-ha (South branch), which indicate players who identify more closely with the Ōsaka Ikuta-ryū (Ko-Ikuta-ryū) and the Tsuguyama-ryū, respectively.[34]

The line of *koto* music from Yatsuhashi Kengyō that divides into further traditions and sub-traditions can be compared to the *dōzoku* (clan/lineage) system with its *honke* (main house) and *bunke* (branch houses). Hsu (1975) relates the historical social processes and organizational structures of Japanese society to the development of the *iemoto* system (*see below*, Group Structure and Hierarchy).[35] There may be any of a number of reasons underlying the division, but the process of organizing a new tradition is one that allows continuity of music and musicians, while at the same time nurturing variation and development of music. Such a process enables musicians to form social units that are integral not only to the transmission of *koto* music, but also to the self-identity of *koto* players.

The *ryū* and *ha* lineage system (*ryūha*) is employed as a means of identifying a player's group affiliation on a large scale. The Miyagi-ha, for example, was established by Miyagi Michio who, according to the lineage chart by Hirano (1989b), is an adherent of the Ko-Ikuta-ryū, itself part of the wider Ikuta-ryū. The Miyagi-ha is a reference to players who belong to the Miyagi-kai (Miyagi group),³⁶ which was formed in 1951 due to the enormous popularity of Miyagi Michio and the subsequent continuation of the group by his successors and students. It describes a highly influential branch of the Ikuta-ryū. The term *ha* in this instance is an indication of the success of the group as an independent entity within the sphere of everyday *koto* performance.

Another example of the application of the term *ha* not included by Hirano (1989b) is seen with the Sei-ha, which was established in 1913 by Ikuta-ryū (Ōsaka Shin-Ikuta-ryū) player Nakashima Utashito (1896-1979). The name Sei-ha is an abbreviation for the group's other names, Sei-ha Hōgaku-kai (Sei-ha Traditional Japanese Music Group) and Sei-ha Ongaku-in (Sei-ha Music School). Another use of *ha* is found in the Yamada-ryū with the organization of groups or factions around some prominent players (e.g., Nakanoshima Kin'ichi and Nakanoshima-ha) (Fujita 1973, 291).

Kei

Leading from the larger traditions of *koto* performance (*ryūha*) are smaller groups or divisions of affiliation to which *koto* players sometimes identify. A term that is sometimes utilized for such a line of musicians is *kei*. With various connotations, *kei* is used in the context of *koto* transmission to indicate a grouping of a larger tradition based on geographic location. Hirano (1989b) lists two examples of *kei*: Kyūshū-kei Ikuta-ryū (a grouping that traces its lineage to Ikuta Kengyō and centered on the island of Kyūshū) and the Chūgoku-kei Ikuta-ryū (a grouping that traces its lineage to Ikuta Kengyō and centered around the western region on Japan's main island of Honshū). Both are loosely classed as Ikuta-ryū. These second-level classifications as indicated by *kei* suffixes are not normally employed as general terms, the players usually preferring to use the term Ikuta-ryū instead.

Suji

The term *suji*, a "sinew" or "lineage" (A. Nelson 1974, 684), is listed three times by Hirano (1989b). It is used solely as a suffix to a performer's name: Tomi-suji, Kiku-suji and Naka-suji, which are lines within Tsuguyama-ryū, Ōsaka Ikuta-ryū and Ōsaka Shin-Ikuta-ryū, respectively. Each lineage belongs to the broader Ikuta-ryū.

Kai

Further levels of affiliation to which *koto* players identify often, but not exclusively, take the form of small-scale groups run by the players. The term *kai* refers to groupings that are found in micro levels of association, especially in the area of private tuition where the student pays a teacher for lessons and generally belongs to the group with direct links to the teacher. The term *kai* is frequently used by *koto* performers in connection with the group of a prominent musician. Fujita (1973) lists nearly 200 representative examples – numerous others exist – most of which function as the immediate group of a teacher and their students. The *kai* might also act as a license giver and performing group with several smaller groupings within it that center around specific teachers and their students. In *koto* performance, as in some other Japanese traditional arts, the term is sometimes utilized for larger groupings (*cf.* O'Neill 1984, 643). The Miyagi-kai, Sei-ha Hōgaku-kai and Chikushi-kai, for instance, are three such examples of well-known larger *koto* groups. The Miyagi-kai and Sei-ha are often referred to as *ha* (faction) to show their importance as sub-divisions of a larger tradition, and the last, Chikushi-kai, as *ryū* because of its influence and size in the northern part of Kyūshū. Each of these *kai* has branch offices throughout Japan.

Shachū

In the Ikuta-ryū the term *shachū* (troupe) is usually reserved for a teacher's immediate performing group and would normally include only the teacher's pupils. In the Yamada-ryū, however, the term identifies the lineage of its musicians on two levels: the present-day *shachū*, of which there are over twenty-five with around 50 to more than 500 members, each headed by an *iemoto* (the head; literally, "house origin") (Read and Locke 1983, 22); and the five historical *shachū*. Read and Locke (1983, 24) list the five historical *shachū* of the Yamada-ryū based on the lineage of the performers: Yamato Kengyō (1782-1863), Yamaki Kengyō (*d.* 1820), Yamase Kengyō (1791-1859), Onagi Kengyō (1791-1851), and Okumura Masago (1841-91). The first four were students of Yamada Kengyō, while Okumura Masago came from the Edo Ikuta-ryū. *Shachū* is employed as a term of reference rather than a group name, and if a group name is applied at this level it would more likely than not use the term *kai* or a similar term as a suffix.

In addition to the terms *kai* and *shachū*, several other labels are used for similar groupings. While most of the main small-scale groups that Fujita (1973) records have the term *kai* as a suffix to their name, other terms such as *sha* (company), *renmei* (league), *renmei-kai* (league/group), *shibu* (branch office), and *kyōkai* (association) are also encountered These alternative terms appear less frequently compared to the other terms (*cf. kai*). In Fujita (1973), *kyōkai* is not used by any Ikuta-ryū group, only once by a Yamada-ryū group and seventeen times by mixed *ryū* groups. Another term, *in* (school or institution), appears when discussing the groupings of *koto* performers, with perhaps the best-known example seen with the Sawai Sōkyoku-in.

Group Structure and Hierarchy

Closer examination of some *koto* performance groups and their organizational structure illustrates the social structure concerning how the instrument and its music are transmitted in Japanese society. As noted above, in the Yamada-ryū, the head of each branch (*shachū*) is called *iemoto*, but the existence of an *iemoto* is not exclusive to the *koto* and is seen in other traditional Japanese arts, such as tea ceremony, flower arranging and calligraphy. As head of a line, the *iemoto* holds the position of greatest respect and is responsible for conveying traditional social codes and conventions to the present day (*see* Hsu 1975; Kumakura 1981; Nishiyama 1997, 198-211; O'Neill 1984; Ortolani 1969; Read 1975; Read and Locke 1983; Yano 1992). According to O'Neill (1984, 635-38) the characteristics of the *iemoto* system (*iemoto seido*) can be summarized as: i) a hierarchical, pyramid-shaped organization; ii) traditional teaching with secret transmission of information; iii) hereditary succession; iv) sense of duty and obligation; and v) permit system.

The *iemoto* system, as well as analogous groupings of *koto* players, provides a social framework that does much to mirror Japanese society. Belonging to a *koto* group provides an organizational framework that is analogous with the extended family. In fact, the very terms *iemoto* (literally, "house origin") and the similarly labeled *sōke* (head family) each signify the concept of house or family in their written script. Each uses the same *kanji* for the words "house" and "family", albeit with a different reading: *ie* (house)/*moto* (origin) and *sō* (head)/*ke* (family). The concept of *iemoto* or a related term for the head of a tradition, therefore, is fundamental to the social structure of the *koto* group. The *iemoto* system in effect creates an extended family and personifies the Japanese concept of the group. The Japanese family system (*dōzoku*) with its hierarchical order of families (*ie*) can be seen as one of the main influences on the *iemoto* system. Emphasis on such concepts as family, stratification, structure, and community have each contributed to the structuring of this system. "The primary function of the iemoto is to preserve and embody the tradition of the shachu" (Read and Locke 1983, 21).

Within the performance group there are social relationships – both horizontal and vertical – that underpin its very existence, and which link it to other Japanese social systems. The vertical relationship noted by Read and Locke (1983, 37) is, from highest to lowest, *iemoto*, teacher, *natori* (when a student receives a performing name), student, and novice student. A strong horizontal affiliation also exists between members of the group who share the same rank. The leader of the group may have an inner circle of students who themselves may have obtained a teacher's license and perhaps even have a group with their own students. A typical license-giving group would function like this where the teacher (*sensei*) has his or her own *shachū* which constitutes part of the larger group. The all-embracing term *sensei* is a form of address by students for their teachers that embodies the hierarchical relationship that is formed between teachers and pupils. This teacher/pupil relationship is comparable with other hierarchical concepts in Japanese society, such as *oyabun/kobun* (parent/child) and *senpai/kōhai* (elder/junior) that were developed in the Edo period based on a family model influenced by neo-Confucianism, which was advocated by Shogun Tokugawa Ieyasu (1543-1616) during the Edo period and was pivotal in helping establish and maintain a socially harmonious Japan throughout that stage of Japanese history.

The *iemoto* system has been pivotal in the transmission of the *koto* and its music. Traditionally a rote-learning context (notation is usually used today), students engage in the teaching method of learning the repertoire of one's teacher, and follow a line of transmission of music interpretation that in the short term seems unchanging.[37] But, as Read and Locke (1983, 28) note, it is not a system that promotes innovation, and "the acceptance of the iemoto's authority, the close and lifelong bond between teacher and student, the strict oral teaching method, the long training period and the formal initiation ceremony [i.e., being accepted as a student] all have helped maintain the continued vitality and integrity of sokyoku as a classical artistic tradition" (Read and Locke 1983, 50). Thus, one wonders how *koto* music can continue to survive in such a rigid social system of learning and performance. The answer is in the very nature of the *ryūha* system, where division into branches occurs as a way of giving identity to a particular performance style, one that is usually based on that of a leading performer. Breakaway groups subsequently often develop into larger groups with their own musical style, after which the process of division would probably repeat itself. This is, of course, contradictory to the idea that members of a group should stay with their teacher and group for life. While many indeed do this, some do in fact leave to establish their own performance group, usually when they have achieved their own significant status as a performer and wish to establish a group with its own musical identity, or when the head of their group dies and there is conflict as to whom the next head should be.

There are also other concepts connected to Japanese group principles and associated with the social groupings of *koto* players. For example, the *tate* (vertical) and *yoko* (horizontal) axes are paramount when considering the place of a *koto* player in their performance tradition. The *yoko* level might be described as being concerned with one's peers, and the *tate* level with one's elders and superiors to whom one shows the greatest respect. Complex levels of group affiliation often occur in a system underpinned by hierarchy on the one hand and group fellowship on the other, and each is a fundamental principle in traditional Japanese society. The macro and micro level groupings that are internally organized are maintained within a structure that emphasizes hierarchy. In connection with authority as characteristic of a hierarchical system in the traditional arts, O'Neill (1984) illustrates organizational structures on comparative and historical levels where clan leaders predating the eighth century are shown in relation to their hierarchical structures. It seems from this that such structures have a deep-rooted historical place in Japanese society and have been transmitted to the present day in various forms in the arts. Many Japanese organizational frameworks exhibit related structures. As Benedict (1946, 55-56) has commented, "every Japanese learns the habit of hierarchy first in the bosom of his family and what he learns there he applies in wider fields of economic life and of government. He learns that a person gives all deference to those who outrank him in assigned 'proper place,' no matter whether or not they are the really dominant persons in the group." One might add to this the process of ancestor worship, which promotes the idea of looking to the past and toward one's elders.

The family, or group that embodies the family model, is placed before individual needs, and loyalty toward parents and elders is expected. The ideology of the family is represented not only in one's immediate household, but also in many other areas of Japanese society. The continuity of the family unit is an important idea that traditionally saw trades passed on through a family line, and in connection with *koto* performance saw the passing on of an art through extended family-like groups. Even in the home itself, the *ie* (family) is represented symbolically by the family *butsudan* (Buddhist altar) where ancestors are remembered. Some families also have a Shinto shrine. At special family celebrations the doors of the family *butsudan* are opened so that ancestors are not left out (Lebra 1976, 27). In a like fashion, the importance of knowing where one exists in *koto* performance traditions, and being able to trace one's ancestry through an acceptable line of performers, is reinforced by the need for good lineage to demonstrate a pure line of descent, or as Lebra (1976, 24) observes, "ambiguity in belonging arouses suspicion or contempt."

Koto groups (i.e., *kai* or equivalent) are usually organized using a hierarchical model that might be represented in a structure similar to the following (from the top down): leader (*iemoto*; or equivalent title such as *kaichō* [group leader], *sensei* [teacher], *sōke* [head family]), committee (*rijikai*), subcommittee (*fukuriji*), administration (e.g., *sōdanyaku* [adviser]), and general members (*kaiin*). Fujita's (1973) list of representative micro level groups includes a summary of the organizational structure of each. They all follow the same basic hierarchical structure, with some differences in terminology. For example, in Fujita's work the term *iemoto* is used only five times: three times in the Ikuta-ryū (two men and one woman) and twice in the Yamada-ryū (two men). The most common term for the leader of the group is *kaichō* (group leader), although the term *sōke* also appears. While the leader of the group may not be labeled *iemoto* in official documents, they may either be referred to as *iemoto* in everyday speech or understood on an implicit level to be representative of an *iemoto*. In such structures, this highest position is occupied by the founder of the group, or the person to whom overall authority has been transmitted. When the leader of a group dies – leadership is for life – the position can be passed on to a blood relation (usually son or daughter), to an adopted heir, to an heir chosen by the group, or it could be that the group divides and forms separate groups.[38] One might relate the idea of transmission of *koto* music to the idea of an unbroken line of imperial descent, where the emperor is (or at least was until the end of World War II) believed to have descended directly from the gods. The traditional Japanese system of dedication toward one's teacher enables learning for life and secures the continuity and survival of the music. Even if one party moves to another region, every effort would be made to sustain the relationship. "The strong sense of belongingness as a stake for self-identity, reinforced by collectivism and conformism, calls for the individual's total commitment and loyalty to his groups" (Lebra 1976, 31).

Continuity of the group and its music goes hand in hand with the sustainable harmony (*wa*) of the group where cooperation and solidarity in social relations through obligation and dedication are paramount to its survival. A student would feel obligation through feelings of *on* (receiving something one wants but does not have), *giri* (social obligation) and *ninjō* (natural inclinations). The frequent lack of a performing soloist who does not have some sort of group affiliation in the world of traditional *koto* performance is perhaps explained by the total solidarity of the performing group. Solo pieces would be performed in a traditional concert, but only in the broader context of the group.[39] "Collectivism thus involves cooperation and solidarity, and the sentimental desire for the warm feeling of *ittaikan* ('feeling of oneness') with fellow members of one's groups is widely shared by Japanese" (Lebra 1976, 25). One learns the instrument as a type of training (*kyōshū*) where artistic development is restricted by the strict following, watching and listening to one's teacher and other members of the group.

It cannot be ignored that the survival and transmission of the *koto* is also connected with the popularity of its music for *koto* players and the wider public. Historically, the instrument has been associated with innovation and change. As mentioned in Chapters 2 and 5, Yatsuhashi Kengyō made a radical move by introducing the *in* scale to the repertoire, thus initiating the "everyday" tradition; Ikuta Kengyō incorporated ideas from popular lyrical *shamisen* playing and forms; Yamada Kengyō used narrative *shamisen* playing; and Miyagi Michio blended ideas from Western tonal music.

Permit Systems

Similar to the historical ranking system used within the Tōdō, modern-day *koto* students normally take the licenses and/or examinations of their tradition or group.[40] Such permit systems are usually known as *menjō* (license) and *shiken* (examination); each helps players distinguish themselves hierarchically from other players within the group. *Menjō* and *shiken* can be used synonymously, or can distinguish between differing test levels. Different performance traditions often have the same type of hierarchical system in granting licenses, although terminology, requirements and fees frequently vary. Students nearly always learn the *koto* in their own time, that is, outside formal education, because traditional Japanese music has until recently rarely been taught in state schools. Certificates are usually awarded by the group that forms part of the larger tradition. Falconer (1995, 116) remarks on the significance of permit systems, stating that "certificates are bought not only for the student's own sense of progress, but as a sort of repayment to one's teacher." A look at the permit systems of several performance traditions – Yamada-ryū, Sawai Sōkyoku-in, Sōkyoku Shūyū-kai, Kikui Sōgaku-sha, and Tōdō Ongaku-kai – would be helpful in delineating similarities and differences, as well as demonstrating how they help contribute to the identity of a player within their group (Tables 16-19).[41]

In the Yamada-ryū, licenses are earned at three levels of ability. From beginner to advanced they are: 1) *Urayurushi* (rear license); 2) *Nakayurushi* (middle license); and 3) *Okuyurushi* (inner license) (Read 1975, 52-53; Read and Locke 1983). However, in the Sawai school of *koto* performance:

> An achieved hierarchy of seven ranks exists with specific requirements for each level. At the lowest levels, the student must play before the direct teacher and a recording is sent to the school office where it is judged. At middle levels, the student must travel to the school headquarters in Tokyo to take a series of tests which take two days to complete. At the upper levels, there is no examination, only a teacher recommendation, but there are requirements to have a minimum number of students of one's own, of which a certain number have to be of a particular rank. The achievement-based ranking system is highly ordered and efficient. (Yano 1992, 77)

The permit system in the performance group Sōkyoku Shūyū-kai, a small sub-tradition of the Ikuta-ryū, consists of licenses that are normally taken once a year by performing specific pieces (Table 16).[42] Unlike the practice of some other groups, the Sōkyoku Shūyū-kai does not have written tests. A student can apply for a license for either the *koto* or the *shamisen*, although it is customary for a student to work toward licenses in both instruments simultaneously. Tests require the playing of pieces and studies. A qualified teacher in the group would receive fifty percent of the licensing fee paid to the head of the group for each student.[43]

Table 16. Sōkyoku Shūyū-kai Licenses

Level	Name of License	Cost (*yen*)
1	*Shoden*	10,000
2	*Chūden*	20,000
3	*Okuden*	30,000
4	*Kaiden*	40,000
5	*Junshihan*	70,000 *
6	*Shihan*	150,000
7	*Daishihan*	200,000

Source: Matsuzaki Shūsetsu, conversations with author, Ogōri, June-July, 1990.
* A performing name is awarded at this level for an additional fee of 10,000 yen. A teacher from this level can then give licenses to their students at levels 1 and 2.

As a performance group, the Kikui Sōgaku-sha, a sub-tradition of the Ikuta-ryū that also identifies itself as part of the Tsuguyama-ryū, has various permits that are awarded to students once they have attained a certain standard. The "tests" of the Kikui Sōgaku-sha are similar to those of other groups and vary only in such details as their names, cost, requirements, and actual number of graded levels. There are three types of tests, each containing different requirements. The initial type of test (*menjō* or license) is awarded to the student by his/her teacher and is given at four different levels of merit (Table 17). The next level of test is the examination (Table 18). Examinations are for students wishing to become a teacher and can only be taken once the fourth license has been awarded. These particular examinations, which during field research in 1991 cost cost 15,000 *yen* each, are held twice a year and must be supervised by the leader of the group, Kikui Shōon. They include both written and aural tests. The final level is the *maki* (literally, "scroll"). This is not really a test, examination or qualification, but a scroll of merit that is given to the disciple showing their lineage through the Tsuguyama-ryū. The *maki* is awarded to students once they have reached a certain level of ability. This is shown by the student having to play a secret piece that belongs to the group in a way that is learned from the teacher.

Table 17. Kikui Sōgaku-sha Licenses

Level	Name of License
1	*Shoden*
2	*Chūden*
3	*Okuden*
4	*Kaiden*

Source: Nakamura Yōichi, conversation with author, Osaka, 1 May 1991.

Table 18. Kikui Sōgaku-sha Examinations

Level	Name of Examination	Cost (*yen*)
1	*Junshihan*	15,000
2	*Shihan*	15,000
3	*Daishihan*	15,000

Source: Nakamura Yōichi, conversation with author, Osaka, 1 May 1991.

In Tōdō Ongaku-kai (abbrev. Tōdō-kai) the tests are analogous with those mentioned above, except for the labels used to describe them (Table 19):

Table 19. Tōdō Ongaku-kai Examinations

Level	Name of Examination
1	*Shōjudō*
2	*Chūjudō*
3	*Daijudō*
4	*Shōkōtō*
5	*Chūkōtō*
6	*Daikōtō*

Source: Kikuhara Hatsuko, conversation with author, Osaka, 23 April 1991.

Within the various traditions of *koto* performance, the classification of repertoire and performer are fundamental to a *koto* player. The importance of the permit system lies in the fact that it gives the players status within their group. The employment of a license system also acts as a method of control for the "safeguard against the possible decay of the tradition" (Adriaansz 1971, 64), as well as providing an income for teachers. *Menjō* usually list some or all the lineage of the tradition together with the level attained. Adriaansz cites an example of a license of the Matsushiro Yatsuhashi-ryū with several regulations clearly stipulated. The regulation about not accepting money for instruction seems particularly to contradict common practice among *koto* teachers today, who operate in a system that is characterized by income-derived instruction:

1. Do not play jōruri [narrative *shamisen* music of Kantō] and kouta [short songs with *shamisen*].
2. Do not teach any person whose character does not show the appropriate qualities.
3. You may teach a person who qualifies through his character, even if he is not very skilful.
4. Do not teach actors, dancers, or geisha.
5. Do not accept any money for your instruction.
6. However, when a person who has been taught the complete repertoire wants to express his gratitude in some tangible form, do not always refuse.
7. Whenever you are invited to perform somewhere, wear clean clothes and be sure that the floor is swept. Only then may you play.
8. If you do not obey these rules, Shinbutsu [the supreme being] will not forgive you. (Adriaansz 1971, 66)

The continuity of *koto* music is today tied closely to the economics of the performance group through a system of tuition and license payment, performing names, licenses, membership of the group, and music performance. The hierarchical system that controls *koto* groups functions according to a model whereby the higher one's place in the group the greater the financial gain for the teacher and head of the group.

Performing Names

A system of ranking *koto* musicians based on their ability was taken up by the Tōdō and is a practice that has continued to the present day, albeit with different terminology and levels. From the highest, the four main ranks were Kengyō (e.g., from Yatsuhashi Kengyō),[44] Bettō, Kōtō, and Zatō. A player might hold several ranks in a lifetime, especially if the performer played other instruments. Each of the four levels was "normally ... attained by merit, not by purchase, although a few cases of its being bought are known" (Adriaansz 1973, 12). When used in the performer's name, these ranks aid in reinforcing hierarchical distinctions through language and symbol.

Like students of numerous Japanese performing arts (*cf.* Nishiyama 1997, 198-211), *koto* students, since the abolition of the Tōdō and depending on their performance tradition, are sometimes awarded a performing name (*natori* or *geimei*) by the teacher once they have attained a certain level of instrumental proficiency. If performing names are used in a group today they will normally be given as a special license. The player will typically use a name, or character (*kanji*), that is in the teacher's name as part of their own and thereby reinforcing the concept of lineage. In program notes of a concert, for example, it is often easy to trace the line of a teacher and his or her pupils through the adherence to one or several *kanji* that are used as performing names. Students can have the same *kanji* as their teacher, but employ a different pronunciation depending on how it fits aesthetically to their full name and individual character. In Kikui Sōgaku-sha, for example, the performing name used by a player would normally include the *kanji* for Kiku, after the line of Kiku-suji. This term is usually used as a prefix to the performer's real name, that is, either the family name or given name.

The focus of this chapter has been on the social level of *koto* playing and transmission. Performing names, certificates and even knowledge of performance practice are given to players as a way of establishing self-identity. Once a player has reached a certain level of performance, a name is awarded to them that can perhaps be seen as a right of passage. As such, the player enters further into the performance tradition to which they identify as a member, as a *koto* player and as an individual within a society that generally interprets "identity" as a means of belonging. The social units that comprise most everyday *koto* performance traditions provide a means by which the *koto* is transmitted in Japanese society; and they also provide a context where the instrument is used in direct connection with cultural or musical identity. It is from this perspective that the next chapter examines the performance contexts in which the instrument is used, places where performers display the instrument and its music in public and private spheres of Japanese society.

Suzuki Harunobu (1725?-70). Two Women by a *Koto*, from the series *Zashiki hakkei* (*The Eight Parlor Views*), *c.* 1776. *Chūban* format color woodblock print, 282 x 205 mm. Rijksmuseum, Amsterdam (1956:617).

5 *Performance*

Analyses of music performance contexts can reveal much about the culture in which that music is played (*see* Johnson 1993, 263-320; Small 1987; Tsuge 1981; O. Yamaguti 1991). Such contexts can provide information on the place of a musical instrument in a cultural milieu, including differences in instrument structure between diverse settings; they can reveal knowledge concerning performers such as social status, amateur/professional standing, playing posture, stage/performance position, and dress codes; and, relating to the music being played, they can unveil much about style, performance practice, instrumental techniques, and learning tools. While several of these areas have already been discussed, the present chapter investigates characteristics of the *koto* in its primary context of music making in order to examine the instrument beyond its physical structure. That is, the study of musical instruments should include a more all-encompassing examination of wider contexts of not only an instrument's form, but also its interrelation to the performer and the context of music performance.

The first section looks at performing contexts and includes a look at the physical space of a live, public performance, including a description of the performer. This is followed by a study of contexts where *koto* music is mediated, and thereby introduces a further aspect of the significance of this traditional instrument in contemporary Japan. As a way of illustrating some of the music-related characteristics of the instrument, the remainder of the chapter examines music notations, instrument tunings, music ornamentation, and genres. This section is not intended to focus on the instrument's vast repertoire per se, but rather is an investigation of the *koto* contexts where its music is heard. As a result, features of the music are introduced so as to reveal the interconnections between instrument, player and music. Indeed, as Stockmann (1991, 326) notes, "musical instruments add different kinds of meaning to a musical performance and its purely musical 'message,' and those who know about it will include this additional information in their decoding strategies. ... the construction of ... instruments may materialize and fix the basic features of a musical system, and their shape and function, moreover, may signify extramusical meaning." The section ends with a survey of the content, development and importance of some of the instrument's music genres, which demonstrates how the primary function of the *koto* in creating music might be viewed as a sonic representation of a meeting and mixing of the physical and social aspects that gel to make the *koto* what it is. It is from this perspective that this chapter extends its study of the *koto* beyond an examination of instrument structure and social transmission to include firstly its wider physical context of performance, and secondly to explore facets of the instrument's wide-ranging material culture.

Performing Contexts

Live performances of the *koto* take place in diverse contexts. The *gakusō*, for example, is typically found in the *gagaku* instrumental sub-genre *kangen*, in ritual Shinto *kagura*, especially at Shinto shrines,[1] and historically as a solo instrument of the imperial household. Many examples of the latter are seen in the eleventh-century *Genji monogatari*. The archaic *chikusō* of the Tsukushigoto was mainly used in ritual performance by Buddhist and Confucian players in northern Kyūshū, although today, apart from being preserved like many other *koto* in museums and archives (*see* Johnson 1999), it is generally found only in reconstructed performances that aim to illustrate a music style of bygone days. Everyday *zokusō* is encountered in far more places – historically and in the present day – be they public or private, due to its greater popularity and wider dissemination over other *koto* types.

Public performances of the *koto*, like music performances in many cultures, take place in amateur, semi-professional and professional contexts. One of the characteristics of belonging to a performance tradition or group is that even absolute beginners might find themselves performing in public as soon as one short and simple piece has been learned. While these beginners would always perform for and usually with their teacher in the learning context, as well as sometimes for other students, the social conditions of learning the instrument often allow a novice the chance of performing in public very early on. The performance does not necessarily showcase the player's technical ability, but is meant to emphasize the horizontal axis in Japanese society of belonging to a group, in this case a *koto* tradition, and of participating in that tradition's cultural and social performances. One might consider such contexts as social spaces that stress the performative dimension of playing the *koto* and articulate how identity in belonging to a tradition is performed socially.[2] This social aspect may in fact occasionally take prominence over the actual quality of the music per se.

The whole process of performance is one type of ritual with players and audiences alike knowing their proper place, and interrelating with each other within a predetermined set of cultural codes (*cf.* Small 1987). Entrances and departures are the dividing points within the ritual space and furnish signals for audience and performers to interact. One of the key features of the organization of most public, amateur *koto* performances is that it is primarily the group itself, by and large consisting of students and their teachers, that functions in undertaking many of the tasks necessary to realize a concert. Individuals take on, or are allocated, appropriate responsibilities that ensure the social harmony of the group and distribute activities and responsibilities, while at the same time instill in all its members sense of duty toward their group.[3]

The importance of viewing the context of musical performance in Japan as one way of comprehending cultural meaning is considered by Tsuge (1983b, 67), who believes that the context articulates "not only musical elements, but also social values and mores as well." Tsuge observed further that non-Japanese at performances of Japanese traditional music often "praise the visual aspects" (1983b, 55). Indeed, Japanese audiences themselves might be said to "read" all the visual images of the event in their totality:

> Initiated audiences of Japanese music … naturally catch many more messages from a single musical performance – not only from the sound of the music but also from other aspects; in particular, visual aspects. The mere sonic events are not the entirety of the music. Indeed, Japanese music cannot be perfect without completeness in its visual aspects. Regardless of skillfulness in articulation, should a performer lack proper manners or make unpleasant facial expressions, then that musical event may not satisfy the audience. Thus a phonograph record conveys very little of an actual performance of music. (Tsuge 1983b, 55)

Each context of *koto* performance has numerous material "signifiers" relating to the instrument, performer, music, the wider performance setting, and the venue. Each allows the performance as a whole to be understood within a language of non-verbal meaning. A live performance of everyday *koto* music, for instance, that aims to create a traditional (usually perceived as pre-Meiji) atmosphere would include the players kneeling toward their instrument on a red mat (*mōsen*). Traditional gold-colored folding screens (*byōbu*), perhaps decorated with iconic scenes from nature, are placed in the background (*cf.* fig. 2)[4] and the names of the pieces being played might be displayed as calligraphy to the side of the stage. A performance that does not include such traditional "signifiers" will have its own codes that facilitate an understanding of the various aspects which usually contrast with traditional performances. Some of the more common signifiers in contemporary and crossover music include high *koto* stands, performers sitting in chairs, colored background lighting or screens, non-traditional dress, and technical effects that are normally associated with the modern world and not with traditional *koto* music. The performances illustrated in figures 70, 74-75, for example, use chairs and high *koto* stands primarily because the genre of music is Western influenced, and from the twentieth-century. Such visual symbols facilitate comprehension of meaning connected with wider contexts of the *koto*, which are generally part of the setting where the instrument is played.

The Performer

The performer's playing position is a signifier that can identify players from different performance traditions. The playing position is partly determined by the playing position of the instrument, the physical capabilities of the player and partly by convention. Players are always positioned near the head end of the *koto*, facing the instrument toward the long side with the instrument head to the player's right. Depending on the performance tradition, players might sit on the floor cross-legged, with one knee raised, kneel (face on or at an angle), sit in a chair, or even stand (*see* figs. 1-2, 70, 74-75).[5] These playing positions, together with the usual arrangement of the movable bridges and position of the fixed bridges, provide the conventional means by which the *koto* is sounded.

The main *koto* performance traditions differ in their playing position, as do the shape of their plectra (the plectra shape is sometimes related to the playing position). An Ikuta-ryū player kneels at a slight angle facing the tail (away from the player), while a Yamada-ryū player kneels directly facing the instrument (fig. 78). By contrast, there are three theories concerning the early playing position in the Tsukushigoto tradition: with the right knee raised (*tatehiza*); with both knees nearly horizontal (*gakuza*); and from a kneeling position with the left leg slightly open and the arch of the left foot touching the calf of the right leg. The latter theory is supported by Wada (1996). As noted in Chapter 2, the Tsukushigoto tradition is now extremely small, and the players are primarily students of other traditions who reconstruct Tsukushigoto music. For example, Miyahara Chizuko (*b.* 1936), who is the main proponent of the Tsukushigoto today, is also a player in Miyagi-kai. She kneels in the Ikuta-ryū style when playing Tsukushigoto music, or sits in a chair with the *koto* placed on a high stand. In *gagaku* during the Nara period, it is thought that the head end of the *koto* was placed on the player's knees while

78 Kneeling positions. *(a)* **Yamada-ryū;** *(b)* **Ikuta-ryū.**

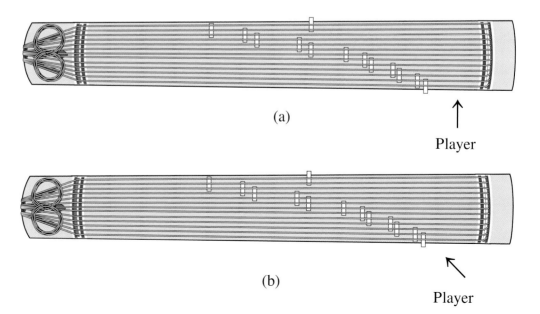

(a)

Player

(b)

Player

sitting cross-legged (Kikkawa 1997, 2). However, *gakusō* players by the Heian period sat cross-legged directly facing the instrument with one side of the *koto* head end immediately in front of them. Kyōgoku-ryū players also sit in this way.

A traditional music performance must conform to traditional dress protocol. A performance of contemporary music, or music seen in contradistinction to *koten* (old or traditional pieces), does not necessarily conform to these forms of etiquette. However, when such music is included in a recital of various genres players usually opt for traditional form. A player might wear traditional or non-traditional dress for a contemporary piece, but seldom wears non-traditional dress for a traditional piece (*cf.* Falconer 1993; 1995, 47). Tsuge (1983b, 55) comments that "it is shocking indeed for a Japanese to see a musician dressed in jeans, or a 'happy [*happi* or workman's livery] coat', to perform a classical piece on the *koto*." When remarking on women's clothing, Tsuge (1983b, 66) notes that "the kimono must be in harmony with the environment and situation – the type of concert, its character (congratulatory or memorial), the musician's position in the given frame (central or periphery), her role and status in the event; it must also agree with the season; it must suit the musician's age; and needless to say, the kimono must state one's sex and marital status." Even the decoration of raiment is understood to be traditional in that it often has motifs and designs similar to those displayed on the *koto* mouth, head cover and brocade.

A female teacher's dress would normally be black and formal, and female students would ordinarily wear the embellished colorful kimono called *hōmongi* (Tsuge 1983b, 65). Older female performers will usually wear more formal and subdued attire. They are normally the more experienced and qualified players to whom younger members show total respect. Formal male dress is called *haori-hakama*, which includes "a dark [black] kimono bearing their family crest called *montsuki* and a pair of striped culottes called *hakama*, ... [and] a short dark half-coat called *haori*" (Tsuge 1983b, 59). The performer's appearance (male and female) is an area that should be considered in connection with stage etiquette, as Tsuge (1983b, 56) explains further: "eye glasses are not supposed to be worn on the stage while performing classical pieces. Rings and wrist-watches should also be taken off. In principle, a performer of traditional Japanese music should not wear any superfluously decorative accessories which support the neck, nose, ears and legs, etc."

Live performances naturally reveal the gender and age of the musicians. Today amateur women dominate most areas of *koto* performance, but not composition (*see* Chapter 4). When a male player does perform, there are no special conventions for his position on the stage or other performance areas. All performers, regardless of gender, are positioned according to their social place within the group. Younger and generally more inexperienced performers will appear earlier on in the event, or, when they play with their seniors, they would normally be positioned to the rear of the stage, which indicates their subordinate position. Such a hierarchy of place reflects the larger context of Japanese society where the individual is always aware of their place in any given context. In the Yamada-ryū, as Read and Locke (1983, 45) have observed, the "senior players ... sit toward the front of the stage:" *tate* (leader), *waki* (second *koto*), *tsure* (the rest of the group), *tome* (rear *koto*).[6] The written program notes that invariably accompany all public, and sometimes private, performances will usually list the hierarchies of performers within the group as a whole (*cf.* Read and Locke 1983, 48). Programs also explain the affiliation or lineage of players within their group by their performing names, if they have one. One can often identify the students of a teacher by the use of a special performance name.

The extent to which an understanding of the performance context is important in appreciating the totality of the event has been summarized by Tokumaru. He demonstrates the significance of examining the interrelationship between the music, musical instrument and performer by noting the transcription made by comparative musicologists Otto Abraham (1872-1926) and Erich M. von Hornbostel (1877-1935) of Sadayakko's (1872-1946) *koto* performance in Berlin in the early twentieth century:[7]

They [Abraham and Hornbostel] must have visually observed Madame Sadayakko playing the *koto*, and on the basis of this were able to discriminate between "the tones raised by pressure on *koto* strings" [indicated with x in their transcriptions; called *oside* (*oshide*; "pushing hand") in traditional terminology] (Abraham and Hornbostel 1975:68) and the unpressed tones. They must have read the facial expressions of the Japanese musicians, because they wrote "we should mention here that the innate politeness of the Japanese makes it very difficult to obtain an unfavourable opinion" (Abraham and Hornbostel 1975:51, footnote 41). (Tokumaru 1986, 111)[8]

Mediated Performance

Performances of *koto* music frequently occur without players and audience meeting face-to-face. Through recordings or live mediation an audience is able to hear the instrument in many other contexts. Such instances of *koto* performance might be seen in two spheres: the private context, or at least a near private setting, and the public context. The latter, which is considered here, might be sub-divided into the public audience who listen because they are there to listen, people who listen because the music has caught their attention, and people who listen implicitly without always consciously being aware of it (e.g., background music).

While *koto* music exists today in what might be viewed as a living tradition of Japanese music, in that its old and new repertoire is part of a flourishing music culture, the instrument is also very much connected with the idea of tradition. That is, the *koto* is usually viewed by the Japanese as a traditional Japanese musical instrument that has its roots in historical Japan (i.e., a Japan before widespread Western influence during the Meiji era). Consequently, many mediated *koto* performances occur in contexts that aim to create a nostalgic sense of traditional Japan. These include such everyday locales as tourist centers, information offices, restaurants, shopping streets, and at times of traditional celebration such as at festivals. The latter also includes New Year celebrations.[9] This was observed by this author at the Kyoto shrine Yasaka Jinja in 1990-91, when the New Year was issued in with a continuous recording of the seventeenth-century instrumental *koto* piece "Rokudan no Shirabe" ("Investigation in Six Sections"), which is attributed to the father of everyday *koto* music, Yatsuhashi Kengyō (1614-85). Another example at this time of year is on the Kyoto subway, which usually plays *koto* music through loudspeakers over the whole of the New Year period (i.e., most of January). Contexts such as these can be viewed as part of a domestic Japanese tourist industry that seeks to establish and perpetuate symbols of traditional Japan, each of which is meant to reinforce a sense of national identity. As J. Nelson (2000, 87) notes, "the domestic tourist industry in the historic city of Kyoto alone, with thirty-nine million visitors in 1997, thrives not because of restaurants, discotheques, or natural scenery; it is, rather, the quaint, 'authentic,' refined, and ... potentially coercive atmosphere of the 'past' that seduces visitors."

There are also contexts where the *koto* is not played, but still evoke an understanding of the instrument as a performance object of Japanese culture. Many Japanese museums, for instance, often exhibit traditional Japanese musical instruments as icons of a bygone age (Johnson 1999). Another context is that of an instrument that could be played but is instead used as decoration, as an ornamental instrument for display, or as a toy instrument. Each is an example of the *koto*, or a version of it, being placed in a context where it is viewed by an observer, and is intended to represent something more than its primary use as a sound-producing object. Here, the *koto* is interpreted as a tangible symbol of traditional Japan. Likewise, an image of the *koto*, or an aspect of it (e.g., movable bridges), is sometimes employed as decoration in many of Japan's traditional arts (*see* Adachi [1913] 1972, 148; Lee 1981, 157, 187).

Notations Systems

There are several different kinds of *koto* notation used to represent sounds or finger positions.[10] While notations are found in most *koto* traditions, their use was not common practice until the late nineteenth century and after. This is explained by the fact that players used to learn primarily by rote, and that during the Edo period, a time when *koto* playing became much more widespread, everyday professional performers did not use notation because they were blind. Today, players very rarely learn by rote, preferring to use notation instead (*see* Halliwell 1994a, 29-31). Needless to say, notations often vary between performance traditions, as do elements of performance practice and instrument type. The importance of studying notation in performance contexts has been emphasized by O. Yamaguti (1986, 31), who mentions that such notations "have much to do with tactile percepts of performance." Ellingson (1992, 156) too stresses the significance of such studies: "the search for an understanding of notations requires a consideration of the musical practices to which they refer and to the concepts and intentions of their users." An understanding of the various types of *koto* notation assists in presenting not only material aspects of the performance context, but also an interconnectedness between the instrument, the performer and the music.

The development of *koto* notations might be divided into two historical periods: those notation systems predating the Meiji era, which follow the traditional vertical writing system (read downward in columns starting from the right of the page – *tategaki*), and those from and after the Meiji era, which are either vertical (as above) or horizontal after Western influence (read from left to right in rows starting from the top of the page – *yokogaki*). They have been divided as such because *koto* notation systems changed and evolved further in the late nineteenth and early twentieth centuries under immense influence from both Western culture and the internal politics of Japan. While notations predating the Meiji era did to a certain extent begin to move toward more descriptive forms of representation, it was only in the late nineteenth century that more detailed features became the norm. Still, *koto* notations are more often than not prescriptive aids for the performers, rather than descriptive scores that contain every utterance of the music. Even if players use notation today, the learning process usually includes much about the intricacies of performance that notation systems could not possibly reveal.

Notation Systems Predating the Meiji Era

Koto tablature (*genmeifu*)[11] has been known since the twelfth century in such works as *Jinchi yōroku* (fig. 79), one of the main historical sources for *gagaku* music.[12] Compiled by the courtier Fujiwara no Moronaga and completed before his death in 1192, the *Jinchi yōroku* tablature lists string names and some ornamentation; rhythm and meter were unclear. The score is read from top to bottom in columns from right to left, in the same way as the principal writing system of pre-modern Japan.[13] As Markham (1983, 63) observes, "the notation consists of a main column of large, primary tablature-signs to the right (occasionally to the left) of which small, primary tablature-signs are written at intervals." This style of notation is still used by *gakusō* players today and reflects the performance practice of this instrument in that it is well suited to represent a type of music with relatively few performance techniques.

In everyday *koto* performance (i.e., *zokusō*) several music sources from the seventeenth and eighteenth centuries serve as useful comparisons with modern-day types of notation. Some *koto* books were not notations per se, but, rather, collections of song texts, evidence that there were sighted amateur players (Kubota 1988, 162). Most Edo-period notations and song texts would have been used by these amateur players. The *Shichiku shoshinshū* (*Collection of Pieces for Beginners of String and Bamboo Instruments*, 1664), *Kinkyoku shō* (*Collection of Koto Pieces*, 1695),

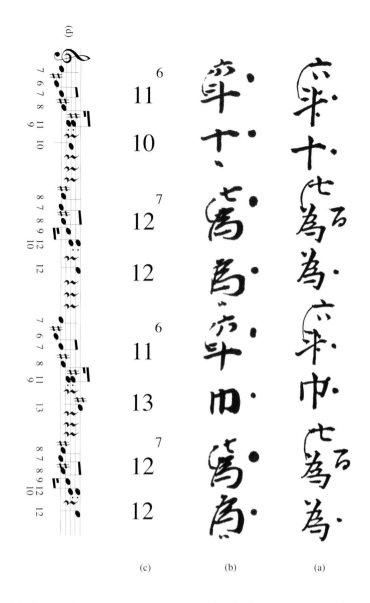

79 Opening of *koto* part of "Etenraku" ("Beyond Heaven Music") in *hyōjō* mode.
(a) *Gakusō* notation as shown in *Jinchi yōroku* (before 1192; this copy dates to the Edo period) (Hirano and Fukushima 1978, 9). Courtesy Fukushima Kazuo;
(b) *Gakusō* notation (Nihon Gagaku-kai 1979). Courtesy Nihon Gagaku-kai;
(c) Transnotation showing string numbers;
(d) Transnotation with actual strings played shown below.

Kinkyoku shifu (*Guide on Koto Music Notation*, 1772, printed 1780), and *Sōkyoku taiishō* (*General Selection of Koto Music*, [1779] 1903) are some of the earliest examples of non-court *koto* notation in the form of vertically-read tablature in columns from right to left. *Shichiku shoshinshū* and *Kinkyoku shō* show string names and/or mnemonic syllables to indicate the notes to be played. *Kinkyoku shifu* is a systematic form of tablature (fig. 80), and is a detailed system that includes string names and beats using a mixture of everyday and special symbols in a grid. *Sōkyoku taiishō* was compiled by the father of Yamada Kengyō (1757-1817), Yamada Shōkoku (act. c. 1772-89), and is a type of articulatory notation, which displays strong and weak beats using large and small circles that indicate the pulse of the music (fig. 80). The tablature is read in columns from top to bottom as vertical notation (*tategaki*), and across the page from right to left. Song texts in this volume were given without any indication of pitch for the vocal line, emphasizing that this part of the music was learned aurally/orally during the teaching process.

With these vertical notations the movement of the player's hand follows the same axis as the printed symbols, as the player reads down the column of notation the hand could be either moving up or down the strings depending on the music. As discussed below, however, the playing movement and the way it reflected the notation system was an important point and one which was given considerable attention in a variety of new notations in the late nineteenth and early twentieth centuries.

80 Vertical notations.
(a) **Opening section (***dan***) of the instrumental piece "Rokudan Sugagaki" ("Sugagaki in Six Sections") as shown in *Kinkyoku shifu* (*Guide on Koto Music Notation*, comp. in 1772, pub. 1780) (Hirano and Fukushima 1978, 190), with transnotation. Courtesy Fukushima Kazuo;
(b) Opening of the *koto kumiuta* "Fuki" ("Rhubarb"). *Koto* tablature as in *Sōkyoku taiishō* (*General Selection of Koto Music* [1779] 1903), with transnotation.**

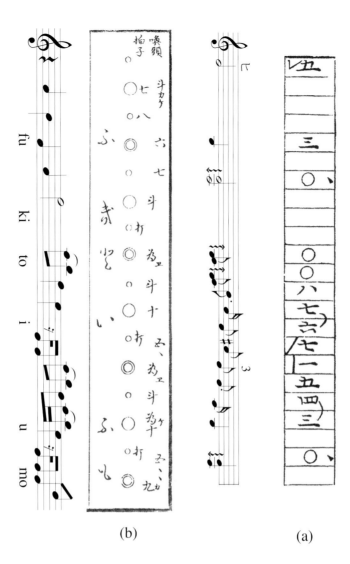

(b)   (a)

Notation Systems From and After the Meiji Era

Over the last two hundred years notation within many traditions and sub-traditions of *koto* performance has undergone change or modification. The type of score that is mainly used today in everyday *koto* performance is slightly more descriptive than those of the late eighteenth century. Why did such changes occur? As mentioned earlier changes occurred during the Meiji era that touched many facets of Japanese society and culture – the *koto* was no exception. A number of new notations were devised, either influenced by Western notation, from earlier Japanese sources, or from a combination of both. The changes that occurred in *koto* notation were mirrored in the increased number of *koto* players, especially of sighted amateur female players, following the official proscription in 1871 of the Tōdō musicians' guild of blind male professional players, who controlled the transmission of *koto* music until this time. Subsequently, as May (1963, 27) has pointed out, "there were ... between fifty and sixty varieties of koto score." This was partly due to the group system of *koto* traditions, where the construction of difference between performers is a primary way of creating identity within the group.

Under Western pressure to trade, the Tokugawa shogunate's policy of seclusion was broken following the Treaty of Kanagawa in 1854; this coincided with a gradual breakdown of the strict social order that had earlier led to Japan's near isolation in the seventeenth century. An important point to consider regarding Japan's contact with colonial powers, in particular the

United States, was that contact with the West was essentially "Westernization" by choice without "colonization" (Eppstein 1994, 4-5). In the latter part of the nineteenth century and the first two decades of the twentieth century, Japan was acutely aware of what was perceived as "Western superiority" and began what can only be described as an almost fanatical obsession with the adoption of Western ideas (Lehmann 1982, 169). As summarized by Lehmann (1982, 166), "in the period 1870-1914 there occurred the most significant and momentous changes which the world had ever witnessed." Even so, there was still an underlying sense of Japanese identity – especially connected with ideas of Japanese nationalism – inculcated in such political slogans as "Western technology, Japanese values" (Hunter 1989, 19). Two main characteristics of this culture contact were "a readiness to try new methods" and "a tenacious adherence to traditional ideals and values" (Tsunoda, de Bary and Keene 1958, 2:133). For Nakane (1970, 115) the Japanese looked "at modernization from the start as a process that has been (or should be) based on and effected by a combination of the Japanese spirit and western knowledge." From the 1870s, with the rise of Japanese nationalism and a search for a new national identity, Japan strove toward modernization (i.e., Westernization), while at the same time looked to traditional Japanese values as a way of adjusting to such radical change. "The basic social structure continues in spite of great changes in social organization" (Nakane 1970, 8). The culture contact that occurred between Japan and the West during the Meiji era was very different to earlier contact, which was highly controlled and limited to certain parts of the country (i.e., Nagasaki). In fact, "many innovations were not really necessary to modernization but were merely imitations of Western customs" (Fairbank, Reischauer and Craig 1973, 523).

Therefore, it goes without saying that Western music was tremendously influential during the Meiji era and continues to be so today.[14] In 1872 the government stipulated that music (i.e., Western music) was to be a principal school subject (*see* Malm 1971).[15] Music educators Izawa Shūji (1851-1917) and the American Luther Whiting Mason (1828-96) were key figures in the transculturation of Western music for use in school education, and Izawa originally aimed to replace Japanese traditional music with Western music (Eppstein 1994, ii). Their influence also included the widespread use of five-line Western staff notation (*gosenfu*), and several *koto* scores were produced using it.[16] Tōkyō Academy of Music (1888), for example, produced the first major *koto* collection to be transcribed into Western staff notation by the Japanese themselves, and a number of other transcriptions and compositions soon followed. Several Yamada-tradition players, such as Yamase Shōin (1845-1908) who later employed a new system of notation influenced by Western staff notation, were involved in the compilation of this work. The Ongaku Torishirabe Gakari (Ministry of Education Music Research Center) published this volume and was actively involved in the modernization of Japanese music. However, while Western staff notation was seen as a possible way of unifying aspects of the nation where its musicians could share, or at least imagine (*cf.* B. Anderson 1991), a common musical language, staff notation was soon associated primarily with Western music or Japanese music composed in a Western style. So-called traditional instruments such as the *koto* sometimes used staff notation, or new Japanese notations were devised having been influenced by it, but it never became the norm outside composition in a contemporary style.

Several new *koto* notations were devised in direct response to Western staff notation. However, while being influenced by the visual design of staff notation, Japanese innovators approached it in a unique way. An example of such a notation is found in Takamatsu (1907), where the score provides two systems of notation, in a type of mirror notation: a "reverse" staff form on the upper staff, and standard Western notation on the lower staff (fig. 81). With this notation the publisher is acknowledging that the player might be conversant with Western staff notation, but recognizes inherent problems in using it entirely for *koto* music. On the one hand, this notation provides an iconic form of representation on the upper staff in that the notes on the lower side of the score are high in pitch, which corresponds to the high notes closest to the player. In other words, if the notation were placed on top of the strings of the *koto*, the position

81 Reverse notations.

(a) **Opening of "Hachidan no Shirabe" ("Investigation in Eight Sections") using "reverse" five-line notation on top row and Western five-line staff notation on lower row (Takamatsu 1907). National Diet Library, Tokyo;**

(b) **Opening of "Rokudan no Shirabe" ("Investigation in Six Sections") using "reverse" five-line notation (Furukawa 1911-12, 1), with transnotation. National Diet Library, Tokyo;**

(c) **Opening of "Rokudan no Shirabe" using six-line "reverse" notation (Ōshima 1929, 40), with transnotation. Courtesy Kinkōdō;**

(d) **Single-line "reverse" notation of opening of a short study ("No. 11") (Kikuyoshi 1901, 28), with transnotation. Miyagi Michio Memorial Museum, Tokyo.**

of pitch on the notation and the instrument would be the same. On the other hand, the score requires a version in Western staff notation for the player to translate or use as required. Another example of this type of "reverse" notation is by Furukawa (1911-12) (fig. 81). One might ordinarily think it is Western staff notation in that it has lines and spaces, and the notes have rhythm. But the notation actually indicates strings rather than pitches, and high notes are at the bottom of the staff and low notes at the top. The notation is iconic in that the *koto* player would see high notes, which are closest to the player on the instrument, at the bottom of the staff. A similar type of notation was used by Ōshima (1929), although in this case it had six lines (fig. 81). This type of notation was also a "reverse" system and read horizontally from left to right, where the seventh string (the central string of the thirteen on the *koto*) was represented by the central space in the stave.

There were several other experimental types of "reverse" notation around the same time. Kikuyoshi (1901), for instance, provides a notation that is read horizontally from left to right (*yokogaki*), and either a single line or three lines are given (figs. 81-82). Like some of the examples already noted, the position of pitch on the staff is the reverse of Western staff notation. In the opening of this score Kikuyoshi comments that the notation is especially helpful for women who have learned the instrument and then after marriage want to go back to it but have forgotten what they have learned. One wonders why Kikuyoshi singles out women, but this might relate to the fact that the *koto* became extremely popular among women in the Meiji era, and the promotion of a notation such as this perhaps reflected the established use of music notation in Japanese music education at that time. A note placed on the single line of the

121

(a)

みやまの　を　く　わ　は　る　な　が　ら

Mi ya ma no o ku wa ha ru na ga ra

(b)

(c)

Hito tsu, hi to ko to, ha na shi wa, hi no ki shi n,

ko-rorin

82 Reverse notations.
(a) Three-line "reverse" notation of "Miyama no Oku" ("Recesses") (Kikuyoshi 1901, 14), with transnotation. Miyagi Michio Memorial Museum, Tokyo;
(b) Opening of *koto* accompaniment of the folk song "Sakura Sakura" ("Cherry Blossoms") using a reproduction of thirteen-line "reverse" notation (*jūsansen-shiki sōfu*), with transnotation;
(c) Opening of *koto* accompaniment of a *mikagura* piece using a "reverse" notation (Tenri-kyō Dōyūsha 1983), with transnotation. Courtesy Tenri-kyō Dōyūsha.

single-line version, and a note placed on the central line of the three-line version, represent the seventh string of the *koto*. Note heads in spaces and lines added above and below the line for the seventh string represent the instrument's lower and higher strings, respectively. In other words, a different space or line is used for each of the thirteen strings of the *koto*.

A notation with thirteen staff lines has been labeled *jūsansen-shiki sōfu* (thirteen-line style *sō* notation). With this notation, the thirteen horizontal lines represent each of the instrument's thirteen strings (fig. 82; *see* Nakajima and Kubota 1984, 161). It was devised by Okada Teiji and Ishide Ichiga, and later used by Yonekawa Kin'ō in 1912 (*see* Kikkawa 1984a, 504). From a player's perspective, a thirteen-line notation or similar "reverse" form provides a form of iconic representation that reflects the player's hand movements between the first and thirteenth strings. What is fundamentally different to Western staff notation or to some other versions of *koto* notation, is that the player's hands move in the same direction as the notes in the tablature. An example of this type of notation is reproduced in a recent collection of essays on the *koto* by Yamaguchi and Tanaka (2002) that is aimed at the recent changes in the national school music curriculum.[17] While several forms of notation are discussed, the authors have chosen to include a thirteen-line staff (*jūsansenfu*), which is extremely unusual and not normally used by *koto* players today. The utilization of this type of notation points to a reinvention of something as a way of investing the *koto* with its own unique Japanese character at a time of cultural nationalism.[18]

"Reverse" notations such as these never became widespread. But a related example that is still used today is preserved in the notation system of the genre *kagura uta* (a genre of Shinto vocal music) of the religious sect Tenri-kyō (e.g., Tenri-kyō Dōyūsha 1983). The notation is read vertically in columns, but with *koto* strings numbered in "reverse" to the standard string numbering (fig. 82). In other words, string number one is closest to the player rather than furthest away. In Tenri-kyō, only six (the highest in pitch) of the thirteen strings of the *koto* are used in *kagura uta*. If a more common notation were employed for this genre it would include a mixture of conventional symbols and the three special *kanji* for strings 11-13. The publisher of this notation states that in order to facilitate learning and avoid confusion, the strings were re-named with only conventional numbers, which correspond to the numbers used for the flute (*fue*) that is also found in the genre *kagura uta*.[19]

Vertical Number Notations

Following the traditional way of reading, vertical notation changed further during and soon after the beginning of the Meiji era. This type of notation had already undergone modification over several hundred years, although the predominant oral transmission of *koto* music meant that it only became more descriptive around the turn of the nineteenth and twentieth centuries when more sighted players were allowed to play the instrument.

The influence of Western notation systems on vertical *koto* tablature was already evident in the 1890s. The notation used by Momotari (1894) indicates rhythm using vertical equivalents to staff notation to the right of the string names (fig. 83). While this type of notation did not indicate measures, one variety of vertical notation that did-was established in 1913. The latter divided every four beats, each beat and each half beat (fig. 83). This type of notation is mostly associated with the Ikuta tradition which, with its numerous sub-groups, is by far the largest *koto* tradition. The publisher Dai Nippon Katei Ongaku-kai, in particular uses this type of

83 Opening of "Rokudan no Shirabe" ("Investigation in Six Sections").
(a) Edition of Momotari (1894, 28). Miyagi Michio Memorial Museum, Tokyo;
(b) Edition of I. Yamaguchi ([1913] 1918, 20), with transnotation. Courtesy Dai Nippon Katei Ongaku-kai;
(c) Edition of Sakamoto (1945, 56), with transnotation. Courtesy Dai Nippon Katei Ongaku-kai;
(d) Edition of I. Yamaguchi ([1913] 1983, 19), with transnotation. (Arrows and text indicating performance directions to the side of the notation have been removed from this reproduction.) Courtesy Dai Nippon Katei Ongaku-kai.

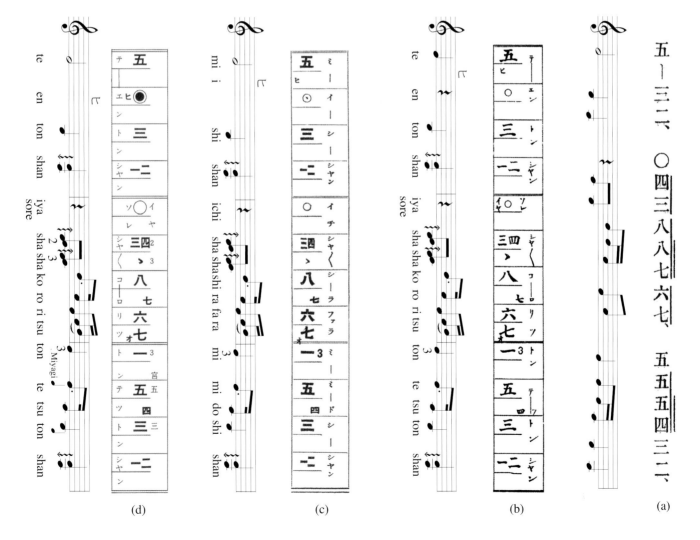

(d)   (c)   (b)   (a)

notation. Still, the front cover of this notation indicates that the version of the music is for both Ikuta and Yamada traditions. While the score follows the style of most Ikuta-tradition notation, it also includes several markings that exemplify the differences between these two traditions. The score is read vertically, in columns from right to left, beats are shown by rectangles within a grid, half beats in the half rectangles, strings and ornamentation are indicated in the center of the column, and *shōga* (oral mnemonics) are specified to the side of the strings using the *katakana* phonetic script. As with some other notations, the grid is a superimposition which falsely divides every four notes into bars – very clearly a Western influence. In connection with the piece "Rokudan no Shirabe" the same publisher later made an alternative addition that is noticeably different (Sakamoto 1945). The later edition includes solfège for most of the notes and some *shōga* for certain ornamentation, rather than using *shōga* throughout (fig. 83). While solfège is widely known and used in Japan today, the solfège edition never became popular and is no longer used. The rejection of solfège is conceivably linked to the historical importance of the oral part of the learning process where the teacher sings notes and idiomatic ornamentation with oral mnemonics. Such a system, while varying slightly between traditions, was historically the main symbolic learning method used in traditional rote-learning. For comparative purposes a later edition of the score is also shown in figure 83. In this version the publisher has returned to the use of *shōga* and even includes an alternative part for the Miyagi tradition, which indicates the increasing popularity of this group of *koto* performance. Also, as seen in the first example in figure 84, the right of each page sometimes indicates each half beat with the *kanji* for right and left, which the teacher might indicate by tapping to help the student keep time. The differences between these three versions of "Rokudan" are slight, but nevertheless provide a visual source to the continuing development of *koto* notation and the way notation is able to

84 Vertical notations.
(a) Opening of "Chidori no Kyoku" ("Song of Plovers") (I. Yamaguchi [1913] 1986, 2), with transnotation. Courtesy Dai Nippon Katei Ongaku-kai;
(b) Opening of "Chidori no Kyoku" (Nakashima 1966, 1), with transnotation. Courtesy Nakashima Yasuko, Maekawa Shuppansha;
(c) Opening of "Rokudan no Shirabe" ("Investigation in Six Sections"). *Honte* (main part, to the right), *kaede* (second part, to the left). Yamada-ryū notation (Yamakawa 1980), with transnotation. Courtesy Dai Nippon Katei Ongaku-kai.

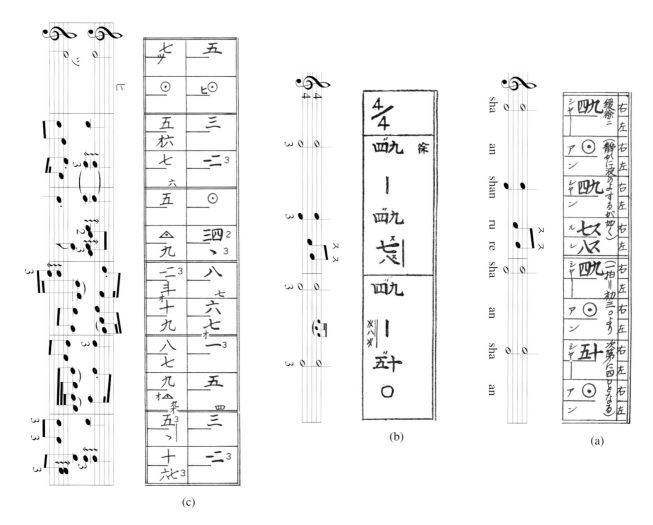

(c)

(b)

(a)

contribute to performance identity. While the piece in these examples does not have a vocal line, when a piece does include singing, which the *koto* player would do, the notation for the vocal line is shown to one side of the column. In *Sōkyoku taiishō*, for instance, the vocal line is seen to the left, but is prescriptive in that no indication of pitch is given, and only the barest information on rhythm and relationship to the *koto* line is provided. However, most *koto* notation nowadays that includes a vocal line does indicate pitch and rhythm in the form of small symbols to one side of the column (or above or below the score in horizontal notation). The pitch of the vocal line is indicated with the same symbols for the *koto* strings, and the rhythm follows the same type of divisions used in the *koto* part.[20]

Several other forms of vertical notation were devised during the Meiji era. Each shared many similarities, such as using *kanji* to represent the strings (the *kanji* for strings one, two and three are sometimes different in divergent notation systems, depending on the tradition), the superimposition of a grid system (usually dividing every four beats, but sometimes sub-dividing every beat and half beat too), and the use of diacritical and ornamental markings to indicate idiomatic techniques and other more descriptive practices. Such notations include those of the Miyagi tradition, the Kyōgoku tradition, which was promulgated by Suzuki Koson (1875-1931) of the Kyōgoku tradition in Kyoto and includes some Western symbols to indicate rhythm (Suzuki 1910), and the Sei-ha tradition, which was designed by Nakashima Utashito (1896-1979) and encloses every four beats and adds symbols derived from the West to indicate rhythm (fig. 84). In the Sei-ha tradition, for example, a single vertical line placed to the side of the *kanji* for the strings indicates an eighth note, and two parallel lines indicate a sixteenth note. Dotted notes have the dot placed just below the *kanji* for the string. Right-hand fingering is shown by a single dash for the index finger, and two dashes for the middle finger.

Most Ikuta-ryū notation is vertical, although there are several types used in the broader sense of the tradition. In connection with the Sawai school, Falconer comments that "beats are represented by horizontal lines; measures are visually divided by these lines, and notes are placed in between the lines, to be played at the point they appear" (1995, 221). "Whole-step presses are indicated with the hiragana symbol for 'o' (an abbreviation of 'osu', to push or press) and half-step presses are indicated with an 'o' from the katakana syllabary. Fingerings are indicated with Arabic numerals; as before, no fingering always means the thumb is to be used; a '2' means to use the first finger and a '3' means to use the second one" (Falconer 1995, 221-22). However, this school sometimes uses the same type of notation as the Sei-ha tradition. In *koto* tablatures, right-hand fingerings – like various ornamental techniques – are indicated with a number of symbols that often differ between the various performance traditions. Such symbols include Arabic numerals ("2": index finger; "3": middle finger); dashes (one: index finger; two: middle finger); and shapes (square: index finger; triangle: middle finger).

While most Yamada-tradition notation is written horizontally, the use of a vertical form is not unheard of. The Yamada-tradition player Yamakawa Enshō (1909-84), for example, edited a vertical form of notation that divided the notes into groups of two beats (fig. 84). This notation uses Ikuta-tradition symbols, but the usual Yamada-tradition system of grouping notes into units of two beats is used.[21]

Horizontal Number Notations

During the intense period of acculturation during the earlier Meiji era, Arabic numerals were adopted as a part of the Japanese writing system, and also used later in Japanese music notations, including some for the *koto*. A form of number notation that was clearly derived from Western principles was introduced in the 1880s to school music education (e.g., Monbushō Ongaku Torishirabe Gakari 1881-84). A few Japanese notations such as those for the *koto* already used Japanese numbers and the application of different symbols to an already extant principle was structurally accessible. May (1963, 80) comments that Luther Whiting Mason favored "a number, dot, and dash system akin to the Paris-Galin-Chevé system."[22] In this number notation,

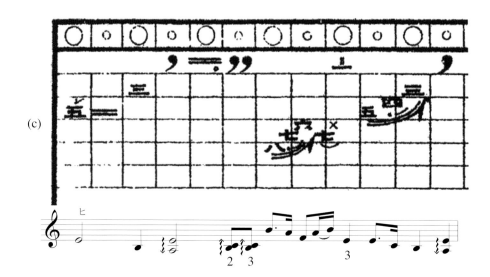

85 Horizontal notations.
(a) Opening of "Sakura
Sakura" ("Cherry Blossoms")
using number notation for the
minigoto (Kinden-ryū
Taishōgoto Zenkoku Fukyū-kai
1995), with transnotation.
Courtesy Kinden-ryū
Taishōgoto Zenkoku Fukyū-kai;
(b) Opening of "Rokudan no
Shirabe" ("Investigation in Six
Sections") using Japanese
numbers to indicate scale
degrees (Machida 1896, 29).
National Diet Library;
(c) Opening of "Rokudan no
Shirabe" using "reverse" grid
notation (Tazaki 1894, 39).
National Diet Library.

numbers represent the degrees of the diatonic scale (i.e., "1" is the root note of the scale, "2" is the second degree, etc.); dots next to notes and lines underneath indicate rhythm; dots above notes show the higher octave; and dashes indicate the extension of notes (i.e., ties). Even today, many Japanese folk song collections still use number notation, often with a double form of notation that includes both Western staff notation and a number system immediately above or below the staff being very common. However, number notation using Arabic numerals was not adopted in most *koto* traditions, and it is normally found only in children's pieces, in particular, miniature instruments such as the *minigoto*. Figure 85 shows the opening phrase of the folk song "Sakura Sakura" with this form of number notation for the *minigoto*. The notation uses Arabic numerals for all of the *koto* strings. Also, a smaller version of the *koto* called *bunkagoto* (culture *koto*) uses a similar system, although it has Arabic numerals for strings 1-10 and standard characters as found in other *koto* notation for strings 11-13 (Zen'on Gakufu Shuppansha 1996).[23]

Perhaps influenced by Western reading practices and number notation, a system for beginners was introduced by Machida (1896) that has Japanese numbers written horizontally, and numbers that correspond to the degree of the scale (fig. 85). Four beats are given to a bar, or superimposed onto the music,[24] and rhythm is indicated by Western notation principles.

Although this notation never became popular, it does exemplify the need at that time for notation and for a system both influenced by Western staff notation and different from it.

Another form of horizontal *koto* notation was devised by Tazaki (1894). It is read from left to right, and its grid imitates staff notation (fig. 85). That is, it has five spaces instead of five lines. It maintains Japanese numerals, uses large and small circles to indicate strong and weaker beats respectively (*cf. Sōkyoku taiishō*), and is another example of a "reverse" type of notation. Of particular importance regarding the underlying idea behind this notation is the comment made by Tazaki that the score was intended to copy the layout of the strings on the *koto*.[25]

An early form of notation that includes many of the conventions in what was to become standard notation in the Yamada tradition was used by Inoue (1911) (fig. 86). It is clearly influenced by Western practices.[26] Using a horizontal type of notation, it is read left to right in rows, has four beats to a bar and has rhythmic indications following Western notation principles. Small phonetic characters, or *shōga*, are placed above the notes using the *katakana* syllabary. On this particular version of "Rokudan" there is an interesting variation on the second beat of the second measure, where, in comparison with other versions, different strings are plucked. This notation had a major impact on future Yamada-tradition notation, but interestingly it was never popular within the Ikuta tradition.

Horizontal number notation consequently became the main notation system of the Yamada tradition (fig. 86). The notation of Nakanoshima Kin'ichi (1904-84), one of the tradition's former *iemoto* or head, for example, includes bar lines that are a superimposition of time under Western influence. The music does not have a regular four-beat pulse (Yamada-ryū notation today is often given two-beats to a bar), and the notation includes Western rhythmic markings, dots and dashes, phrase marks, a time signature, and Arabic numerals to indicate some plucking fingers. Syncretism in this notation is extreme, and the cultural logic of the pre-Meiji reading system has been challenged in that the notation, while using a number system known in most *koto* notations, has not only changed the way the score is read, but it also includes many ideas that have a distinct Western origin and superimposes them onto traditional Japanese music.

In the late Meiji era, the Japanese government promoted nationalism in an attempt to rally feelings of national cultural identity, while at the same time drawing from the West in an attempt to achieve this. As stated in the Imperial Rescript on Education (Kyōiku Chokugo) of 1890 "the goal ... to instill among young Japanese a sense of Confucian moral duty and respect for the emperor, society, and the family while promoting a sense of national tradition and heritage, national identity, and patriotism" (Parisi, Thompson and Stevens 1995, 107). Furthermore, "after about 1890, textbooks ... were carefully scrutinized for evidence of undesirable kinds of foreign influence" (Beasley 1990, 96). One wonders firstly how Western music managed to continue to be so influential on Japanese musical life at a time when opinions about acculturation were changing and the country was witnessing increased imperialism, and secondly why new notations based on Western ideas continued to be devised during an era when Western influence was actually being challenged. A possible explanation for the latter might be that the new notations still mainly used Japanese characters. Ironically, the use of Western staff notation elsewhere never seemed to have been challenged.

Just like many other characteristics of the instrument, *koto* notation too is frequently perceived as belonging to a "traditional Japan", even though in actual fact much about it is relatively modern. Some features in the types of *koto* notation are very similar (e.g., numbers), although variation in, for example, ornamentation symbols, the direction of the score and the division of beats, often vary between performance traditions. Today, there is indeed a pluralistic coexistence of notations, and this pluralism reflects the diverse make-up of *koto* traditions, with each often having their own version of notation in a culture that emphasizes groupism on the one hand and difference on the other.

86 Horizontal notations.

(a) Opening of "Rokudan no Shirabe" ("Investigation in Six Sections"). Edition of Inoue (1911, 9), with transnotation. Miyagi Michio Memorial Museum, Tokyo;

(b) Opening of "Rokudan no Shirabe". *Honte* (upper line), *kaede* (middle line) and *kaede* (lower line, octave lower than middle line). Yamada-ryū notation (Nakanoshima 1996), with transnotation. Courtesy Nakanoshima Hiroko, Hōgakusha;

(c) Opening of "Rokudan no Shirabe". *Kaede* (upper line) and *honte* (lower line). Yamada-ryū notation (Yamada-ryū Sōkyoku Kyōju-kai 1975, 1), with transnotation. Courtesy Hakushindō.

(a)

(b)

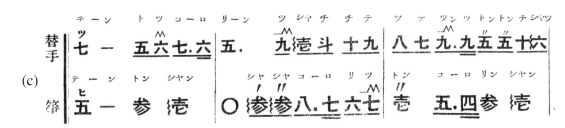

(c)

kaede

koto

Oral Mnemonics

Koto music includes a system of oral mnemonics (*shōga* or *kuchishōga*) that is sung by the teacher as an aid for the student (Kamisangō 1986; Kawada 1986). These oral mnemonics are based mainly on an onomatopoeic system that relates directly to the numerous ornamental techniques that are an inherent part of *koto* music. *Shōga* is occasionally written within the notation using either of the two Japanese phonetic syllabaries (*hiragana* or *katakana*). Some *koto* notations, such as *Shichiku shoshinshū* and *Kinkyoku shō* mentioned above, mostly employ this system.

The fact that most everyday professional *koto* musicians before the late nineteenth century were blind might have led to the development of *shōga*. Since blind musicians could not read notation they relied on a mnemonic system to help them memorize the music.[27] As Tsuge (1986a, 256) writes, "because most musicians involved in this genre were blind, these notations [i.e., tablatures] were obviously not used in practice. It was no doubt a mnemonic system called *kuchijamisen* or *kuchishōga* which was actually used in teaching and learning." *Shōga* does not indicate pitch, but does include "onomatopoetic indicators of the kinds of tones to be played" (Kamisangō 1986, 297). *Shōga* for the *koto* includes the following sounds: *t, ts, s, r, n, k, y, (ji); i, e, a, o, u,* and palatalization (Kawada 1986, 162).[28] Several of these sounds are used in connection with ornamentation (figs. 83-84, 86).

Tunings

The *koto* has several tunings.[29] While each of the *koto* strings has the same tension without movable bridges, a tuning is established when a movable bridge is placed under each of the thirteen strings and positioned appropriately along the upper surface of the soundboard. Several tunings are used by *gakusō* in court music (fig. 87), and many more by *zokusō* in everyday *koto* music. There are also *koto* tunings used in Tsukushigoto, which are derived from *gakusō* tunings (i.e., *taishikichō*),[30] in *koto* music unique to Okinawa (fig. 88), and several others, either devised for specific pieces of music or utilized in *koto* music from and after the Meiji era.

The two main *zokusō* performance traditions, the Ikuta-ryū and the Yamada-ryū, each have a number of *koto* tunings specific to this style of music (fig. 89). Many tunings are shared between the traditions, albeit sometimes referred to by a different name. Read (1975, 374-78) lists thirty-five such tunings relating to the Yamada-ryū, although only a few of them such as the *hirajōshi* and *kumoijōshi* – two of the main tunings in the Ikuta-ryū – are actually used on a regular basis.[31] Much *koto* music employs the tuning called *hirajōshi*, which was established in *zokusō* music by Yatsuhashi Kengyō.

Tunings may begin on any note, which is usually indicated at the beginning of a piece of notated music. While the first string is often tuned in unison to the fifth string, it is sometimes tuned an octave lower, even though this lower pitch is more difficult to obtain in lower-pitch tunings. If the pitch is not indicated in the score, it would be decided by the player, or, if the piece has a vocal line, it would normally be sung by the *koto* player, depending on the player's vocal range. Whereas a fixed tuning provides many of the melody notes in a piece of *koto* music that are characteristic of the instrument's repertoire, notes outside those of a tuning can be made by pressing down on the strings behind the movable bridges (tail end). Sometimes the tuning is adjusted during a piece by altering the position of one or more of the movable bridges.

The tunings in figure 89 are representative examples of some used by *zokusō* (Ikuta-ryū names appear first). Other tunings and alternative names are known, but those in figure 89

87 *Gakusō* tunings.
(a) *Ichikotsuchō*;
(b) *Sōjō*;
(c) *Taishikichō*;
(d) *Hyōjō*;
(e) *Ōshikichō*;
(f) *Banshikichō*.

(a)

(b)

(c)

(d)

(e)

(f)

serve to illustrate the diversity of the instrument's fixed tunings. As Hirano (1989a) has demonstrated, everyday *koto* tunings were sometimes devised for specific pieces and a number of variant names have been used in different source materials. In addition are glimpses of outside culture contact in the use of names and the notes found in a specific tuning, even though in theory the Japanese policy of isolation during the Edo period generally restricted large-scale trade and Western influence. For instance, a tuning for the *koto* called *orandajōshi* (Holland tuning) or *orugōrujōshi* (orgel tuning; the word *orgel* is from the Dutch meaning "organ") was devised under Dutch influence especially from the seventeenth century onward, and this tuning's "peculiar quality derives from the fact that there is only one half step in it and, also, from the bright major-mode feeling" (Kikkawa 1997, 103). The tuning was initially utilized in *koto* music by Ichiura Kengyō (act. *c.* 1804-17) in Osaka in his piece "Oranda Manzai" ("Dutch Long Life"). This piece was also the first for *koto* to employ the *kaede* (or *kaete*) style, which is a melodic second line that differs slightly from the main part and often includes heterophonic movement between the parts. Even later, the late nineteenth and early twentieth centuries too witnessed new *koto* tunings for specific pieces or styles of music (*see* Kikkawa 1997).

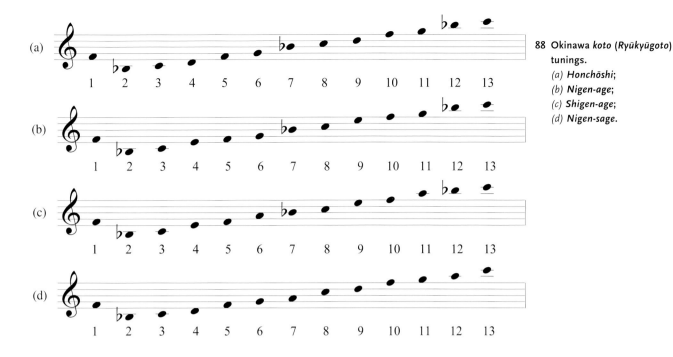

88 Okinawa *koto* (*Ryūkyūgoto*)
tunings.
(a) *Honchōshi*;
(b) *Nigen-age*;
(c) *Shigen-age*;
(d) *Nigen-sage*.

The nature of music played on the *koto* is influenced by the structure of the instrument.
The music must be written within a certain range and its aesthetic quality decided with the aid
of sound production. Likewise, the physical capacity of the performer and the intermediary
devices used in performance also contribute directly to the ideal structure of the sound itself:

> In musical instruments, we can find cultural values and concepts overtly and/or covertly
> represented in various forms and at various levels. For instance, the structure of instruments
> (for example, the arrangements of strings or fingerholes) is in itself thought to suggest an
> essential portion of the music theory which has been deeply embedded in the musical
> thinking of a people. (O. Yamaguti 1986, 30)[32]

When the movable bridges are placed on the soundboard they form a different visual
pattern for each tuning system. The physical space between each movable bridge reflects the
interval between the notes of the tuning. The space between the movable bridges is reduced
slightly as the pitch of the strings rises, that is, a half step between two strings in the lower
register has a wider gap between the movable bridges than the same interval in the higher
register. Just as visual forms of notation may today be used by the performer as a means of
aiding memory, other means of representation are also found during a performance that help
both the audience and the performer to understand visual forms through other sensory means.
By having the thirteen strings of the *koto* tuned with the assistance of thirteen movable bridges,
a visual structure of the tuning of the piece is made available to those able to see it. This
structure also allows the player not only to see the structure of the tuning, but also physically to
feel the position of each movable bridge and vibrating/non-vibrating string with their hands in
order to create a conceptual map of their position and to facilitate changes in tuning if required.
Such occurrences have been observed by Yamaguti who remarks that:

> The strings of the *koto* are all of the same thickness and should be tightened to almost the
> same tension, according to tradition. Therefore, before a performance, when the *ji* or *kotoji*
> ("pillars" or "pillars for the *koto*"; movable bridges) are erected underneath the strings tuned
> in one system, or when – even during performance – some of them are moved so as to be
> retuned in another, the visual images of the arrangements of *ji* can unmistakably indicate the

89 *Zokusō* tunings.
(a) Kumoijōshi;
(b) Honkumoijōshi;
(c) Nakazorajōshi (called *akebonojōshi* in the Yamada-ryū);
(d) Kataiwatojōshi (Yamada-ryū);
(e) Nijūkumoijōshi (called *iwatojōshi* in the Yamada-ryū). Another form exists with the 1st string raised one tone and/or the 13th string one octave above the 8th string;
(f) Hirajōshi;
(g) Akebonojōshi (also called *nijūnakazorajōshi;* and *iwatojōshi* in the Yamada-ryū);
(h) Hankumoijōshi (called *katakumoijōshi* in the Yamada-ryū);
(i) Shiagari hankumoijōshi (called *hankumoijōshi* in the Yamada-ryū);

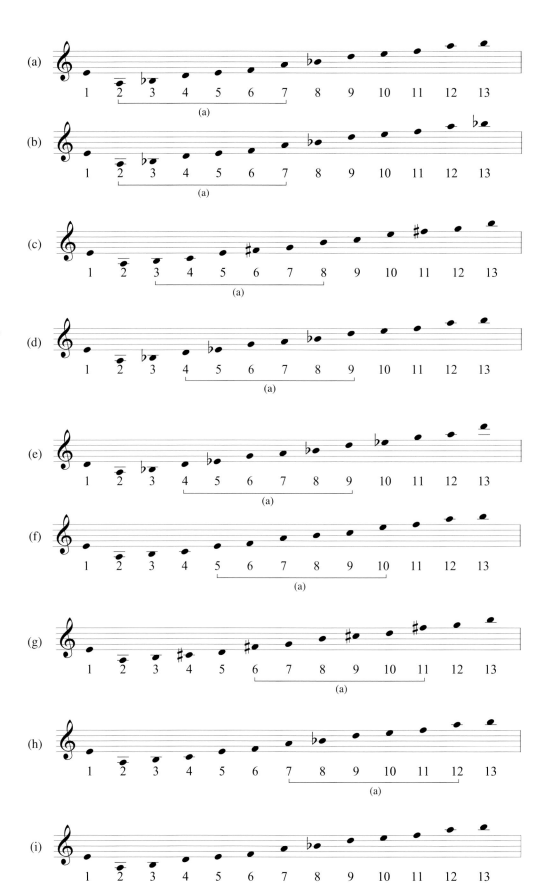

132

(j)

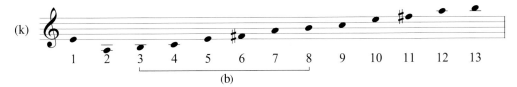

(k)

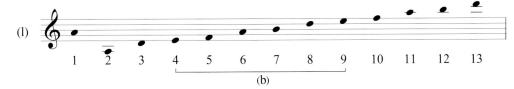

(l)

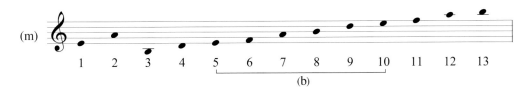

(m)

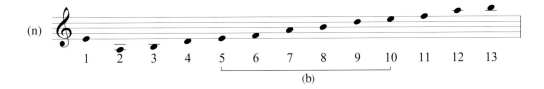

(n)

(o)

(p)

(q)

(r)

89 (j) *Rokutoagari kumoijōshi* (also called *nijūkumoijōshi*, and *han'iwatojōshi* or *sekishōjōshi* in the Yamada-ryū);
(k) *Rokuagarijōshi* (also called *hannakazorajōshi*; and *nakazorajōshi* in the Yamada-ryū);
(l) *Akikazejōshi*;
(m) *Kokinjōshi*;
(n) *Shikuagarijōshi* (also called *katakumoijōshi*);
(o) *Shikuagari nakazorajōshi*;
(p) *Orugōrujōshi* (also called *orandajōshi*);
(q) *Hanakumojōshi* (also called *ōgakujōshi*; and *higurashijōshi* in the Yamada-ryū);
(r) *Nogijōshi*;

89 (s) *Akinojōshi;*
(t) *Gakujōshi* (also called
kariganejōshi and *shin-
kariganejōshi*);
(u) *Sōfurenjōshi;*
(v) *Natsuyamajōshi;*
(w) *Gaisen rappa jōshi.*

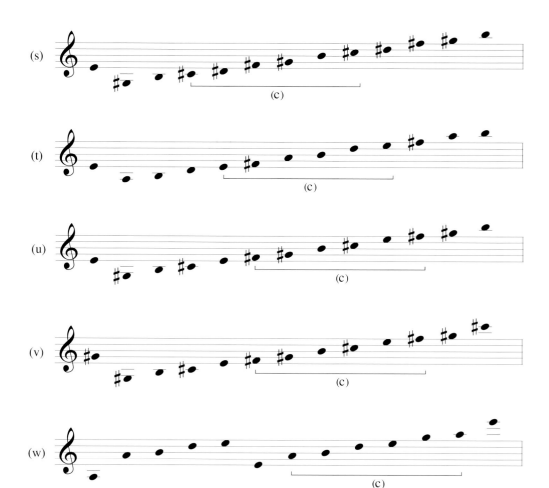

particular tuning system applied at any given moment. It follows then that a theoretical
foundation of performance on the *koto* is established primarily in the sphere of tactility;
however, it should be noted that the whole process as well as the result of this theoretical
foundation inevitably involves visual and aural perceptions. At any rate, this kind of process
and the results of tactile theorization on an instrument can be regarded as representations of
a culture value which requires the performer to conform to the specificity of the tradition.
(O. Yamaguti 1986, 30)

The grouping of the movable bridges usually follows a pentatonic scale either with or
without semitones. Today, the scales used have intervals that are basically the same as those
used in Western music. However, half-steps or semitones are sometimes slightly smaller in *koto*
music (Adriaansz 1973, 40; Koizumi 1977, 74).[33] *Koto* tunings with half-steps were first used in
the instrument's tunings and repertoire by Yatsuhashi Kengyō. The scale he employed as the
basis of his tuning (e.g., *hirajōshi*) – the *in* scale – was until this time considered unsuitable for
koto music as it was used primarily by common or everyday people. Hence, the term *zokusō* or
everyday *koto* music was used for the instrument and repertoire from the time of Yatsuhashi
(*see* Chapter 2). Today, the tuning of *koto* strings usually follows predetermined pitches that
decide the register depending on the physical boundaries of the instrument, But in *kumiuta*, as
Tsuge (1986a, 256-57) notes, "importance is not attached to absolute pitch. Rather, the
instrument is tuned in the register best suited to the singer's voice. It is assumed, moreover,
that *hirajōshi* ("common tuning") based on the *miyakobushi* [or *in*] scale is to be used."

The tunings shown in figure 89 divide into three main groups: (a) those indicating tunings
with the descending version of the five-note *in* scale; (b) those indicating tunings that include a
scale related to the *in* scale; and (c) those indicating tunings that include the five-note *yō* scale.

While several tunings are illustrated, only a few of them are actually used extensively. *Hirajōshi* is by far the most common, and is generally the tuning first established on the *koto* as a foundation from which to find others. The tuning labeled *orugōrujōshi* or *orandajōshi* is a special case and does not include any of the scales already mentioned.

The placement of the movable bridges to follow a particular tuning creates an ordered terrain that influences the pitch structure of the instrument's music according to the physical capabilities of the performer. This idea has been explored by O. Yamaguti:

> Plucking techniques on the strings of the *koto*, for instance, are usually schematically conceptualized as basic patterns which support the whole performance, to be undertaken properly in context. One of the basic plucking techniques is applied with the tsume ("fingernail"; here, plectrum or pick) on the thumb, plucking two or more adjacent strings in succession, to produce a descending melodic movement which may be posited as a basic motif of koto music, one which provides it with a ground for establishing culturally recognized order. This plucking with the thumb is easily accomplished because the arrangement of the strings is from high to low, away from the body of the performer. This accords comfortably with the natural physical movement of the thumb plucking toward the inside of the hand (palm). (O. Yamaguti 1986, 30)

Fixed tunings are an inherent aspect of *koto* music and instrument form. The instrument's outer appearance has a characteristic feature of movable bridges placed along the upper surface of the soundboard, and the player's position and their movement is influenced by the tunings.

Ornamentation

Gakusō

Gakusō playing techniques today include the plucking of single strings and several idiomatic patterns that typifiy most *gagaku* instrumental music. Some of the right-hand ornamental techniques of *zokusō* are related to those of earlier traditions such as *gakusō* in court music (*gagaku*). However, the *gakusō* has far fewer ornamental techniques than the *zokusō*, and today left-hand manipulation of strings is no longer seen.[34] Three ornamental techniques form the basis of music played on the *gakusō* (fig. 90). The prescriptive notation shows only the octave pattern, while performance practice dictates that other notes are played. The technique *shizugaki* is by far the most common in the *kangen* (wind and strings) repertoire of *gagaku*, and *sugagaki* is found primarily in formalized introductions and endings. These techniques were influential in later *koto* genres and are still encountered in very similar and related *zokusō* techniques, such as *kakezume*, *hankake* and *hayakake*.

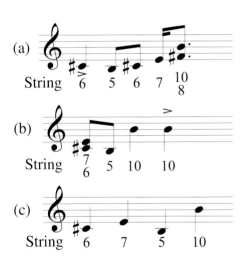

90 *Gakusō* techniques.
(a) *Shizugaki*;
(b) *Hayagaki*;
(c) *Sugagaki*.

Zokusō

Zokusō ornamentation forms part of the idiomatic language of traditional *koto* performance. In addition to techniques that were influenced by Western music, which have become part of modern-day *koto* music – including arpeggio, tremolo, harmonics, staccato, pizzicato, vibrato, and various percussive effects on the strings (either side of the movable bridges and on other parts of the instrument) – there are several widely used techniques and melodic patterns that

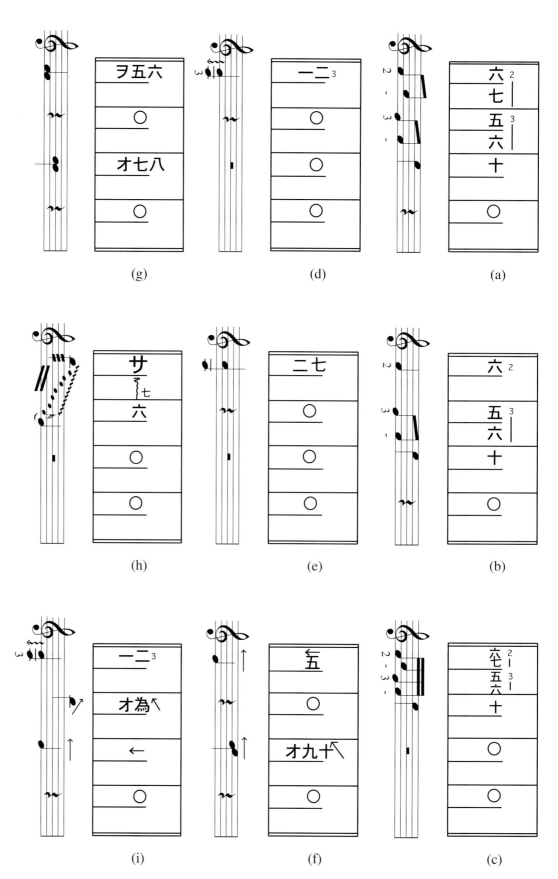

(g)

(d)

(a)

(h)

(e)

(b)

(i)

(f)

(c)

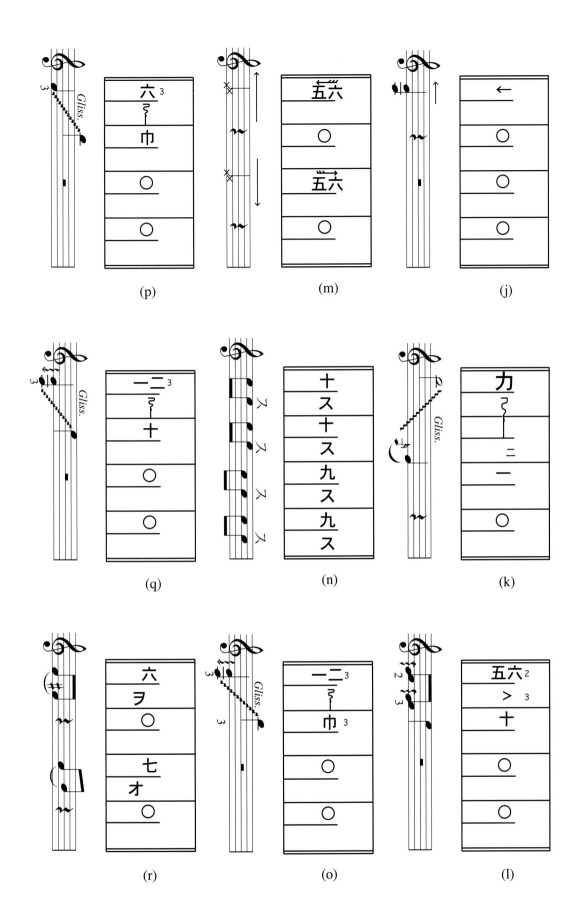

(p)

(m)

(j)

(q)

(n)

(k)

(r)

(o)

(l)

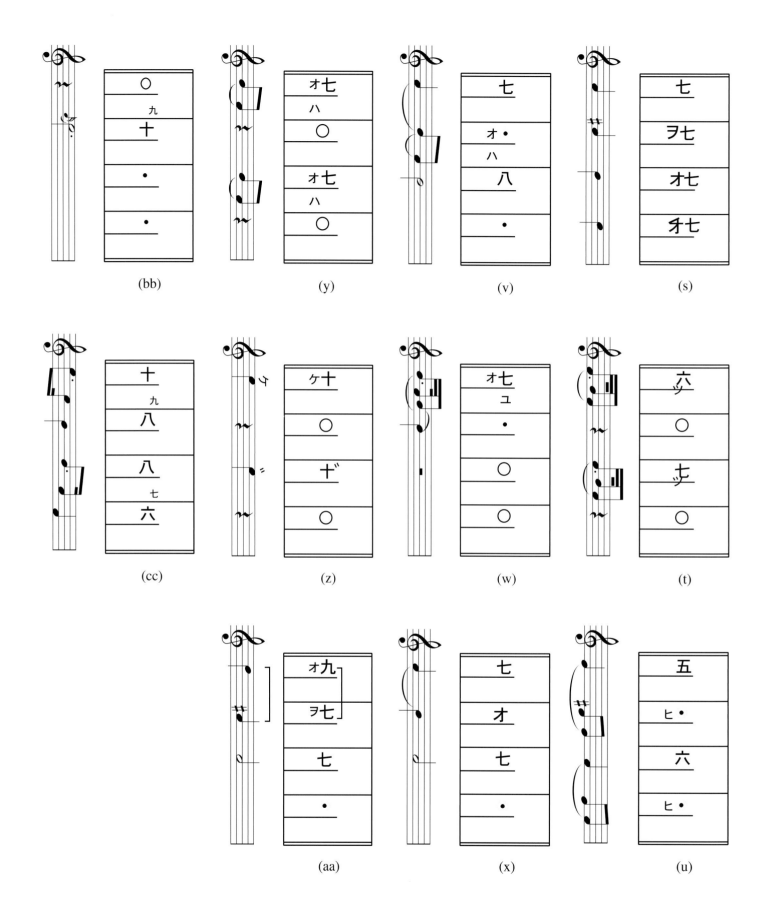

(bb) (y) (v) (s)

(cc) (z) (w) (t)

(aa) (x) (u)

are often found in both traditional and contemporary music. These techniques and the written symbols in the notation can vary slightly between different performance traditions, as do the diverse onomatopoeic names describing them.

The *Sōkyoku taiishō* ([1779] 1903), regarded as a major treatise on *zokusō* (fig. 91), describes twenty-five techniques of ornamentation (*see listing below*): seventeen for the right hand and eight for the left hand. While this historical work gives a concise explanation on how to play the techniques, the inclusive explanation given below of each of them is intended to cover the possible performance practices of several present-day performance traditions in order to present various ways in which the techniques are played nowadays. These descriptions, shown below, closely follow Andō's (1986, 195) own outline of the techniques, together with his clarification of performance practice and onomatopoeic names that are based on the Ikuta-ryū. While not all performance traditions can be covered fully, the examples given are meant as a general outline of some possible types of ornamentation. The techniques of the other main everyday tradition of *koto* performance, the Yamada-ryū, are displayed in figure 97; they are based on the scores of the former *iemoto* Nakanoshima Kin'ichi. These techniques and their symbols are either the same or very similar to those delineated for the Ikuta tradition.[35]

The techniques shown in figure 91 use a notation of the Ikuta-ryū, and those in figure 97 that of the Yamada-ryū. Both utilize the *hirajōshi* tuning. In the notations right-hand fingering is expressed with "2" (index finger), "3" (middle finger). Most notes without a number are played by the thumb, which except for the first string, usually rests on the string below the one just plucked. When the thumb does not rest on the next string the technique is called *kozume*. As well as the diverse alternative terminology used for the techniques, well-known onomatopoeic words and phrases are indicated in parenthesis. These are usually found in everyday speech, with slight variations occurring between different performance traditions.

(a) *Kakezume* (dispersed plectra) (*tonren tonren ten* or *kara kara ten*). A melodic pattern that uses the thumb, index and middle fingers. Usually, the index finger plays one string followed by the next string above it; the middle finger then plays the string below the first one played, followed by the next one above it; the thumb then plays the note an octave above the first string played by the middle finger.

(b) *Hankake/hangake* (half *kake*; i.e., half *kakezume*). A variation of *kakezume* that has fewer notes. In any of the variants, grace notes might be played by the middle finger before the thumb plays (*to to ten* or *ka ka ten*). Three types are found:
   (i) *Mukōhan* (*ton ren ton ten*). The index finger plays two strings followed by the middle finger playing one.
   (ii) *Tanhan* (*ton ton ren ten* or *ton ka ra ten*). The index finger plays one string and the middle finger two, as in the illustration.
   (iii) *Kaihan*. Both the index and the middle finger play one string each.

(c) *Hayakake/hayagake* (fast *kake*; i.e., fast *kakezume*) (*kara kara ten*). This is a variation of *kakezume* that plays the sequence at twice the normal speed.

(d) *Kakite* (scratch hand); *kakizume* (scratch plectra) (*sha, shan*). The middle finger plucks two adjacent strings (usually the first and second strings) in one fast stroke. The plucking motion is toward the player so that the string furthest away is played first. One sound is heard when played quickly, although two separate notes can sometimes be heard when played slowly. The plectra might come to rest on the next string above the two that were struck. Adriaansz (1973, 51) comments that in the Yamada-ryū the player "may (not 'must') continue the movement of...[the] finger in the same direction until it stops against the next string." Ikuta-ryū players today usually play *kakite* in the same way as the Yamada-ryū.

92 *Awasezume* koto technique. Player: Yamakawa Tamae (Miyagi-ha, Ikuta-ryū). Dunedin, 1996. Photograph by the author.

93 *Chirashi/namigaeshi* koto technique. Player: Yamakawa Tamae (Miyagi-ha, Ikuta-ryū). Dunedin, 1996. Photograph by the author.

(e) *Awasezume* (meeting plectra) (*shan*) (fig. 92). The thumb and (usually) middle finger play simultaneously (usually in octaves), although the middle finger might occasionally play momentarily before the thumb.

(f) *Chirashi* (scatter); *chirashizume* (scatter plectra) (*shu'*). This technique, which varies considerably between different traditions, is played by scraping the right side (as viewed from the top of the hand) of the middle plectrum along one, two or more strings (depending on the tradition) in a sweeping motion from right to left (*cf. waren*). It is often indicated by a horizontal arrow above the string, or strings.

The term *chirashi* might also be used to describe a technique that is played by scraping the strings with the end of the index and middle plectra along two adjacent strings, the lower of which is often pressed in order to raise it to the pitch of the upper string (fig. 93). In this instance, the technique is sometimes called *namigaeshi* (wave return). In such cases, the technique is notated with either a curved or a straight arrow pointing to the left (either horizontally or to the upper left). In some modern music the technique might be played with the plectra scraping to the player's right, in which case the arrow points to the right.

(g) *Oshiawasezume* (push, meeting plectra); *oshiawase* (*ryan*; *shan*). Two adjacent strings are plucked simultaneously by the thumb, the lower of the two being raised by pressing it down to match the pitch of the upper string (shown in the example with a *katakana "wo"* for a half tone and an *"o"* for a whole tone).

(h) *Ren* (progression); *uraren* (back progression) (*sārarin*). The plectrum on the index finger plays a tremolo on the thirteenth string (unless indicated otherwise) and then this finger and the middle finger alternate rapidly to play a glissando from high to low. This technique usually ends with a grace note on the string immediately before the final note in the progression. In the Yamada-ryū the tremolo is not usually played. Instead, the player hooks the index and middle finger plectra around the string to produce a scraping sound and then plays the glissando from high to low (Read 1975, 380-81).

(i) *Namigaeshi* (wave return) (*shan shu' shū*). This technique is interpreted in several ways. Sometimes it is played with a pattern of three techniques, as shown in the example, which begins with *kakite*, then *chirashi* (scraping with the tips of the index and middle plectra along two adjacent strings), and finally *waren*. Another method is to play the technique in the same way as one of the versions of *chirashi* (scraping with the extremity of the index and middle plectra along two adjacent strings).

(j)   *Waren* (ring movement) (*shū*). The side of the middle finger plectrum sweeps across the first string with a quick movement from the player's right to left, sometimes just touching the second and even the third strings as well, in order to produce a scraping sound (cf. *chirashi*). In the Ikuta-ryū the technique is notated by either a horizontal arrow pointing left (either above the notation of the first and second strings, or on its own without any indication of strings, but signifying the first two), or by a *katakana* "*wa.*"

(k)   *Nagashizume* (flowing plectra) (*kārarin*). This technique consists of a glissando played by the thumb plectrum from high (usually from the thirteenth string, unless indicated otherwise, and emphasizing it and the string below it – the lower string is not indicated) to low, very often leaving out or playing very quietly the strings between start and finish. The technique usually ends with one or two grace notes before the final note. It is sometimes called *hanryū* (half flowing), if it begins on a lower string.

(l)   *Warizume* (dividing plectra) (*sha sha*). The index finger plays two adjacent strings very quickly beginning with the lower, followed by an identical pattern on the same strings by the middle finger (in the example a repeat sign occupies the second half of the beat). The thumb usually continues by playing a string an octave higher than the lower of the two adjacent strings, in which case the technique is labeled onomatopoeically as *sha sha ten*.

(m)   *Surizume* (scraping plectra); *urazuri* (backward scraping) (*zū zū*) (fig. 94). The index and middle plectra scrape with their right side first from right to left along two adjacent strings, pause, and then scrape from left to right along the same strings. The technique is usually notated with arrows indicating the direction of the plectra.

(n)   *Sukuizume* (backward plectra) (*ri; ru; re; ro*). A backward stroke by the thumb that produces a slight scraping sound (indicated by a *katakana* "*su*"). When played slowly the ring on the index plectrum may hold onto the thumb ring in order for the technique to be played louder and preventing the thumb ring from falling off. The same technique is used on the *shamisen*, which is played with a backward stroke of the plectrum.

(o)   *Hikiren* (pulling progression) (*shān rin*). The middle finger plays a glissando from low to high. The first part usually begins with *kakite* on the first and second strings, followed by very quiet notes before the final string (sometimes with a grace note, *kasanezume*, in front of it).

94 *Surizume koto* technique. Player: Yamakawa Tamae (Miyagi-ha, Ikuta-ryū). Dunedin, 1996. Photograph by the author.

(p) *Hanhikiren* (half pulling progression) *(shān rin)*. A version of *hikiren* that begins on a higher string than *hikiren*.

(q) *Hikisute* (pulling, give up) *(shān toton)*. A version of *hikiren* that ends on a string lower than the thirteenth string.

(r) *En* (cover, or shade); *atooshi* (after push). After a string has been plucked, it is pressed behind its movable bridge by left-hand fingers (thumb, index and middle fingers) to raise the pitch (portamento). The string is usually pressed on the part of the beat indicated, although the exact point is usually learned through one's tradition, as is the point of release unless it is shown specifically in the score.

(s) *Kō* (push); *oshide* (push hand); *oshiiro* (push, color). A string is pressed behind its movable bridge by the left hand to raise the pitch either by a half tone, a whole tone or one and a half tones. A related technique called *kakeoshi* holds down two strings at the same time.

(t) *Tsuki* (thrust); *tsukiiro* (thrust, color). A string is pressed immediately after a note is played (usually raised about one tone), and then released straight away. The technique is indicated with a *katakana* "tsu" in the score.

(u) *Jū*;[36] *hikiiro* (pull, color) (fig. 95). A string is pulled toward the player's right (usually about a half tone) and then released. It is usually pulled on the beat following the one played and released on or before the half beat before the next. The technique is indicated with a *katakana* "hi" in the score.

(v) *Jūkō* (layered pushing); *kasaneoshi* (layered pressing). Repeated pushing and releasing of a string, or raising an already pushed string further.

(w) *Yōgin* (shake, song); *yuriiro* (shake, color). Usually releasing a pushed string and pushing it again immediately (the opposite of *tsuki*). The technique is indicated by a *katakana* "yu."

95 *Hikiiro koto* technique. Player: Yamakawa Tamae (Miyagi-ha, Ikuta-ryū). Dunedin, 1996. Photograph by the author.

96 *Keshizume koto* technique. Player: Yamakawa Tamae (Miyagi-ha, Ikuta-ryū). Dunedin, 1996. Photograph by the author.

(x) *Kōkyō* (push reverberation); *oshihibiki* (push reverberation). After an open string is played it is pressed on the next beat to raise its pitch before the open string is played again. The motion is slower than *en* (*atooshi*).

(y) *Kōhō* (push release); *oshihanashi* (push release). Releasing a pushed string. Indicated in the notation by a *katakana* "ha".

In addition to these standard techniques, several others can be used in both traditional and modern music. These include *keshizume*, *yokozume*, *kasanezume*, and *kōrorin* (fig. 96). The technique of *keshizume* (stopped plectra; also called *soede* [added hand]; or *soezume* [added plectra]) is played by placing the nail of the left-hand index finger under a string just in front of the movable bridge in order to produce a buzzing sound when the string is plucked by a plectrum. This is indicated in the notation by either a *katakana* "*ke*" or two dashes. The technique of *kakeoshi* (held push) is played by pressing two strings simultaneously – indicated in the score with a bracket (fig. 91, aa). In *yokozume* (side plectrum) the thumb plectrum scrapes along a string (or strings) from right to left (indicated in the score with the *katakana* symbol for "*yo*" or "*yoko*"). For *kasanezume* (fig. 91, bb) the middle-finger plectrum plays a grace note from one string to the next one above it (indicated by a smaller symbol for the string). *Kōrorin* (an onomatopoeic term) involves a pattern of three notes, the second of which is a grace note (indicated by smaller symbols, *see* fig. 91, cc). The use of the left hand (bare fingers, one or more) or right hand (little finger or ring finger) to pluck the strings has become increasingly more frequent in *koto* music since the Meiji era. Kikuzuka Yoichi (1846-1909), for example, included new techniques to play the *koto* such as left-hand plucking, which influenced later composers for the instrument to adopt such a technique.

Yamada-ryū Techniques

Yamada-ryū ornamentation exhibits similar techniques and, while varying from the Ikuta-ryū in that they are read from left to right in the tablature, use similar or the same symbols.[37] The examples listed below are described by Nakanoshima (1956), and they illustrate firstly the ornamental language of the music of the tradition, which shares much with other *zokusō* traditions, and secondly how they are represented in notation. Further explanation of the techniques is given only when they differ considerably from those already described:

(a) Right-hand fingering. "1" (thumb); "2" (index finger); "3" (middle finger); "4" (ring finger).
(b) Left-hand fingering. "1" (thumb); "2" (index finger); "3" (middle finger); "4" (ring finger); "5" (little finger).
(c) *Kakizume*.
(d) *Warizume*.
(e) *Awasezume*.
(f) *Uraren*.
(g) *Hikiren*.
(h) *Hikisute*.
(i) *Nagashizume*.
(j) *Namigaeshi*. The second note has *uraren*.
(k) *Waren*.
(l) *Chirashizume*. The side of the middle finger plectrum usually scrapes the string.
(m) *Sukuizume*.
(n) *Furizume/sukuizume*. Played rapidly in succession.
(o) *Surizume/urazuri*.
(p) *Hajiki*. The string is plucked quickly with the back of the index finger plectrum.
(q) *Kozume* is a backward stroke by the thumb and then raising the pitch by pushing with the left hand.
(r) *Uchizume* (struck plectra) (*ten*, *shan*). The rings of the index and middle plectra on the palm side of the hand strike the strings percussively.
(s) *Otoshi/nagashi*. Pluck slowly and gradually get faster.
(t) *Oshiiro*.
(u) *Oshihanashi*.

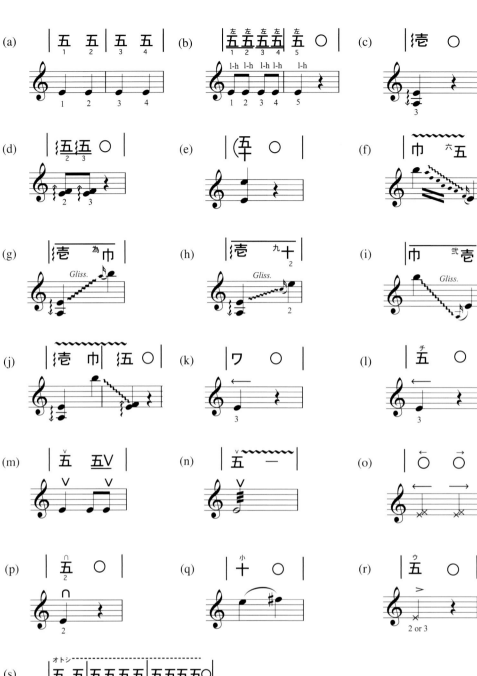

(v) *Oshidome.* Press the string after plucking, usually where the triangle is placed in the notation.

(w) *Oshidome hanashi.* Release after playing *oshidome*.

(x) *Oshihibiki.*

(y) *Yuriiro.*

(z) *Oshiawase.* (Arrow is reversed when played by index finger.)

(aa) *Tsukiiro.*

(bb) *Hikiiro.*

(cc) *Soezume.*

(dd) *Keshi.* A staccato (the note being stopped with the left hand very quickly).

(ee) *Kakeoshi.*

Genres

Koto music (*sōkyoku*) dating from the time of Yatsuhashi Kengyō falls into four broad categories: *danmono* (instrumental pieces); *kumiuta* (song cycles with *koto* accompaniment); *jiuta sōkyoku* (songs with *koto* accompaniment), which often use the *tegotomono* form (alternating voice and instrumental sections); and *shinkyoku* (new music). *Shinkyoku*, by the very nature of the term, is concerned primarily with music dating from the Meiji era. Music from this time might either relate directly to the music language of historical *koto* forms, or include a modern, crossover or experimental music style. The sub-styles referred to as *Meiji shinkyoku* (new music of the Meiji era) and *shin-nihon ongaku* (new Japanese music), both of which emerged after considerable Western influence in the late nineteenth century, are two examples of new Japanese music that contrast a traditional style. Such composers as Miyagi Michio (1894-1956), Nakanoshima

Kin'ichi and Sawai Tadao (1937-97) are perhaps three of the best-known composers of *shinkyoku* in the twentieth century, and their music – especially that of Miyagi Michio – is sometimes referred to as "traditional" in that it is now very much part of the soundscape of traditional Japanese music. These composers and others were much inspired by techniques of composition found in Western music, while maintaining a Japanese identity for the instrument. The *koto* is also found in numerous other genres of contemporary music. It is found in jazz, rock and a variety of crossover styles, and is commonplace in the contemporary world of Japanese traditional culture.[38] In such genres it might be played in a variety of ways that use traditional and/or experimental techniques.

Most *zokusō* traditions share a wide range of repertoire (usually referred to as *koten*: old pieces), as well as often having pieces unique to a particular group. The two main everyday traditions of the Ikuta-ryū and the Yamada-ryū have many traditional pieces in common, which usually differ slightly according to performance practice. Within the numerous sub-traditions or groups of both, one can often find a repertoire that is played due to an influential player of that specific tradition. The Yamada-ryū, for example, also has its own genres, as well as playing the tradition repertoire of *kumiuta*, *danmono* and *jiuta sōkyoku* (Read 1975, 42-43).[39] Some of these genres include *utamono* composed by Yamada Kengyō, adapted compositions from the Ikuta-ryū, and arranged compositions (primarily from *jōruri*). Read (1975, 65) states that the Yamada-ryū divides their *koto* repertoire into the following categories, many of which have origins in the repertoires of other instruments:

> *Utamono* (literally, "singing piece").
> *Kumiuta* (song cycles with *koto* accompaniment).
> *Danmono* (instrumental pieces) and *kinutamono* (instrumental pieces).
> *Sangenmono* (*shamisen* pieces) and *kokyūmono* (*kokyū* pieces).
> *Shinsōkyoku* (new *koto* music) and *Meiji shinkyoku* (new music of the Meiji era).
> Pieces arranged from *jiuta* (lyrical *shamisen* music of Kansai).
> Pieces arranged from *jōruri* (narrative *shamisen* music of Kantō).

The significance of *danmono*, *kumiuta* and *jiuta sōkyoku* in the repertoire of *koto* music today is such that they are understood to be representative traditional genres. The performance of such pieces is exemplary of a continuing tradition of playing an established historical repertoire. Each of these three styles is summarized below as a way of illustrating their form and highlighting their relevance in the history of *koto* music.[40]

Danmono

The instrumental genre called *danmono* or *shirabemono* has been known since the seventeenth century, especially relating to the repertoire of Yatsuhashi Kengyō (fig. 98; Adriaansz 1967, 1970, 1973). As an important instrumental piece in the *danmono* repertoire, the well-known "Rokudan no Shirabe", has also been used as an added part to several other pieces where it is superimposed on another melody in a style called *dan'awase* (literally, "*dan* [section] meeting").[41] As Read (1975, 70) has pointed out, it is found in several compositions by Yamada Kengyō: "In three of his compositions, 'Hototogisu,' ["Cuckoo"] 'Sumiyoshi' [a shrine in Osaka] and 'Yaegaki,' [literally, "Multifold Fences"] Yamada-Kengyō included an *ai no te* [an instrumental interlude] in which the *ji* (second *koto* part) is the first *dan* of *Rokudan*." "Rokudan" is also found in one form or another in the pieces "Akikaze no Kyoku" ("Autumn Wind Music") by Mitsuzaki Kengyō (*d.* 1853), "Kumoi Rokudan" ("Six Sections, Kumoi [Tuning]")[42] by Chiyoda Kengyō (*d.* 1863), and "Aki no Nanakusa" ("Seven Flowers of Autumn"). "Aki no Nanakusa" is thought to have been composed by Yamato Shōrei (1844-89) and then revised by Yamase Shōin (Tsuge 1983a, 160).[43] The *koto* player and composer Fukumori

98 Opening *dan* of "Rokudan no Shirabe" ("Investigation in Six Sections") (Miyagi 1996, 3), with transnotation. Courtesy Miyagi Kazue, Hōgakusha.

Toshiko has also written the piece "Rōritsu no Sato"[44] (1986), which inserts "Rokudan" as its second part.

A characteristic feature of *danmono* pieces is a structure of several sections (*dan*) with 104 beats in them. This is interpreted today as twenty-six measures with four beats in each in the Ikuta-ryū and usually fifty-two measures with two beats in each in the Yamada-ryū.[45] The first section has an extra four beats for a total of 108 beats. While "Rokudan" has six sections, the *danmono* repertoire consists of several pieces that are named after the number of sections that

te n ton shan   sha sha ko ro ri chi   ton ten ton shan chin te tsu ko ro ri chi

ton ten ton shan   shan te n sha sha chi n to te tsu u n   sha sha te tsu sha sha te tsu

ton ko ro rin shan tsun te tsu ko ro ri chi   tsu to ko ro rin shan tsun ten chin chiin

te tsu ko ro rin tsu te tsun shan ten sha sha tsun to te tsun te tsu sha sha ko ro rin ten

ton ka ra te tsu sha sha ko ro rin ten ton ten ton ten tsun ten ko ro rin chi tsu te chi

tsun ten tsun te tsu sha sha te chi tsun ten ko ro rin ri n chi ton ko ro rin tsu te

![music notation]

tsun chi tsu chi tsu te chi tsu te tsu te ko ro ri chi ton ten ton shan

divide the overall piece: "Godan" has five sections, "Hachidan" has eight sections, "Kudan" has nine sections, and "Kumoi Kudan" has nine sections. In the latter piece, the tuning of strings of the *koto* is also indicated in the title of the piece, that is, *kumoijōshi*. An exception to such naming of the pieces is the work entitled "Midare" ("Confusion"). Generally classified as part of the *danmono* repertoire, it has several forms and is sometimes called "Jūdan" ("Ten Sections") and "Jūnidan" ("Twelve Sections") in the Ikuta-ryū and Yamada-ryū, respectively.

As a piece of music seen to be representative of the *koto* repertoire, "Rokudan" is frequently a favorite in performances. "Rokudan" is played habitually in *koto* performance and it is a work that all everyday *koto* players would be expected to learn regardless of tradition (*see* Falconer 1995). Many performance traditions require it for a license, and it is often included in competitions – sometimes with several *dan* removed – or heard at times of celebration. In effect, this traditional piece has become symbolic of both the *koto* and its repertoire. In order to remain as an embodiment of the *koto* with layers of cultural meaning, however, "Rokudan" must be played on a form of the instrument that allows this particular piece to be preserved in its true traditional form. Hence, the need for the structure of the *koto* to remain unchanged in a form that is appropriate and authentic for its music.

Kumiuta

Kumiuta evolved in the seventeenth and eighteenth centuries, and at present has a repertoire of fifty-three pieces (Tsuge 1986a, 256), most of which are played in both the Ikuta-ryū and the Yamada-ryū.[46] It was Yatsuhashi Kengyō who helped establish much of the traditional repertoire for the instrument. Yatsuhashi developed Tsukushigoto pieces to form a repertoire that included thirteen *kumiuta* and several *danmono* ("Kudan" and "Rinzetsu").[47] This transformation between performance traditions was also a change in social milieu, which was reflected in the music in Yatsuhashi's use of the *in* scale. The genre of *kumiuta* is an historically important form of *koto* music and often associated with secret pieces. Even "when the prohibition against free distribution of the secret pieces was lifted in the Meiji period, kumiuta by then had become so limited to only specialists that in effect not much was changed: the secret pieces remained practically unknown" (Adriaansz 1973, 14).

Koto kumiuta assumed their current form with Yatsuhashi Kengyō in the seventeenth century (fig. 99).[48] Based on the texts and music of the Tsukushigoto, Yatsuhashi's thirteen *kumiuta* song cycles symbolize the advent of modern-day *koto* music, that is, everyday performance as opposed to court or religious music.[49] *Koto kumiuta* are usually performed by a solo *koto* player who sings as well. For example, the *koto kumiuta* "Fuki" ("Rhubarb") as shown in figures 80 and 99 even has a melodic line based on the *gagaku* piece "Etenraku" ("Beyond Heaven Music") (Miyazaki 1972):[50]

> A popular pastime of the nobility during these periods [Kamakura and Muromachi] was the improvisation of *imayō* ('contemporary songs'). Such 'noble *imayō*' (distinct from 'common *imayō*'; popular religious songs sung by the common people) often used the melody *Etenraku* as a vehicle for their poetry. Then, as now, *Etenraku* was one of the most popular compositions of *gagaku*. Such *entenraku-imayō* are the prototypes of the song cycles with *koto* accompaniment (*kumiuta*) of *tsukushi-goto*. *Fuki*, the oldest and most influential *kumiuta*, has been shown to be a direct descendant of such poetic improvisation on a section of the music of *Etenraku*. (Adriaansz 2001, 827)

The importance of the transmission of *kumiuta* in the late seventeenth century was such that the genre is classified at different levels that reflect the ability of the performer:

> The Shoku-yashiki [Tōdō] would not accept the Ikuta-ryū as a new school unless kumiuta were classified as the main work of the school; the other, later forms [*jiuta*] were considered as less important. ... Ikuta Kengyō arranged kumiuta according to difficulty into four classes: *omote-gumi* [outside pieces], *ura-gumi* [inside pieces], *naka-yurushi* [interior pieces], and *oku-yurushi* [deep interior pieces]. The popularity of kumiuta, however, declined and the form became more and more a concern of specialists. (Adriaansz 1973, 13)

Furthermore:

> By way of illustration, it may be helpful to imagine these categories as representing the structure of the imperial palace or a *Shintō* shrine with outer and inner walls, and further inside, the outer and inner sanctuaries. It should also be mentioned that these categories represent stages of a student's progress in the learning of the *koto* repertoire, and are regulated by the issuing of diplomas along the way. (Tsuge 1983a, 3)

99 Opening song of "Fuki" ("Rhubarb") (Kikuhara 1987), with transnotation. Courtesy Kikuhara Kōji, Hakusuisha.

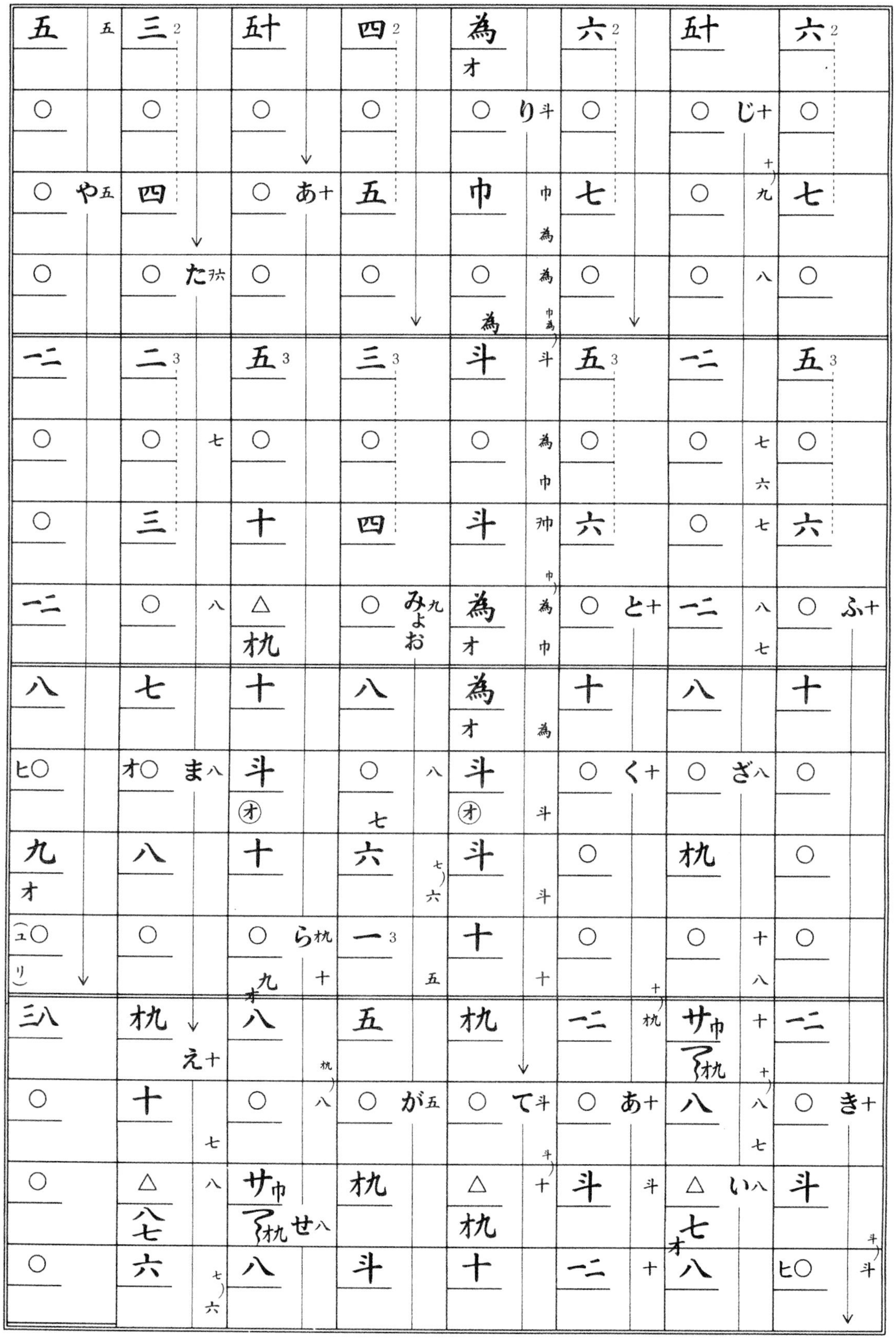

五　｜　三　｜　斗　｜　四　｜　為オ　｜　六　｜　斗　｜　六

○　｜　○　｜　○　｜　○　｜　○　り斗　｜　○　｜　○　じ十　｜　○

○　や五　｜　四　｜　○　あ十　｜　五　｜　巾　｜　七　｜　○　十九　｜　七

○　｜　○　た杤　｜　○　｜　○　｜　○　為　｜　○　｜　○　八　｜　○

二　｜　二　｜　五　｜　三　｜　斗　｜　五　｜　二　｜　五

○　｜　○　七　｜　○　｜　○　｜　○　為巾　｜　○　｜　○　七六七　｜　○

○　｜　三　｜　十　｜　四　｜　斗　｜　六　｜　○　｜　六

二　｜　○　八　｜　△枕　｜　○　みよお九　｜　為オ　｜　○　と十　｜　二　八七　｜　○　ふ十

八　｜　七　｜　十　｜　八　｜　為オ　｜　十　｜　八　｜　十

ヒ○　｜　オ○　ま八　｜　斗オ　｜　○　八　｜　斗オ斗　｜　○　く十　｜　○　ざ八　｜　○

九オ　｜　八　｜　十　｜　六　七六　｜　斗斗　｜　○　｜　枕　｜　○

ユ○リ　｜　○　｜　○　ら枕九オ十　｜　一三十五　｜　十斗十　｜　○　｜　○　十八十　｜　○

三八　｜　枕　え十　｜　八　枕八　｜　五　｜　枕　｜　二　枕　｜　サ巾了枕　十八十　｜　二

○　｜　十　七　｜　○　｜　○　が五　｜　○　て斗斗十　｜　○　あ十　｜　八　八七　｜　○　き十

○　｜　△　八七　｜　サ巾了枕せ八　｜　枕斗　｜　△　枕　｜　斗斗　｜　△　い八七オ　｜　斗

○　｜　六　七六　｜　八　｜　斗　｜　十　｜　二十　｜　ヒ○　斗斗

Here, one may relate concepts that are external to *koto* music to a wider sphere of Japanese society. Entering further into the world of *koto* music by learning to play pieces that are considered technically more difficult is analogous to entering other areas of Japanese society or culture through different layers. This in turn is similar to the concepts of wrapping and unwrapping Japanese culture through its many material and conceptual layers.

Concerning the structure of *koto kumiuta*, Tsuge (1986a, 254) commented that "although a song cycle is usually composed of six songs, the text of each song is self-contained and thus the six songs within one *kumiuta* are not necessarily related to each other in terms of subject

matter. ... the musical form of *koto kumiuta* is remarkably regular and symmetrical: each song is composed in a fixed frame of 32 measures or 64 beats, and consists of 8 phrases of 8 beats each." The *koto* part and vocal line are sometimes heterophonic in that their melodic lines might be similar, but with slight variations between them. However, as in figure 99, there are different ways of conceptualizing the structure of this form. In this figure, which is the first song of "Fuki", there are 64 measures or 256 beats.

100 Opening page of "Chidori no Kyoku" ("Song of Plovers") (Miyagi 1996, 16), with transnotation. Courtesy Miyagi Kazue, Hōgakusha.

155

101 Opening of *tegoto* section from "Chidori no Kyoku" ("Song of Plovers") (Miyagi 1996, 24), with transnotation. Courtesy Miyagi Kazue, Hōgakusha.

Jiuta Sōkyoku

Kumiuta declined in popularity in the late seventeenth century. As such, Ikuta Kengyō developed a more popular style of playing based on *shamisen jiuta* (regional songs) of the Kansai region. *Jiuta sōkyoku* soon developed a structure called *tegotomono* (figs. 100-1; *see* Burnett 1980; Wade 1976), which consisted of long and complex instrumental interludes. Such pieces in this form characteristically used a three-part structure: *maeuta* ("front song" accompanied by *koto*); *tegoto* (instrumental interlude); and *atouta* ("after song" accompanied by *koto*). This style flourished in Osaka in the late eighteenth and early nineteenth centuries. Typically when found in ensemble or *sankyoku* (*shamisen, koto* and *kokyū* or *shakuhachi*),[51] it is the *shamisen* that often has the main melodic role.[52] However, the music texture is often heterophonic in that there might be a simultaneous presentation of a melody by the instruments, but varying slightly in terms of the exact notes played by each instrument (e.g., melody, ornamentation and rhythm). The structure of the *tegotomono* form has been compared to the *jo-ha-kyū* concept (introduction, exposition, rushing), which is a typical aesthetic structuring concept in traditional Japanese music, both within each of the three main sections and for the entire piece of music (Burnett 1980). The first page of the *maeuta* of *jiuta tegotomono* "Chidori no Kyoku" ("Song of Plovers") is reproduced in figure 100, while the opening of the *tegoto* instrumental interlude is in figure 101.

O. Yamaguti (1986, 33) notes that in *jiuta tegotomono* "we can observe a parallelism of speech thinking and music thinking, for the (speech) term [*tegotomono*] precisely denotes that "hand" [*te*] manipulations are the major concern of (music) performance." Here, Yamaguti directly links the instrument to the way it is played and the way that its genres are conceptualized. *Jiuta* soon started to include interludes (*ai no te*), which, as the instrumental component of the music began to be increasingly emphasized, gradually became extended into a structure called *tegotomono*. The Osaka musician Minezaki Kōtō (act. *c.* 1785-1805) was a key figure in the development of *tegotomono*.[53] The earlier emphasis on the *shamisen* in *jiuta* soon changed in later styles so that the *koto* and the *shamisen* functioned more interdependently. In the music of Ichiura Kengyō, for example, a style evolved that saw the increased use of two parts (*honte* [main part]; *kaede* [second part]), one of which was superimposed on the other using a compositional technique called *uchiawase*. The use of a main part and other part became a distinguishing feature of *koto* music in the nineteenth century, and later composers even re-worked older pieces to add a *kaede* part to popular compositions such as "Rokudan" (*see* fig. 86).

From the Meiji era onward *koto* music underwent rapid change. Such composers as Mitsuzaki Kengyō of Kyoto and Yoshizawa Kengyō (1800 or 1808-72) of Nagoya looked to older forms (e.g., *kumiuta*) in a search to revive *koto* music as opposed to placing an emphasis on the *shamisen* in ensemble. They were, as Adriaansz (2001, 829) asserts, working in a so-called "neo-classical movement." Yoshizawa's "Chidori no Kyoku", which used the *tegotomono* structure with its three-part form, as well as using *honte* and *kaede* parts, is a well-known example of this style. The *tegoto* in this piece provides a paradigm of not only this genre, but also the interplay between two *koto*.[54] But perhaps the most dramatic changes in the *koto* repertoire occurred with the works of Miyagi Michio, who blended ideas from Western music to traditional Japanese music in the aforementioned *Meiji shinkyoku*. Miyagi's works are a striking contrast to that of Suzuki Koson, who "attempted in his works to combine modern poetry and romantic feeling with classic practices of the Heian period" (Adriaansz 2001, 830).

The twentieth century witnessed many other changes in *koto* music. The traditional repertoire or *koten* does not cease to play a seminal part in the music of many *koto* traditions. At the same time many twentieth- and twenty-first century composers continue to contribute to the instrument's extensive contemporary repertoire, and to challenge the role of a so-called traditional instrument in modern Japan. Players and composers such as Nakanoshima Kin'ichi, Sawai Tadao, Miki Minoru, and others have been successful in expanding the borders of the *koto* repertoire and musical language, as well as question our perception of the instrument in today's world.

The select pieces, genres and composers mentioned in this chapter serve to illustrate several important styles of music that have been maintained as part of a traditional repertoire for a traditional musical instrument. The *koto* is not restricted to its more traditional genres of *kumiuta*, *danmono* and *jiuta sōkyoku*, even though this repertoire is established and bound by social institutions that help perpetuate the music as a traditional form but in a modern context. The *koto* is a traditional Japanese musical instrument and its historic music helps it to retain a traditional form and structure that only changes within limited conceptual and physical boundaries. However, in the same way that the instrument's historic repertoire is emblematic of "traditional Japan", so does its modern repertoire stand for "non-traditional Japan". With a history in Japan of more than thirteen hundred years, the *koto* has passed through many social and cultural contexts – from high art to folk art, from the secular to the sacred, and from a solo instrument to an accompanying role, there are a myriad of music genres and styles intermeshed with it.

Keisai Eisen (1791-1848). "Kumoi of the Tsuruya", from the series *Keisei dōchū sugoroku – Mitate Yoshiwara gojūsantsui (Courtesans as the Board Game Sugoroku Along the Highway – The Yoshiwara as the Fifty-three Stations)*, c. 1825-26. *Ōban* format color woodblock print, 371 x 253 mm. Published by Tsutaya Kichizō. Rijksmuseum voor Volkenkunde, Leiden (1-4470-S).

6 Conclusion

The importance of the *koto* in Japanese culture since its introduction to the archipelago from China some thirteen hundred years ago has been maintained by its use in various performance contexts, and by its role in other social and cultural spheres. The *koto* is imbued with rich cultural meaning as *a* special traditional Japanese musical instrument. This is not to forget that today other instruments like the *shamisen*, *shakuhachi*, *taiko*, and *biwa* exist as emblems for traditional Japan on local, national and international levels. Even though these instruments could be interpreted as quintessential material objects of traditional Japanese culture, they are also very much part of the world of contemporary Japanese music in that their inherent historic associations and representations intensify their meaning as modern icons of the past.

As an instrument fundamentally unaltered in form since Heian times, the *koto* is, at least on one level of study, typically defined as a *hōgakki* or *wagakki* – a traditional Japanese musical instrument. The place of the instrument in Japanese literature and the arts, its physical structure, decoration, various classifications and names, reinforce its role as an object of a real or an imagined traditional Japan. The representation of a certain decorative motif on the *koto*, or the manufacture of a part of the instrument in a particular way, may add a further layer of traditional or symbolic meaning to the physical structure of the instrument. Added to this is the fact that the instrument is often played in a context that itself underlies and resonates with a nostalgic search for an idealized past. As Creighton (1997, 242) points out succinctly, "images of the past are invoked to refute the perceived threat of cultural loss to which the processes of modernization and Westernization have subjected modern Japan." It is this "culture of difference" that does much to strengthen notions of tradition and nostalgia, and ultimately determines the place of the traditional *koto* in historical and contemporary Japan.

Even though the *koto* has recognized origins in China and at the same time is viewed as an object of traditional Japan, aspects of its form, transmission and performance are in constant flux. Such change is nevertheless prescribed so as to maintain and perpetuate the place of the *koto* in traditional culture, or to juxtapose that tradition with the modern world. There is, therefore, a sense that the *koto* is very much a vestige of Japan's heritage, yet, and ironically, much of the so-called traditionalism of this instrument is actually relatively recent. That the *koto* is subject to such a perception might be linked to the idea of inventing – or reinventing – and nurturing a sense of tradition (*see* Hobsbawm and Ranger 1983). As Hobsbawm (1983, 1) states, "'traditions' which appear or claim to be old are often quite recent in origin and sometimes invented." The invention of tradition occurs "more frequently when a rapid transformation of society weakens or destroys the social patterns for which 'old' traditions had been designed, producing new ones to which they were not applicable, or when such old traditions and their institutional carriers and promulgators no longer prove sufficiently adaptable and flexible, or are otherwise eliminated" (Hobsbawm 1983, 4-5). Consequently, there are many facets to the *koto* that are indeed not as "traditional" as might first appear. Instrument design and materials, quantity, quality, and types of parts added to the main body, performance practice, repertoire, notation/tablature systems, and social and cultural contexts of performance have all been influenced in varying degrees in response to a social need necessitating cultural transformation.

In his discussion of *koto* and *shamisen kumiuta*, Ackermann (1990, 37-39) introduces the concepts of *dentō* (tradition) and *denshō* (transmission, handing down) as terms that should be examined in relation to understanding the transmission of the repertoire of these two instruments. While Ackermann (1990, 37) notes that "there is probably no concept in any Western language that corresponds exactly to the Japanese *denshō* and *dentō* and all that these expressions imply," the terms may be viewed as key concepts of *koto* performance where players necessarily construct ideas of place and identity. One thing that is certain to the existence of a tradition of *koto* performance is that it is transmitted from generation to generation through a system of hereditary (or adopted) transmission of skills and knowledge. In order for this process to take place there must be a social structure and mechanism for the music to be continued – or at least perceived as continuing – without the threat of extinction or intervention from outside influence. In this sense, *koto* performance traditions follow a path set by recognized codes of behavior that are deeply rooted in Japanese society. A study of performance practice itself generally reveals an emphasis on a systematized way of learning that takes the student through several levels of ability, rather than one with a focus on artistic creation. *Denshō* and *dentō* are concepts which are seen to underpin the existence of *koto* performance traditions, and should be seen as constructs that permeate most facets of the instrument.

The transmission of *zokusō* or everyday *koto* music – its instrument and music – from its beginnings in the seventeenth century to the present day has been influenced by numerous changes in the surrounding cultural milieu, and in social changes regarding who could play the *koto*. This is evinced in the Edo period when *koto* performance was controlled by professional blind male musicians, a situation that was transformed from the mid-Meiji onward with sighted amateur women assuming the prominent role. Be it Edo, Meiji or contemporary Japan, however, underlying social structures have inevitably inculcated players with a sense of place and identity within *koto* performance traditions. This has been achieved through a projection of "groupism" onto *koto* traditions and through an understanding of the importance of group continuity. Continuity, for example, allows present-day performers of everyday *koto* music to trace their lineage to the founder of that tradition, Yatsuhashi Kengyō, and even to the traditions of Tsukushigoto and *gagaku* that antedate him. Macro to micro levels of group structure instill a notion of place and identity, where such aspects as the need for group affiliation, hierarchical structures within those groups and the transmission of a group's music are seen as essential concepts for the survival and continuity of *koto* music. This in turn has secured the place of the *koto* as one of *the* Japanese traditional musical instruments par excellence in the twenty-first century.

For most *koto* players identity is constructed within a performance group that stresses uniqueness or difference when compared to other *koto* traditions. The process of knowing or tracing one's lineage through the numerous contexts and associations of *koto* performance in effect establishes an individual's identity within several levels of affiliation. The importance of lineage on a macro level is reflected in the essential hierarchical structuring of the group from its leader to its newest or most junior members. These and other structuring aspects of performance groups concretize the historical and present-day place and identity of its members.

Such concepts as *uchi* (us/inside) and *soto* (them/outside) are often found in anthropological studies on Japan, and they are equally applicable in a discussion on the *koto*. In a performance tradition a player is part of the *uchi*. Outsiders, and this includes *koto* musicians both from related and more distantly related traditions, constitute the *soto*, at least on one level. It is the social make-up of such traditions and the ways they reflect characteristic traits of Japanese society that encourage life-long dedication by their members and create what is seen as a social center. By contrast, other traditions are perceived as peripheral, hence the various ethnographies of specific *koto* traditions in the literature on the instrument.

Koto performers follow a rigid social system that frequently dictates who can learn the instrument and what they learn. The longer one studies in a specific tradition, especially with one teacher, the deeper one is immersed in the social network of the obligations and allegiances of a *koto* performance group. For the researcher of Japanese music who learns in such groups, it is more difficult to compare one tradition with others through first-hand experience. In my own field research on the *koto*, which requires comparative study of different performance traditions, I have always been surprised at the way teachers and students alike have a wealth of knowledge that is focused on their own performance tradition. But very rarely do they have contact with performers from other traditions or possess in-depth knowledge about them. This is perhaps due to the unique characteristics of performance practice – despite often being the same traditional music – within groups, a facet that contributes to their own sense of identity. The bonds made with one's own group are not simply based on loyalty, but are also driven by practicality. This means that the various traditions share the organizational and structural features of aspects of Japanese society in the very make-up of the group. But it is the subtleties of music performance and the subsequent transmission of the music through teacher to pupil in a rigid system of learning and dedication by the student to the teacher and group that creates a group culture on the one hand, and a "culture of difference" (in this case, different groups) on the other. When one learns in this manner it is extremely difficult to perform even the same piece of music with musicians from another group due to the sometimes quite intricate differences that are handed down within and through the traditions during the oral/aural/literate learning context.

An attempt at understanding the *koto* necessitates an understanding of broader aspects of Japanese culture. What is the significance of the form and decoration of the *koto*? Why do *koto* players form performance traditions? What are the contexts of *koto* performance? Do these contexts interrelate with the instrument and/or its player? While questions such as these reflect the different foci and chapters of this book, it should be stressed that this work is merely an introduction to many facets of the *koto* and its culture. After all, the instrument, its meanings and classifications exist, like other instruments and ensembles, as part of what Margaret Kartomi would describe as "a seamless web of cultural knowledge" (1990, 271).

While considering all of the above, it is evident that the cultural meaning of the *koto* is multilayered. The *koto* has an abundance of cultural meaning. In the numerous institutions of everyday *koto* performance there are several key concepts that have contributed to the successful (and sometimes unsuccessful) continuity of the instrument and its music to the present day (e.g., group harmony, succession, social control, popularity, tradition, transmission, and economics). These topics stand out among many, and the examination of a few has served to outline some of their underlying features in connection to *koto* performance. When examined closely, this instrument, just like any object of material culture, divulges unique information about its specific culture through various modes of verbal and non-verbal discourse and meaning. Attempts at generalizations regarding the *koto* are extremely difficult. However, an examination of the instrument results not only in information concerning different instrument types, performance traditions and contexts of performance, but also about its meaning in a number of social and cultural contexts. The aim of this book, therefore, has been to uncover *some*, but by no means *all*, aspects of the *koto* connected with the physical form of the instrument, its transmission through performance traditions and its contexts of performance.

Notes

Introduction

1 The term *zokusō* can also refer to the type of *koto* associated with this music.

2 Kishibe (1982a) and Tanabe and Hirano (1982), which are found in the music dictionary *Ongaku daijiten* (*Music Dictionary*), are reproduced in the specialized dictionary on Japanese music, *Nihon ongaku daijiten* (*Japanese Music Dictionary*) (*see* Hirano, Kamisangō and Gamō 1989).

3 *See* Tsuge (1986b) for an annotated bibliography of non-Japanese writings on Japanese music, which includes numerous references to the *koto* and its music (*see* Reese's 1987 review for several additional references). *See also* Kubota (1983) for a guide to some of the literature on *koto* music.

4 Adriaansz' various writings on the *koto* have covered many diverse areas and have done much to introduce a number of topics to English readers.

5 Related terms include *Nihon bunkaron* (unique Japanese culture), *Nihon shakairon* (unique Japanese society) and *Nihon ron* (unique Japan).

Chapter 1: *The Setting*

1 Sometimes referred to as *ue* (top, i.e., head) and *shita* (bottom, i.e., tail).

2 *See* Fairbank, Reischauer and Craig (1973, 324-57) for an examination of Japanese cultural borrowing at this time, and Garfias (1975) for a discussion of the transmission and development of *gagaku*, and for a summary of some of the non-Japanese (i.e., Korean and Chinese) music genres and musicians transmitted to Japan.

3 Other numbers of strings are found on *zheng*, as with some of the other Asian zithers, but it would have had thirteen at the time it was first transmitted to Japan. Japan's other main historical zither, the six-string *wagon* (Japanese zither, or *yamatogoto* [Japanese zither]), has a longer history in Japan than the *koto*.

4 The term *hōgaku* is sometimes used to refer to Japanese popular music vis-à-vis Western popular music, which is labeled *yōgaku*. In this context traditional Japanese music is referred to as *junhōgaku* (pure, traditional Japanese music).

5 Japan's isolation is a regular feature in discourses on Japanese history of the Edo period. For a critique of this topic, *see* Jansen (1992), who looks at Japan's contact with China during this period.

6 *See* Adriaansz (1973, 3-21) and Wade (1976, 1-17) for further discussions on the social history of *koto* performance traditions.

7 *See* Fujita (1973) for lists of membership of some groups (over 82,000 members for the Ikuta-ryū and over 9,000 for the Yamada-ryū, and mixed *ryū* at over 12,000). These figures often include *shamisen* (three-string lute) players, some *shakuhachi* (end-blown flute) players, and some players may be listed several times according to their various affiliations. Also, the listing of groups might not take into consideration all such groups and membership. There are also players outside Japan (Japanese and non-Japanese) and independent players who have no affiliation to groups, although the latter is rare.

8 The *Kojiki* is an account of Japanese history based on myth, legend and historical fact (*see* Philippi 1968). The importance of this book has been noted by Philippi (1968, 3) who describes it as "a nation's origins," and that it is "the earliest source book in Japanese literature and history." *See also* the related work, *Nihongi*, which gives an early account of non-Japanese musicians in Japan with Koreans playing at the funeral of Emperor Ingyō in 453 (*see* Aston [1896] 1956).

9 On music and musical instruments in *Genji monogatari*, *see* Lieberman (1971).

10 It is interesting to note, however, that so-called traditional Japanese music often uses instruments that were imported from the Asian mainland and have been Japanized over hundreds of years.

11 Prints that show the *koto* in Kyrova et al. (2000) include Yashima Gakutei (1786?-1868): "Sankyoku" ("Three Instruments", triptych, 1822), which shows three women playing *koto*, *kokyū* (bowed lute) and *shamisen*; a print of a lady-in-waiting by a *koto* in the series *Katsushikaren Gakumen Fujin Awase* (*A Series of Ladies in Framed Pictures for the Katsushika Poetry Club*, 1823); and "Hisakataya gobantsuzuki" ("A Set of Five Prints for the Hisakataya Poetry Club", late 1820s), depicting a poetry club of five female instrumentalists; Yanagawa Shigenobu (1787-1832): an untitled *surimono* (a de-luxe privately published Ukiyo-e print) of a female *sankyoku* ensemble; Katsukawa Shuntei (1770-1820): a print of young women playing the *koto* in a garden setting from the series *Hanagasaren shichifukujin* (*The Seven Gods of Good Fortune for the Hanagasa Poetry Club* 1821); Suzuki Harunobu (1725?-70): a print from his series *Zashiki hakkei* (*Eight Parlor Views*, c. 1766) that

portrays two young women with a *koto* (one player is interestingly reading a book entitled *Kinkyoku shū*, perhaps indicating the need for music notation, or simply a song text, by the sighted female amateurs; *see* Chapter 5); Tsukioka Yoshitoshi (1838-92): "Gosechi no Myōbu" ("Lady Gosechi", 1887) playing the *koto* to two men; "Sagano no Tsuki" ("Saga Moor", 1891), showing Lady Kogō playing the *koto* – both are from the series *Tsuki no hyakushi* (*One Hundred Aspects of the Moon*); Utagawa Kunisada II (1823-80): "Hahakigi no maki" ("The Chapter Hahakigi"), from the series *Genji monogatari* (*Tale of Genji*, c. 1834-37), depicting a court lady playing the *koto*; Utagawa Kunisada (1786-1865): *Bijin awase gojūsantsugi* (*Fifty-three Stations of Beauties Compared*, late 1820s), showing a courtesan leaning over a *koto*; Katsushika Hokusai (1760-1849): "Uki-e Genji jūnidan no zu" ("Perspective Print of Genji Practising", c. 1785), from an untitled series, showing the young Princess Jōruri playing the *koto*; Utagawa Toyokuni (1769-1825): untitled diptych (1812), of a scene from the play *Chūshin kōshaku* ("Retainer's Story") with a woman playing the *koto*; Keisai Eisen (1790-1848): a print from the series *Keisei dōchū sugoroku – Mitate Yoshiwara gojūsantsui* (*Courtesans as a Board Game Along the Road – the Yoshiwara as the Fifty-three Stations*, c. 1825-26) of a courtesan in a Yoshiwara brothel with *koto* adjacent; and one from the series *Keisei rokkasen* (*Courtesans as the Six Classical Poets*, late 1820s) of a courtesan in a brothel with *koto* behind her; and Kitagawa Utamaro (1753-1806): "Tsūgen" from the series *Enchū hassen* (*A Romantic Vision of the Eight Immortals*, c. 1793), showing a courtesan in a brothel with a *koto* behind her. The only print showing a *koto* that includes a man, which is by Okumura Toshinobu (c. 1717-50), is an untitled single-sheet work (1724) depicting the instrument in the *kabuki* play *Yomeiri Izu nikki* (*Marriage at Izu Diary*). *See also* Green (1985; 2001) for a study of blind musicians – mostly men – of the Edo period as seen in Ukiyo-e. Prints by Utagawa Hiroshige (1797-1858) of around 1840-42 and Utagawa Toyokuni of around 1800 show blind male musicians teaching the *koto* to young sighted women.

12 "Rokudan no Shirabe", often abbreviated to "Rokudan" ("Six Sections"), is an instrumental piece understood to have been arranged/composed by Yatsuhashi Kengyō (1614-85); "Haru no Umi" was composed by Miyagi Michio (1894-1956) in 1929 for *koto* and violin (or *shakuhachi*); and "Sakura" (or "Sakura Sakura") is a popular folk song, but not specific to the *koto*.

13 On the *koto* and its associations with cultural nationalism *see* Johnson (2004). *See* Vlastos (1998) in connection with invented traditions in modern Japan. *See also* Bestor (1989) on the invention of tradition, and Hendry (1987, 164-67) for a summary of nostalgia as a significant concept in understanding Japanese society.

1 One only has to look at important Japanese dictionaries and encyclopedias to realize that the instrument is classified in several ways. For example, in *Nihon ongaku daijiten* (*Japanese Music Dictionary*) the instrument is listed under "Sō", whereas in *Hōgaku hyakka jiten* (*Encyclopedia of Traditional Japanese Music*) the entry "Sō" is a general explanation about zithers (see Hirano, Kamisangō and Gamō 1989 and Kikkawa 1984a, respectively). In the latter work, the instrument is explained in detail under the entry "koto", which is listed using *hiragana* phonetic script as well as two *kanji* for the instrument.

2 The Hornbostel and Sachs ([1914] 1961, 22) system of musical instrument classification labels the *koto* a half-tube, heterochord zither (classification: 312.22). While not actually having a half-tube shape, the soundboard does have a curved shape across its widthwise axis, the arch of which helps to form the upper part of the sound chamber; and the strings, which are attached to the body, run along most of the upper surface of the soundboard. Some scholars label the *koto* a true board zither (classification: 314.122) (e.g., Yamaguchi and Emmert 1977, 190), which indicates that the strings run along a board. On various classifications of the *koto*, see Johnson (1996-97).

3 *See* especially van Gulik ([1940] 1969, 217-49) for a discussion of the *kin* (also called *shichigenkin*: seven-string *kin*) in Japan. In China the instrument is called *qin* or *guqin* (old *qin*). The term *kin* is a Sino-Japanese reading (*on'yomi*) of one of the character used for the word *koto*, which is the native *kun'yomi* reading of the character. In connection with the confusion this character sometimes causes, Picken and Mitani (1979) and van Gulik ([1940] 1969, 217-49), for example, discuss the possible instruments (*koto* or *kin*) to which this character might refer in the eleventh-century book *Genji monogatari* and some other Japanese literature.

4 While the character for *sō* was excluded from the 1946 official list of 1,850 Japanese characters for daily use, it was included in a later, 1981, official list of 1,945 characters. The 1946 list is called *tōyō kanji* (characters for daily use) and that of 1981 *jōyō kanji*, also translated as "characters for daily use."

5 In her discussion of the character for *kin*, Falconer (1995, 115) notes that "the top part of this character ... is 'king' written twice, and the bottom part ... means now, the present. ... The top part was chosen to visually represent the strings stretched across the koto while the bottom part is the sound resonating within the hollowed soundbox of the instrument." *See* Adriaansz (1973, 22-23) for a brief account of possible origins of the word *koto*.

6 One of Japan's other zithers, the *wagon* (six strings), also includes this *kanji* in its name. The first part of the word *wagon*, *wa*, denotes "Japan", as does the term "Yamato" in this instrument's other name, *yamatogoto* (Yamato zither). One may presume that the suffix is used to refer to the instrument as an indigenous Japanese zither vis-à-vis imported zithers such as the *sō no koto* (koto). The term *gon*, which is the second *kanji* in the word *wagon*, is another reading of the *kanji* for the word *koto*. Several other string instruments were transmitted to Japan, although no longer used, and show their place or origin in their name, together with a suffix using the character for string instruments. Two examples are the *kudaragoto* (Kudara string instrument [i.e., harp]) and *shiragigoto* (Shiragi string instrument [i.e., zither]). Some of Japan's earlier zithers have been discussed by, for example, Department of Performing Arts, National Theater of Japan (1994), Hughes (1988), and Miyazaki (1993). Miyazaki provides a useful source for Japanese zithers depicted in Tomb-period *haniwa* (clay figures). On

the remains of *koto* and other zithers held in the Shōsōin, *see* Hayashi (1964), Kishibe (1984), Harich-Schneider (1973, 59-68), and Shōsōin (1967, 1989).

7 The term *kinsō* is used to describe East Asian zithers in general.

8 The Japanese language uses a variety of terms when counting different types of object. McClain (1981, 235-41) notes that over fifty such counters are used. The counter used when talking about numbers of *koto* is *men*. In a context when one has established that the *koto* is the object under discussion, one might count one *koto* as *ichimen* (one *men*), two *koto* as *nimen* (two *men*), and so on. The connection between the term *men* and *koto* might be explained in that the term *men* is used for several other objects including surfaces and sides (A. Nelson 1974, 951). The nearest connection the *koto* has with the literal meaning of this counter is that of a "surface" (the *koto* has a long upper surface that is a dominant feature of the instrument).

9 Both terms are used today to describe traditional Japanese musical instruments.

10 The term "pipe" is a literal translation of the term *kan*, which in this context means a wind instrument.

11 The *kanji* for the word *chiku* in *chikusō* has the alternative reading *tsuku* in the name Tsukushi.

12 The *chikusō* and *zokusō* are sometimes referred to as *utagoto* (song *koto*) vis-à-vis the *gakusō* (Nakajima and Kubota 1984, 56). The term *utagoto* indicates that the voice is a major part of the repertoire.

13 Other names and terms are also used for all of these instruments. For example, the *Yamadagoto* might be referred to as *Yamada-ryū-goto* (Yamada-tradition *koto*) or *Yamada-ryū no koto* (*koto* of the Yamada tradition). Such name combinations sometimes use the term *sō* as a suffix.

14 A more recent *gakusō* made in 1976 and held at Osaka College of Music (B03-0906) even has tuning pegs inside its mouth, a feature that only appeared in the twentieth century and is more common to beginners', electric, larger and smaller *koto*.

15 Miyahara Chizuko, conversation with author, Kitakyūshū, 30 March 2000.

16 The term Tsukushi was sometimes used for the whole of the island of Kyūshū. Mabuchi (1991) provides an analysis of the reported origins of Tsukushigoto. *See also* Kishibe and Hirano (1971) and Miyazaki (1972, 1995), who have carried out extensive research on Tsukushigoto.

17 Miyahara is based in Kitakyūshū, Kyūshū, and has just two students. She is also a player in the Miyagi performance tradition, so named after Miyagi Michio (1894-1956). Miyahara Chizuko, conversation with author, Kitakyūshū, 30 March 2000.

18 Social stratification during the Edo period is usually divided into four general groups. From top to bottom were samurai, farmers, artisans, and merchants (*shi-nō-kō-shō*), although two further divisions might be added: nobility above samurai, and outcasts below the merchants (Fairbank, Reischauer and Craig 1973, 406-7). For most blind musicians, their position was at the lower end of the hierarchy, although the officially recognized guild of blind musicians, Tōdō, enjoyed support from the samurai class, whereas the *mōsō* (blind priests who used the *biwa* lute for accompaniment), for example, did not (*see* Ackermann 1990, 61-64, and also Nishiyama 1997 for a survey of Edo-period arts as relates to their social context).

19 Outside *zokusō*, women did play the *koto* professionally during the Edo period as geisha (female entertainers). A useful source for this is the popular woodblock prints of the time, which often depict geisha playing the *koto* or *shamisen*.

20 The Tōdō had a system of ranking their musicians and assigned special names accordingly. Within this system the four main levels were (beginning with the highest): Kengyō (e.g., Yatsuhashi Kengyō), Bettō, Kōtō, and Zatō (*see* Chapter 4).

21 The *in* scale is sometimes referred to as *miyakobushi*. Several *koto* tunings use this scale, as shown in Chapter 5. On the *in* scale and the historic role of Yatsuhashi Kengyō, *see also* Picken (2000).

22 The term *sōgaku* (*sō* music) is an older term for *koto* music, but is no longer used today. Although the term *kinkyoku* (*kin* music) is sometimes applied for *koto* music, it is confusing because the word *kin* also refers to the seven-string Chinese *qin* (Kikkawa 1997, 12).

23 *See* Adriaansz (1984) and Kikkawa (1997) for summaries of *koto* genres and styles.

24 *See* Ackermann (1990, 53-68), Adriaansz (1971) and S. Yamazaki (1977) for further discussion of the Yatsuhashi-ryū.

25 Hiroshima Kenritsu Kōgei Shikenjō (1987, 45) notes that about 97% of players use the *Yamadagoto* and about 3% the *Ikutagoto*. During this author's fieldwork it was observed that many Ikuta-ryū players who have *Ikutagoto* prefer to use their more recent *Yamadagoto*. Fukumori Toshiko, conversation with author, Kyoto, 20 May 1991; Kikuhara Hatsuko, conversation with author, Osaka, 23 April 1991; Kikutsuka Atsuko, conversation with author, Kyoto, 27 May 1991; Nakamura Yōichi, conversation with author, Osaka, 1 May 1991; Tsuda Michiko, conversation with author, Kyoto, 10 May 1991.

26 1 *shaku* (30.3 cm) is made up of 10 *sun* (1 *sun*: 3.03 cm), which itself consists of ten *bu* (1 *bu*: 3.03 mm). The *koto* is traditionally about six *shaku* long (*c.* 182 cm).

27 *See* Kishibe, Kondō and Kishibe (1971) for a comprehensive biography of Yamada Kengyō.

28 The unadorned soundboard of the modern *koto* can be directly correlated to the aesthetics of the wood that decorates the rooms of traditional Japanese houses and is appreciated in terms of its natural beauty.

29 *See* Hikone-jō Hakubutsukan (1996, 84, 111) for a brief description of this instrument and others held by the museum (*see also* Miyazaki 1979).

30 *See* Nakajima and Kubota (1984) for representative lists of the main pieces of the traditional repertoire together with their various classifications.

31 On small and large *koto*-type instruments *see* Katsumura (1986) and Johnson (2003).

32 Musashino Ongaku Daigaku Gakki Hakubutsukan (1985, 20-21) has a *koto* that folds in half; it is 143 cm long.

33 An instrument with such a device was observed belonging to Nakagawa Shūsui (Nakagawa Kimi, *b.* 1919), who is head of the Ikuta sub-tradition called Sōkyoku Shūyū-kai (often abbreviated to Shūyū-kai). One of her instruments has an added tuning device on its first string. This extends the string length, and is especially useful for contemporary music that might require a lower tuning on the first string. Nakagawa Shūsui, conversation with author, Fukuoka, 17 July 1990.

34 Observed on an instrument belonging to Hayashi Kimiko. Hayashi Kimiko, conversations with author, Kyoto, October 1991.

35 On Western influences on music in Japan *see* Harich-Schneider (1973), Komiya (1956), Malm (1971), May (1963), Pecore (2000), and Tanabe (1931).

36 *See* Howe (1997) for a study of Mason's contribution to music education.

37 Ōsaka Ongaku Daigaku Fuzoku Gakki Hakubutsukan (1984, 92-93) has four *ayamegoto* ranging from 69 cm to 135 cm. An alternative term, *ryōsō* (enjoyable *sō*), is also given.

38 The instrument is sometimes called *tankin* (small *kin* - an alternative reading of one of the *kanji* for *koto*) (*see* Chiba 1989b).

39 Fujita Fusahiko, conversation with author, Fukuyama, 18 June 1997.

40 The term *neo-koto* is normally written in *rōmaji* (romanized script), presumably to emphasize a meaning of "new".

41 Sometimes referred to as *ōgoto* (big *koto*), *daikoto* (big *koto*), *jūnanagen* (seventeen strings), *jūshichigensō* (seventeen-string *sō*), and *jūshichigengoto* (seventeen-string *koto*). A version of the instrument recently marketed is labeled *Imamuragata jūshichigen* (Imamura-style 17 strings), which has its strings attached to sliding block at the head end for ease of tuning and maintenance (*see Hōgaku Jānaru* 2001, 53).

42 In 1920 Miyagi Michio and Motoori Nagayo (1885-1945) presented a concert of new music entitled "Shin-Nihon Ongaku Dai-Ensōkai" ("A Great Concert of New Japanese Music"). The term *gendai hōgaku* (contemporary, traditional Japanese music) was later used to describe progressive traditional music.

43 Naitō Masako, letter to author, 2004. On this instrument and its innovator, *see* www.pop-corn.co.jp.

44 Several types of *jūgogen* (fifteen strings) have been made (*see* Katsumura 1986, 171; Kikkawa 1984a, 503-4; Tanigaitō 1989, 287).

45 *See* Wade (1994) for analysis of some of the early compositions for this instrument.

Chapter 3: *Manufacture and Component Parts*

1 From 1984 to 1992, for example, FHSKK's *koto* production increased annually from 12,600 to 14,900 instruments, falling slightly in 1993 to 13,400 instruments. Figures for numbers of *koto* produced after this date are not available, but income reduced from over 1,000,000,000 *yen* in 1995 to 800,000,000 *yen* for each of the years 2000 to 2003. Fukuyama Shōkō Kaigisho, letters to author, 1994; 2004. This might be a result of a decline in the Japanese economy during these years and possibly an increased amount of *koto* production by other makers. For further discussion of FHSKK and *koto* manufacture *see* Hirata and Kaihara (1988), Hirata (1994, 1996), Hiroshima Kenritsu Kōgei Shikenjō (1987), Sumita (1986), and O. Yamaguti (1994, 60). On *koto* manufacture, *see also* Johnson (1996b) and the summary by Kishibe (1967).

2 The term *shiburoku* means literally "four parts to six" and refers to strips of wood each side of the fixed bridges.

3 The construction of *koto* outside Japan and China should also be mentioned. For example, the American, John Wittersheim, Professor of Art at Siena Heights University in Adrian, Michigan, made three instruments in 2001 (John Wittersheim, letter to author, 18 January 2003; *see also* Wittersheim 2002). As an artist he has explored various materials and construction techniques, perhaps differing from Japanese makers mostly in that rather than carving out a soundboard from a single piece of wood, he assembles pieces to create the arched surface of the soundboard. The materials he used for his *koto* include Douglas Fir, Curly Maple, Sitka Spruce, Black Walnut, and anodized aluminum (this instrument has nickel strings). As well as working closely with Japanese musicians outside Japan, Wittersheim also undertook research with the *koto* maker Noda Masaaki from Kanazawa.

4 *See* Tsuge (1978) for discussion of zoomorphism and Asian musical instruments. Compare also the Chinese seven-string *qin*, which includes in its nomenclature terms for both the dragon and the phoenix (van Gulik [1940] 1969; Tsuge 1978).

5 Sometimes the measurement of the length of *koto* is misleading because the instrument's length might be taken in two possible places: along the center of the soundboard from end to end; or along its long sides, which would exclude the slight curvature at the tail extremity (this is especially prominent on the *Yamadagoto*).

6 *See also* Yoshida (1955, 66-68).

7 The term *ma* is an alternative reading of the *kanji* for *ken*, as in *honken*.

8 This term also relates to the type of *koto* called *nagaiso* (long side).

9 The term *sō* should not be confused with one of the instrument's names. The terms use different *kanji* and have a different meaning.

10 *Koto* are sometimes referred to according to the grain pattern on the upper surface of the soundboard. For example, *itamegoto* (grain *koto*) and *masamegoto* or *masagoto* (straight grain *koto*).

11 *See also* Kishibe (1982a, 1364) and Nakajima and Kubota (1984, 58).

12 Shinwa Kingaku, conversation with author, Fukuyama, 17 June 1997.

13 In the Nara period, the main body of the *koto* was made from several pieces of wood in the form of a box (Tanabe and Hirano 1982, 1350). It was not until the time of the *zokusō* that the standard instrument came to have several supports (*dōbari*) put across the width to strengthen the body (Tanabe and Hirano 1982, 1350). The actual exterior shape of the instrument has remained the same since the Nara period.

14 The *shamisen* and the *zheng* (the Chinese version of the *koto*) also often have similar carvings.

15 These terms are often used without the suffix *bori* (*hori*).

16 Chūjō and Hotta (1985, 214) note that an instrument with no

grooves is labeled *hiradō* (plain body) or *maruuchidō* (clear body).

17 Kikuhara Hatsuko, conversation with author, Osaka, 23 April 1991.

18 The term *tomekō* (scooped-out soundboard) is sometimes used instead of *tomezuke*.

19 For discussions of the acoustic properties of the *koto*, *see* Adriaansz (1973, 29-30), Hirata and Kaihara (1988, 97-100) and Obata and Sugita (1931). On plucking movements and acoustics, *see* Andō (1982).

20 Ogawa Gakki Seizō, conversation with author, Fukuyama, 16 June 1997.

21 The Kasuga Shrine in Nara has a Heian-period *koto* in its Treasure Hall that is labeled *makiegoto* (lacquered *koto*). Unlike some instruments (i.e., *gakusō* and other non-*Yamadagoto*) that occasionally use this label, all of its upper surface has lacquer work with designs of landscapes, flowers and insects.

22 The instrument is referred to as a *koto* (general term), and no other information about it is known. *See also* Aston ([1896] 1956, 269).

23 The oak leaf design is occasionally called *santake* (three peaks) or *kashiwaita* (oak board).

24 Shōsōin (1989, plate 126) shows a Nara-period *wagon* with an oak leaf design on it, although *wagon* today never have one. A similar pattern is found on some Buddhist decoration where it can be seen on doors, pillars, and banners.

25 *Cf.* also Hendry's (1993, 75) discussion of the wrapping of garments known as *jūnihitoe*, which have twelve layers and are worn by ladies of the Heian-period court. *See* Oka (1967, 1975, 1988) for numerous examples of wrapping and Japanese packaging.

26 The term "fixed bridge" is used here to differentiate these two bridges from the movable bridges that are placed at points under the strings along the *koto* surface to establish and adjust the tuning. The term "fixed bridge" also follows a translation of the Japanese term for these parts (fixed bridges and movable bridges are referred to as types of *koma* or "bridge"). While the fixed bridge at the tail is more like a nut, the fixed bridge at the head helps partly to transmit vibrations into the main body. It is at this end that the strings are plucked, just a few centimeters to the left of the fixed bridge.

27 The term *i no me* refers to a decorative shape in Japanese architecture, which is like that on the sides of the *koto*, but that usually points upward - especially on temple roofs - rather than downward as on the *koto*.

28 When a string is pressed behind (tail end) the movable bridge to raise its pitch, the bridge below that string might move slightly towards the head end. The player often has to reposition such movable bridges during performance.

29 The flying geese formation is a well-known art motif found in such works as "Descending Geese at Katata" ("Katata no rakugan") in the series *Eight Views of Lake Biwa* (*Ōmi hakkei no uchi*, *c*. 1834) by Utagawa Hiroshige (1797-1858).

30 The word "Okayasu" is the composer's name, and "Ginuta" (*kinuta*) is the name of a wooden block that was used historically to soften clothes.

31 Ackermann (1990, 347) notes that "wild geese in autumn are associated with the idea of coming, returning. The opposite image would be wild geese in spring, associated with the concept of leaving, flying off to the north, from where they will return again in autumn."

32 A common weight of a *koto* string is 17.5 *monme* (65.63 grams), although players might use a slightly different size according to personal preference (usually between 16-19 *monme*).

33 *Sōkyoku taiishō* of 1779 explains the names for strings 11-13 as onomatopoeia (*see* Adriaansz 1973, 471).

34 It is interesting to note that the first two strings in this nomenclature use the same characters as the first two in the title of the twelfth-century documentary source of *gagaku*, *Jinchi yōroku*.

35 Different colored strings are sometimes used, especially on instruments used by beginners so that, for example, one or two strings can be easily found.

36 A high stand (*sōkyōdai* [*sō* reverberating stand]) which uses microphones and the performer controlling the volume with a switch with the left hand and the reverberation with a pedal with the left foot was introduced in the early 1950s by Nakashima Utashito (1896-1979), although it made little impact (*see* Tanabe 1964, 244-47).

37 On Japanese design motifs, *see* Adachi ([1913] 1972), Blakemore (1978), Hibi and Niwa (2001), and Lee (1981). *See* Asquith and Kalland (1997) for anthropological discussions of the uses of nature in Japan.

38 *See also* Andō (1986, 17) and Chūjō and Hotta (1985, 54-58) for further examples of grades of *koto*. Ogawa Gakki Seizō list a single type of *nagaiso* instrument priced at 2,000,000 *yen* and above in 1990-93, and 2,200,000 *yen* and above in 1997-2004 (1990-93, 1; 1997-2004, 1). This instrument is listed separately.

1　The *koto* is found not only throughout Japan and the Japanese diaspora (some *koto* traditions have overseas members and even branch offices), but also in some non-Japanese contexts, especially universities and museums.

2　Many large-scale performance traditions use the suffix *ryū* in their name (not to be confused with the homonym, but different character and meaning, used as a suffix for many of the instrument's component parts – "dragon"; *see* Chapter 3). While this term is often translated in English as "school" (as in a school of performance), in this book the term "tradition" is used instead in order to reinforce the idea of handing down ideas through generations, which is typical in the transmission of *koto* music. When the term "school" is used in this text it refers to organizations of musicians that use an alternative term in the name of their group (e.g., the suffix *in*), which is more suited to such a translation. The term tradition is also used for some of the other levels of group affiliation to which players usually belong, unless the context of the discussion requires the use of a further differentiating term (e.g., group or troupe).

3　Adriaansz (2001) summarizes some of the main points concerning *koto* performance traditions and the transmission of their repertoires in relation to the social milieu of the time.

4　On lineages of *gakusō* musicians, *see* S. Nelson (1986, 12-13).

5　*See also* Garfias (1975, 28-34) regarding *gagaku* performance inside and outside the Imperial Palace.

6　Both *tōgaku* (*gagaku*) pieces.

7　At a time of Chinese influence on Japan during the Muromachi period, examples of Chinese painting depicting the *qin* are well known and were imitated by Japanese artists (Holvik 1992, 452).

8　The *hosodono* is the side of the palace for ladies-in-waiting.

9　The *Kōkiden* is the living quarters within the palace for court ladies.

10　Other *koto kumiuta* song texts that refer to this classical work include "Koryū Shiki Genji" ("Genji in the Four Seasons – Old Version"; either Yatsuhashi Kengyō or Ikuta Kengyō), "Kō Genji" ("Prince Genji"; Anonymous, attr. Tsuguyama Kengyō, *d.* 1697), "Akashi" (place name; Kitajima Kengyō), "Hana no En" ("Festival of the Cherry Blossoms"; Ishizuka Kengyō, act. *c.* 1755), "Hashihime" ("The Bridge Maiden"; unknown, arr. by Mitsuhashi Kengyō, *d.* 1760), "Hatsune no Kyoku" ("First Song of the Year"; Yamada Kengyō), "Otsu no Kyoku" ("Second Piece"; anonymous; the text is identical to "Koryū Shiki Genji," although the music is different), "Tamakazura" ("Jeweled Chaplet"; Mitsuhashi Kengyō), "Tōryū Shiki Genji" ("Genji in the Four Seasons – New Version"; Anonymous), "Ukifune" ("A Boat Upon the Water"; Mitsuhashi Kengyō), "Utsusemi" ("The Shell of the Locust"; Kitajima Kengyō), and "Wakaba" ("Young Grasses"; attr. to Kitajima Kengyō, or Makino Kengyō).

11　Fritsch (1996) provides a detailed history of blind musicians in Japan. On the history of the blind in Japanese society, *see* Katō (1974). Hall and Jansen (1968) provide a comprehensive discussion of the influences on Edo-period social institutions, especially in terms of feudalism. For a comparison of organizations in other arts *see*, for example, Moeran (1987). *See* Hirano and Tanigaitō (1980) and Kubota (1974) in connection with the genealogy of blind musicians.

12　On *hinin*, *see* Groemer (2001, 280, 288), who notes that singing and other performance activities were sometimes part of their livelihood. *See* Ohnuki-Tierney (1987) on special-status people in Japanese society.

13　In the Edo period, when everyday *koto* performance developed,

artisans were positioned at the bottom of a four-tiered (*shi-nō-kō-shō*) social system that consisted from highest to lowest: samurai (warriors, *shi*), peasants/farmers (*nō*), artisans (*kō*) and merchants (*shō*).

14　Yoshino and Murakoshi (1977, 41) make reference to a list of occupations in which *hinin* could engage.

15　The Bettō rank was included with Kengyō.

16　A different *kanji* for the word Tōdō is used by this group.

17　Of the prints that depict the *koto* in Haags Gemeentemuseum (1975) and Kyrova et al. (2000), for example, all but one show the instrument either being played by women or in a context with women present. *See also* Green (1985; 2001) who looks at blind musicians of the Edo period as depicted in Ukiyo-e. It was mostly blind men (including *koto* players) who were shown in these commercial prints.

18　On the world of the courtesan in Yoshiwara, *see* Seigle (1993).

19　Compare authors who critique the group model in Japan, such as Befu (1980), Dale (1986), Mouer and Sugimoto (1986), Sugimoto (1997), and Sugimoto and Mouer (1989).

20　There are a number of well-known professional solo *koto* players, but it is the norm for students to enter a performance tradition early in the learning process. Only later might a player of professional standard embark on a solo career, but very often maintaining an association in one way or another with their earlier tradition.

21　*See also* Fritsch (1996).

22　Mixed performances are occasionally found today, where members from different *koto* traditions join together for a special or celebratory concert. Such performances might include, for example, the meeting of players from different sub-traditions (e.g., from within the Ikuta-ryū), or from different traditions (e.g., from the Ikuta-ryū and the Yamada-ryū).

23　Such occurrences usually create very bad social relations between the players.

24　One example is given by Tsuda (1983, 141), who traces the genealogy of the Kyō Ikuta-ryū. Many other contemporary traditions have similar lineage charts.

25　The term Tsukushi-ryū started to be used at the beginning of the nineteenth century when several other traditions (*ryū*) emerged (Adriaansz 1973, 468).

26　Hirano and Kubota (1989, 489) classify seven main *koto* traditions, in this case dating from Tsukushigoto as it was a non-court tradition: the Tsukushi-ryū (or Tsukushigoto), the Ikuta-ryū, the Ikuta-ryū (i.e., Tsugaru Ikuta-ryū), the Tsuguyama-ryū, the Yatsuhashi-ryū, the Yamada-ryū, and the Kyōgoku-ryū.

27　The term Okinawa *sōkyoku* is used to describe *koto* music of Okinawa, rather than a performance tradition per se. Like Tsugaru Ikuta-ryū, several genres of performing arts in Okinawa that include the *koto* have been designated an Intangible Cultural Property (*mukei bunkazai*): traditional dances; Nomura-ryū (traditional music); Afuso-ryū (traditional music); Tansui-ryū (traditional music); Okinawa *sōkyoku*; Yaeyama folk music (Okinawa Prefectural Board of Education 1998, 22-33).

28　Tsugaru Ikuta-ryū is a label used for a tradition of *koto* performance found in the Tsugaru district of Aomori Prefecture in northern Honshū. This tradition is maintained by Kasai Harue (*b.* 1917) and just a handful of her students (*see* Kasai 1999; Kishibe 1975; Kishibe and Sasamori 1976; M. Yamazaki 1995). Tsugaru Ikuta-ryū has been designated an Intangible Cultural Property (*mukei bunkazai*).

29　In the 1970s there was just one teacher of this tradition, Sanada Shin (1883-1975). On Sanada Shin's repertoire, *see* S. Sanada (1970). On the Yatsuhashi-ryū and this sub-tradition *see* Kikkawa

(1967) and Y. Sanada (1980).

30 The affiliation is by name only, although there is an Ikuta-ryū Association (Ikuta-ryū Kyōkai).

31 In the early 1970s Fujita (1973, 340) noted that the Yamada-ryū Sōkyoku Kyōkai had 1,600 members. This included only those who directly belonged to the organization and not some students or even students of students who were not full members.

32 This group was by far the largest of nearly 200 listed by Fujita (1973). It also calls itself Chikushi-kai (Chikushi group) and in 1973 had nearly 40,000 members (Fujita 1973, 261).

33 On the Kyōgoku-ryū, *see also* Kichimi (1984) and Wada (1995).

34 Both *ha* play the Nogawa-ryū style of *jiuta shamisen*.

35 For a comparison of the role of the *iemoto* and organizations in connection with *chadō* (tea ceremony), *see* J. Anderson (1987).

36 On the Miyagi-ha, *see* Ayer (1997) and Prescott (1997).

37 For descriptions of *koto* lessons, *see* Falconer (1995), Halliwell (1994a), Malm (2000), and Piggott ([1909] 1971).

38 Preservation societies (*hozonkai*) exist in many of Japan's traditional arts, including *koto* performance (*cf.* Fujie 1986 on festivals in the Tokyo area, and Hughes 1985 in connection with folk music).

39 Soloists are more popular today with the international market for world music giving prominence to the soloist musician, and the experimentation with contemporary music that often emphasizes the idea of a solo performer.

40 Tanigaitō (1994) provides a brief discussion of *koto* playing licenses based on an exhibition held at the Miyagi Michio Memorial Museum.

41 When known, fees are indicated in the tables, although such information was not always readily available during field research. The level and cost in each of the tables is shown from the lowest to highest.

42 The name of this group is often abbreviated to Shūyū-kai. The group is centered mainly in the north of Kyūshū and the south of Honshū and was formed in the mid-1960s by Nakagawa Shūsui. Field research was undertaken with members of this group in 1990. The group, which is structured with several smaller groups of teachers and students, has a female *kaichō* (group leader; Nakagawa Shūsui), *riji* (committee; 4 people), *fukuriji* (sub-committee; 6 people), and *sōdanyaku* (1 person). The group Sōmei Ongaku-kai, for example, which is also part of the Ikuta-ryū in a wider sphere, has the same number of certificates. Hayashi Kimiko, conversations with the author, Kyoto, October 1991.

43 On the cost of examinations *see also* Falconer (1990, 472), who notes that some Ikuta-ryū teaching examinations can cost between 300,000-600,000 *yen*.

44 Yatsuhashi Kengyō was also known by at least three other names, reflecting his affiliation and level, or rank, of expertise: Jōhide, Yamazumi Kōtō, Uenaga Kengyō (Ackermann 1990, 58). *See* Hirano and Tanigaitō (1980) for a discussion of the title Kengyō as relates to the genealogy of blind musicians.

Chapter 5: *Performance*

1 The *zokusō* type of *koto* is sometimes used at Shinto shrines during *kagura* (Shinto song and dance), as a modern-day replacement for the *gakusō*.

2 The concept of space in connection with the *koto* is explored by Elkinton (1990), who looks at the Japanese concept *ma* (space) in connection with the form of the *koto*, performance practice and music.

3 Performances of the *koto* outside its normal cultural contexts (e.g., outside Japan or by non-Japanese performers) might proceed according to a different set of rules and conventions for players and audience.

4 On aspects of studying such contexts, *see* Tokumaru (1997).

5 When playing in the *sankyoku* ensemble the *shamisen* (called *sangen* in this context) player is usually positioned to the *koto* player's left, and the *shakuhachi* or *kokyū* player to the *shamisen* player's left.

6 Several different positions may be taken during lessons: the two instruments might face each other; the instruments may be next to each other; or a row might be formed with the teacher either in front or behind. It should be noted that the pupil would also sometimes begin to learn the repertoire of their teacher while waiting for their lesson. Lessons often overlap with several students arriving at the same time and listening to each other while they are at their teacher's house.

7 Sadayakko was the wife of Kawakami Otojirō (1864-1911), who led a troupe of touring Japanese performing artists, and visited Berlin in 1901. She was known by several different names or spellings of these names (e.g., Sada Yacco).

8 In connection with the *shamisen*, *see* Tokumaru (1986, 116), who shows the importance of the practical position of the pitch and the player's fingers; *see also* Baily (1977) for a related study in connection with movement patterns while playing the *dutār* (a long-necked lute from Afghanistan).

9 J. Nelson (2000, 11) notes that about 72% (86.9 million people) of the population visited shrines and temples over the 1998 New Year period.

10 On notations, *see* especially Fukushima and Nelson (1983), Harich-Schneider (1973), Hirano and Fukushima (1978), Kubota (1988), S. Nelson (1986), Tsuge (1986a), and Wade (1976). Johnson (2002) looks at Meiji-era and post-Meiji-era *koto* notations. Nakajima and Kubota (1984, 163-66) provide a comparison of the symbols used in seven different types of *koto* notation: Western staff notation, *shōga* (oral mnemonics), *yoko-shiki* (a horizontal tablature, especially used in the Yamada-ryū), *Sei-ha-shiki* (a vertical tablature, especially used in the Sei-ha tradition), *Katei-shiki* (a vertical tablature, especially used in the Ikuta-ryū), *Sōkyoku taiishō* (a notation book of 1779 using a vertical tablature), and *Kinkyoku shifu* (a notation book of 1772 using a vertical tablature).

11 The term "tablature" defines a notation system that allows the player to relate the visual signs directly to the physical form of the instrument. With most *koto* notations, string numbers are shown in the tablature, rather than indicating directly the pitch of those strings.

12 Markham (1983) provides a useful interpretation of *Jinchi yōroku* in connection with the *koto* (i.e., *gakusō*) used to accompany *saibara* (a genre of court songs). *See also* Condit (1976), Garfias (1974) and Picken and Mitani (1979).

13 Japanese can be written in several ways: in columns from right to left (traditional style); and across the page from left to right (Western style). Some short scripts are even read horizontally from right to left.

14 On Western music (*yōgaku*) in Japan, *see* especially Eppstein (1994) and Galliano (2002). Galliano also writes on contemporary Japanese music that includes traditional instruments.

15 *See also* May (1963), who gives a study of Meiji-era school music, and Pecore (2000), who provides a study of the internationalization of the Japanese school curriculum.

16 Some composers, for example Sawai Tadao, might even write their music in Western notation and then have it transcribed to a traditional form for publication (Falconer 1995, 85).

17 Two chapters look specifically at notation. One introduces notation and the other shows several music transcriptions (Katō and Ueno 2002; Yonekawa 2002).

18 For a summary of the current political milieu, *see* Yoshino (2002).

19 Shimizu Kuniharu, letter to author, 15 July 2003.

20 Some Ikuta-ryū sub-traditions today still use a form of vertical notation that does not indicate rhythm (e.g., Tsugaru Ikuta-ryū).

21 *See also* the vertical notation system used in Okinawa *sōkyoku*, which is found in the volume called *Kunkunshi*. This type of notation divides each beat into a rectangular unit and includes the standard symbols used in other historical forms of *koto* notation (*see* Okinawa Sōkyoku Hozonkai 1995).

22 A number notation was used in Europe by, for example, J. J. Rousseau in the eighteenth century, and later by Aimé Paris (1798-1866), Pierre Galin (1786-1821), and Joseph Maurice Chevé (1804-64).

23 The Arabic numerals "11", "12" and "13" are sometimes found in number notation for the *koto*, especially for use by children.

24 Machida later used Japanese numbers horizontally and included two beats to the bar (e.g., 1914).

25 The preface to this notation notes that the writer belongs to the Yamada tradition.

26 A later example by Inoue (1917) mixes this type of notation with Western staff notation and *shōga*.

27 *See* Garfias (1975) for a discussion of solmization of *gakusō* music.

28 *See also* Gunji (1986) for an examination of the relationship between timbre, solmization and onomatopoeia in Japanese music in general.

29 *See also* Hirano (1989a) and Nogawa (1994).

30 Tsukushigoto tunings include a system called *jūnichōshi* (twelve tunings), where the same intervallic space between each string is maintained through the twelve pitches of the octave. Beginning with the note "A", the names of the twelve Tsukushigoto tunings are: *ichikotsuchō, tanginchō, hyōjō* (the *gagaku* scale *taishikichō* is called *hyōjō* in the Tsukushigoto), *shōsetsuchō, shimomuchō, sōjō, fushōchō, ōshikichō, rankeichō, banshikichō, shinsenchō,* and *kamimuchō*. Miyahara Chizuko uses two tunings in her Tsukushigoto repertoire. Each is established by sliding the movable bridges after establishing the *zokusō* tuning *hirajōshi*. The player moves strings four and nine up one tone, and strings six and eleven up a half tone; the other moves strings, four, six, nine, and eleven up a half tone. The former is referred to as *gakujōshi*, which is the same tuning as the *gagaku* tuning *hyōjō*, and the latter corresponds to the *gagaku* tuning *taishikichō*. Miyahara Chizuko, conversation with author, Kitakyūshū, 30 March 2000. *See also* Miyazaki (1995).

31 On Yamada-ryū tunings, *see* especially Kishibe (1973), and also Nakajima and Kubota (1984, 87-98).

32 This idea has also been explored by Tokumaru, who notes that the *shamisen*'s "fingerboard [is] ... an ordered terrain of pitches" (1986, 114), and a "somatic and conceptual frame of reference" (1986, 116).

33 On Japanese scales, *see* Koizumi (1977).

34 Picken and Mitani (1979) provide a useful discussion of left- and

right-hand finger techniques of the *koto* (i.e., *gakusō*) of the Heian period, although the precise date when *gakusō* left-hand techniques ceased to be used is not known (*see also* Garfias 1974, 1975). *See* Markham (1983) in connection with the *koto* used to accompany *saibara* court songs. Kubota (1980) examines the influence of *gagaku* on everyday *koto* music. *See also* Harich-Schneider (1953, 1965) on aspects of court music. *See* Miyazaki (1995) on ways of playing Tsukushigoto.

35 On performance techniques of several different *koto* performance traditions, *cf.* Andō (1986), Chūjō and Hotta (1985), Kishibe (1973), Read (1975), Tsuda (1983), and S. Yamazaki (1977).

36 This term means literally leg or shin and does not immediately describe how the technique is played.

37 The Ikuta-ryū and the Yamada-ryū sub-traditions often vary their performance practice of techniques and ornamentation.

38 Falconer (1995, 265-82) examines the world of modern *koto* music that looks beyond restrictions of cultural boundaries.

39 On the music of the Yamada-ryū, *see also* Ackermann (1986).

40 For further discussion of the history of these and other genres of *koto* music, *see* especially Adriaansz (1984) and Kikkawa (1997).

41 *See* Adriaansz (1973), Hirano (1978) and Halliwell (1994b) for further detailed analyses of this piece and its prototype "Sugagaki". *See* Gutzwiller (1992) on the idea of polyphony and a separation of parts in the version of "Rokudan" for two *koto* (*honte/kaede*). Ackermann's (1979) study of the interrelationship between voice and *koto* (i.e., the player sings and plays the instrument in the same piece) concludes that together they provide one continuous line.

42 The second *koto* part of this duet uses the tuning called *kumoijōshi*.

43 "Aki no Nanakusa" ("Seven Flowers of Autumn") has "Rokudan" in the first interlude (*ai no te*) and the piece was included in a book of *koto* music transcribed into Western staff notation (*see* Tōkyō Academy of Music 1888). This book was a teaching resource compiled by Ongaku Torishirabe Gakari (Music Study Committee). Both Yamase and Yamato were members of the committee and Yamada-ryū *koto* players.

44 This is an old name for an area in Ōhara, Kyoto.

45 Thrasher (1995) discusses *danmono* and related structures in Chinese and Japanese instrumental music.

46 The Ikuta-ryū play fifty-two and the Yamada-ryū fifty-three. Only "Hatsune no Kyoku" ("First Song of the Year") is played by the Yamada-ryū. *See also* Adriaansz (1973) and Tsuge (1981, 1986a), and for a study of *kumiuta* song texts, *see* Ackermann (1990).

47 These two *danmono* were the models of "Rokudan" and "Midare", respectively.

48 *Kumiuta* are also found for the *shamisen* (*see* Ackermann 1990).

49 The Tsukushigoto repertory has ten *kumiuta* by Kenjun, the texts of which were drawn from high-art literary sources, and the song verses juxtaposing often unrelated texts.

50 *See also* Adriaansz (1971) for musical analyses of different versions of "Fuki", and Holvik (1992) for a cultural analysis of its text. *See* Thompson (2001) for a survey of *koto* music in Ryūkyū, which shows a connection between the Yatsuhashi tradition and the music of these southern islands.

51 From the Meiji era the *kokyū* was often replaced by the *shakuhachi*.

52 Such music in Osaka was collectively called *Ōsakamono* (Osaka pieces), and in Kyoto it was called *Kyōmono* (Kyoto pieces).

53 Burnett (1989) provides a musical analysis of Minezaki's piece "Zangetsu" ("The Setting Moon"), which shows it to be somewhat different to the composer's other *jiuta tegotomono* pieces.

54 "Chidori no Kyoku", like many other pieces, is often played by a variety of instruments, sometimes in the *sankyoku* ensemble, and sometimes not.

Tables

Table 1. Instruments and Traditions.
Table 2. Classifications According to Outer Surface Decoration.
Table 3. Frequently Shared Features of *Gakusō*, *Chikusō* and Early Forms of *Zokusō*.
Table 4. Comparison of Ikuta-ryū, Yamada-ryū and Their *Koto*.
Table 5. Modified, Smaller and Larger *Koto*.
Table 6. Comparison of Instrument Sizes.
Table 7. Curvature and Height of a *Yamadagoto*.
Table 8. String Names and Symbols.
Table 9. Ancient String Nomenclature.
Table 10. Note Names.
Table 11. Grades of *Koto* (Ogawa Gakki Seizō).
Table 12. Grades of *Koto* (Mishima Gakki).
Table 13. Grades of *Koto* (Shinwa Kingaku).
Table 14. Grades of *Koto* (Oda Koto Seisaku-sho).
Table 15. Grades of *Koto* (Makimoto Gakki).
Table 16. Sōkyoku Shūyū-kai Licenses.
Table 17. Kikui Sōgaku-sha Licenses.
Table 18. Kikui Sōgaku-sha Examinations.
Table 19. Tōdō Ongaku-kai Examinations.

Chronology

Jōmon	*c.* 8,000 B.C.E to *c.* 200 B.C.E.
Yayoi	*c.* 200 B.C.E.- *c.* C.E. 300
Yamato (Kofun or Tomb)	*c.* 300-710
Nara	710-94
Heian	794-1185
Kamakura	1185-1333
Muromachi (Ashikaga)	1333-1568
Azuchi-Momoyama	1568-1600
Edo (Tokugawa)	1600-1868
Meiji	1868-1912
Taishō	1912-1926
Shōwa	1926-1989
Heisei	1989-present

Select Character List

A

Afuso-ryū 安富祖流

ajiro 網代

ai no te 合の手

akebonojōshi 曙調子

akikazejōshi 秋風調子

akinojōshi 秋野調子

aku 灰汁

arashi 嵐

arutogoto アルト箏

asagatabori 麻型彫り

ashi 足

atarashii koto 新しい箏

atoashi 後足

atooshi 後押し

atouta 後歌

atozuke 後付け

awasezume 合わせ爪

ayamegoto 菖蒲箏

ayasugibori 綾杉彫り

B

banshikichō 盤渉調

bēsugoto ベース箏

beta べた

betamaki べた巻

betazuke べた付け

Bettō 別当

bibu 尾部

bunkagoto 文化箏

bunke 分家

byōbu 屏風

C

"Chidori no Kyoku" 「千鳥の曲」

Chikushi-kai 筑紫会

Chikushi-ryū 筑紫流

chikusō 筑箏

chirashi 散らし

chirashizume 散らし爪

chūden 中伝

Chūgoku-kei Ikuta-ryū 中国系生田流

chūjudō 中授導

chūkōtō 中勾当

D

daijudō 大授導

dai-jūshichigen 大十七弦

daikoto 大箏

daikōtō 大勾当

daishihan 大師範

dan 段

dan'awase 段合せ

danmono 段物

denshō 伝承

dentō 伝統

dōbari 胴梁

dōzoku 同族

E

Edo Ikuta-ryū 江戸生田流

erekutorikkugoto エレクトリック箏

"Etenraku" 「越殿楽」・「越天楽」

F

fuchi 縁

Fujiike-ryū 藤池流

"Fuki" 「菜蕗」・「蕗菜」・
「蕗」・「富貴」

fukuriji 副理事

fukuro 袋

Fukuyamagoto 福山琴

Fukuyama Hōgakki Seizōgyō Kyōdō Kumiai
福山邦楽器製造業協同組合

furizume 振り爪

Fushimi-ha 伏見派

fushōchō 鳧鐘調

G

gagaku 雅楽

Gagakuryō 雅楽寮

gaisen rappa jōshi 凱旋ラッパ調子

gakki 楽器

gakujōshi 楽調子

gakusō 楽箏

gakuza 楽座

geimei 芸名

geisha 芸者

gendai hōgaku 現代邦楽

gengakki 弦楽器・絃楽器

Genji monogatari 源氏物語

Genjo 玄恕

genmeifu 弦名譜

genmeigakki 弦鳴楽器

gogo 五五

gogō kinkuchi 五号金口

gogō kōki kinkuchi uwazunomaki 五号紅木金口上角巻

gohachi 五八

gosenfu 五線譜

goshakugoto 五尺箏

H

ha 派

hachigō tamabuchi 八号玉縁

hachijūgen 八十弦

Hagi Yatsuhashi-ryū 萩八橋流

hajiki 弾き

hakuhan 薄板

hanakumojōshi 花雲調子

hanhikiren 半引き連
han'iwatojōshi 半岩戸調子
hankake 半拘・半掛
hankumoijōshi 半雲井調子
hannakazorajōshi 半中空調子
hanryū 半流
hansō 半箏
han'uwazuno 半上角
han'uwazunomaki 半上角巻
hariita 梁板
"Haru no Umi" 「春の海」
hayagaki 早掻
hayakake 早拘・早掛
higurashijōshi ひぐらし調子
hikiiro 引き色
hikimono 弾物
hikiren 引き連
hikisute 引き捨て
himegoto 姫箏
hinin 非人
hiradō 平胴
hirajōshi 平調子
hishi 菱
hōgakki 邦楽器
hōgaku 邦楽
honchōshi 本調子
honjitategoto 本仕立て箏
honjōshi 本調子
honke 本家
honken 本間
honkumoijōshi 本雲井調子
honte 本手
hori 彫り
Hossui 法水
Hōsui 法水
hozonkai 保存会
hyōjō 平調
hyōjuntekiji 標準的柱

I

ibota 疣取
ibotarō 疣取蝋
ichigō beta 一号べた
ichigō semikiri 一号背見切
ichikotsuchō 壱越調
ichimen 一面
ie 家
iemoto 家元
iemoto seido 家元制度
ikakō イカ甲
Ikutagoto 生田箏
Ikuta Kengyō 生田検校
Ikuta-ryū 生田流
Ikuta-ryū 郁田流

imayō 今様
inketsu 音穴
i no me 猪の目
iso 磯
isogata 磯型
itame 板目
itamegoto 板目箏
ito 糸・弦
itokaeshi 糸返し
itomakura 糸枕
ittaikan 一体感
iwatojōshi 岩戸調子

J

ji 柱
Jinchi yōroku 仁智要録
jiuta 地歌・地唄
jū 臑
jūgogen 十五弦
jūhachigen 十八弦
jūkō 臑押
jūnanagen 十七弦
junhōgaku 純邦楽
jūnichōshi 十二調子
junshihan 準師範
jūrokugen 十六弦
jūsangen 十三弦
jūsansenfu 十三線譜
jūsansen-shiki sōfu 十三線式箏譜
jūshichigen 十七弦
jūshichigengoto 十七弦箏
jūshichigensō 十七弦箏

K

kaede 替手
kai 会
kaichō 会長
kaiden 皆伝
kaihan 皆半
kaiin 会員
kakeoshi 掛け押し
kakezume 拘爪・掛爪
kaki 掻き
kakite 掻き手
kakizume 掻き爪
kakko 羯鼓・鞨鼓
kakumaki 角巻
kamiashi 上足
kamimuchō 上無調
kangen 管弦
kanmuri 冠
kansō 乾燥
karakusa 唐草
kari 雁
kariganejōshi 雁音調子

karin 花林・花梨

karin betamaki 花林べた巻

kasaneoshi 重ね押し

kasanezume 重ね爪

kashiwaba 柏葉

kashiwagata 柏型・柏形

kashiwaita 柏板

katakumoijōshi 片雲井調子

kataiwatojōshi 片岩戸調子

Katei-shiki 家庭式

kazarigoto 飾り箏

kazune 和音

kei 系

keifu 系譜

keikogoto 稽古琴

ken 間

Kengyō 検校

Kenjun 賢順

keshi 消し

keshizume 消し爪

kikkō 亀甲

Kiku/kiku 菊

Kikuike-ha 菊池派

Kikuike-ryū 菊池流

Kikui Sōgaku-sha 菊井箏楽社

Kiku-suji 菊筋

kin 琴

kindai 琴台

kinji 巾柱

kinkuchi 金口

kinkyoku 琴曲

Kinkyoku shifu 琴曲指譜

Kinkyoku shō 琴曲抄

kin no koto 琴のこと

kinsō 琴箏

kiri 桐

kiri mon 桐門

Kisaragi-kai 如月会

kō 甲

kō 押

kōboku 紅木

kobun 子分

kogatagoto 小型箏

kōhai 後輩

kōhō 押放

Ko-Ikuta-ryū 古生田流

koji 小柱

kojin shugi 個人主義

kōki 紅木

kōki kinkuchimaki 紅木金口巻

kōki nijūmaki 紅木二重巻

kokinjōshi 古今調子

kōki tamabuchimaki 紅木玉縁巻

kōki uwazunomaki 紅木上角巻

kokutan 黒檀

kōkyō 押響

koma 駒

komochi ayasugibori 子持綾杉彫り

kosei 個性

koto 琴・箏

Kōtō 勾当

kotoji 琴柱

koto kuyō 琴供養

koto matsuri 琴祭

kouta 小唄

Ko-Yatsuhashi-ryū 古八橋流

kōzukuri 甲造り

kozume 小爪

kuchimae 口前

kuchimae bukuro 口前袋

kuchimae kabā 口前カバー

kuchimae nejizuke 口前ねじ付け

kuchimae sakku 口前サック

kuchijamisen 口三味線

kuchishōga 口唱歌

kuchizuno 口角

kuchizunomaki 口角巻

kumiuta 組歌

kumoijōshi 雲井調子

Kunkunshi 工工四

kurikō 刳甲

kurumagoto 車箏

Kyōgoku-ryū 京極流

Kyō Ikuta-ryū 京生田流

kyōkai 協会

Kyōma 京間

Kyō-ryū 京流

Kyōto Kami-ha 京都上派

Kyōto Shimo-ha 京都下派

Kyōto Tōdō-kai 京都當道会

Kyūshū-kei Ikuta-ryū 九州系生田流

M

ma 間

maeashi 前足

maeuta 前歌

maki 巻

makie 蒔絵

makuraito 枕糸

makurazuno 枕角

maruguchi 丸口

maruuchidō 丸打胴

masagoto 柾箏

masame 柾目

Matsushiro Yatsuhashi-ryū 松代八橋流

Meiji shinkyoku 明治新曲

men 面

menjō 免状
mijikai koto 短い箏
minichuagoto ミニチュア箏
minigoto ミニ琴
Miyagi Michio 宮城道雄
miyakobushi 都節
mokume 木目
monme 匁
montsuki 紋付き
mōsen 毛氈
mōsō 盲僧
mukadeashi 百足足
mukōashi 向足
mukōhan 向半
Murai Rei 村井れい

N
nagaashi 長足
nagaisogoto 長磯箏
nagaisohonjitategoto 長磯本仕立て箏
nagashi 流し
nagashizume 流し爪
nagasō 長箏
Nagoya Ikuta-ryū 名古屋生田流
Nakanoshima-ha 中能島派
Naka-suji 中筋
nakayurushi 中許
nakazorajōshi 中空調子
namigaeshi 波返し・波帰し
namiken 並間
namikō 並甲
nanagō han-tamabuchi 七号半玉縁
nanagō kurikō kōki tamabuchimaki,
kuchimae zōge
七号刳甲紅木玉縁巻, 口前象牙
nanagō kurikō tamabuchi zōgemaki 七号刳甲玉縁象牙巻
nanagō tomekō kōki tamabuchimaki 七号止甲紅木玉縁巻
natori 名取り
natsuyamajōshi 夏山調子
nekoashi 猫足
neo-koto ネオ箏
nibankō 二番甲
nigen-age 二弦上げ
nigen-sage 二弦下げ
nigō-jō shitan kuchizunomaki 二号上紫檀口角巻
nigō kuchizuno 二号口角
nigō shitan kuchizunomaki 二号紫檀口角巻
Nihonjin ron 日本人論
Nihon Tōdō-kai 日本当道会
Nihon Tōdō Ongaku-kai 日本当道音楽会
niigoto 新箏
nijūichigensō 二十一弦箏
nijūnakazorajōshi 二重中空調子
nijūkumoijōshi 二重雲井調子

nijūgen 二十弦
Nogawa-ryū 野川流
nogijōshi 乃木調子
Nomura-ryū 野村流

O
ōgakujōshi 大楽調子
oginu 尾絹
ogire 尾布
ōgoto 大箏
okuyurushi 奥許
okuden 奥伝
omote-gumi 表組
omoteita 表板
onketsu 音穴
orandajōshi オランダ調子
orugōrujōshi オルゴール調子
Ōsaka Ikuta-ryū 大阪生田流
Ōsaka Shin-Ikuta-ryū 大阪新生田流
Ōsaka Yatsuhashi-ryū 大阪八橋流
oshiawase 押し合せ
oshiawasezume 押し合せ爪
oshide 押し手
oshidome 押し止め
oshidome hanashi 押し止め放し
oshihanashi 押し放し
oshihibiki 押し響き
oshiiro 押し色
ōshikichō 黄鐘調
otoana 音穴
otoshi 落とし

R
raden 螺鈿
rankeichō 鷺鐘調
ren 連
renmei 連盟
renmei-kai 連盟会
renshūgoto 練習箏
rijikai 理事会
rissōdai 立奏台
rōei 朗詠
rokuagarijōshi 六上り調子
"Rokudan no Shirabe" 「六段の調」
rokugō nijū 六号二重
rokugō nijūmaki (kinkuchi) 六号二重巻（金口）
rokushakugoto 六尺箏
rokutoagari kumoijōshi 六斗上り雲井調子
ryōsō 涼箏
ryū 流
ryū 竜・龍
ryūbi 竜尾
ryūde 竜手
ryūfuku 竜腹
ryūgaku 竜額

ryūgan 竜眼
ryūha 流派
ryūhai 竜背
ryūkaku 竜角
ryūken 竜瞼
ryūkō 竜口
ryūkō 竜甲
ryūkyaku 竜脚
ryūkyō 竜頬
Ryūkyūgoto 琉球箏
ryūshi 竜趾
ryūshin 竜唇
ryūshu 竜手
ryūsoku 竜足
ryūtō 竜頭
ryūzetsu 竜舌
ryūzu 竜頭

S

sabi 寂
sagari さがり
sakura 桜
"Sakura Sakura" 「桜桜」・
「さくらさくら」
Sanada Shin 真田しん
sanbankō 三番甲
sangō han'uwazuno 三号半上角
sangō shitan han'uwazunomaki 三号紫檀半上角巻
sanjūgen 三十弦
sankyoku 三曲
sanshakugoto 三尺箏
santake 三岳
satsuki beta karinmaki 皐月べた花林巻
Satsuma Yatsuhashi-ryū 薩摩八橋流
Sawai Kazue 沢井一恵
Sawai Tadao 沢井忠夫
Sawai Sōkyoku-in 沢井箏曲院
Sei-ha Hōgaku-kai 正派邦楽会
Sei-ha Ongaku-in 正派音楽院
Sei-ha-shiki 正派式
seiza 正座
seizai 製材
sekiita 関堰・関板
sekishōjōshi 夕鐘調子
sekkai 石灰
sensei 先生
sha 社
shachū 社中
shaku 尺
shakuhachi 尺八
shamisen 三味線
shiagari hankumoijōshi 四上り半雲井調子
shiage 仕上げ
shibu 支部

shibui 渋い
shiburoku 四分六
Shichiku shoshinshū 糸竹初心集
Shichiku taizen 糸竹大全
shigen-age 四弦上げ
shihan 師範
shiken 試験
shikuagarijōshi 四九上り調子
shikuagari nakazorajōshi 四九上り中空調子
shimoashi 下足
shimomuchō 下無調
shin-Fukuyamagoto 新福山箏
shin-kariganejōshi 新雁音調子
shinkyoku 新曲
shin-nihon ongaku 新日本音楽
shin-nihon ongaku-undō 新日本音楽運動
shi nō kō shō 士農工商
shinsenchō 神仙調
shinsō 新箏
shinsōkyoku 新箏曲
Shin-Yatsuhashi-ryū 新八橋流
shinza 芯座
shirabemono 調べ物
shitan 紫檀
shitan han'uwamaki 紫檀半上巻
shitan kuchizunomaki 紫檀口角巻
shita no ana 下の穴
shizugaki 閑掻
shōchikubai 松竹梅
shoden 初伝
shōga 唱歌・証歌・正歌・声歌
shōji 小柱
shōjudō 少授導
shō-jūshichigen 小十七弦
shōkōtō 少勾当
Shoku-Kengyō 職検校
Shokuyashiki 職屋敷
shōsetsuchō 勝絶調
sō 箏・筝
sō 槽
sōdanyaku 相談役
soede 添手・副手
soezume 添爪・副爪
sōfurenjōshi 想夫恋調子
sōgaku 箏楽
sōke 宗家
Sō-kengyō 総検校
sōkyōdai 箏響台
sōkyoku 箏曲
Sōkyoku Shūyū-kai 箏曲秀友会
Sōkyoku taiishō 箏曲大意抄
Sōmei Ongaku-kai 倉明音楽会
sō no koto 箏のこと・箏の琴

sopuranogoto ソプラノ箏
Sōrokuyashiki 惣録屋敷
sōshoku 装飾
soto 外
sudaremebori 簾目彫り
sugagaki 清掻・清攪・菅掻・菅垣
sugotojitategoto 素箏仕立て箏
suhama 洲浜
suji 筋
sukuizume 掬い爪・掬い爪
Sumiyama-ryū 隅山流・住山流・
澄山流
sun 寸
surizume 摺り爪

T
tagayasan 鉄刀木
tagensō 多弦箏
taishikichō 太食調
tamabuchi 玉縁
tamado 玉戸
tamamoku 玉杢
tanginchō 断金調
tangoto 短箏
tanhan 短半
tankin 短琴
tan-nijūgen 短二十弦
Tansui-ryū 湛水流
tategaki 縦書き
tatehiza 立て膝
tatsu 竜・龍
tegoto 手事
tegotomono 手事物
tei-nijūgen 低二十弦
teion-nijūgen 低音二十弦
teion-nijūgogen 低音二十五弦
tenjinza 天人座
tōbu 頭部
Tōdō 当道
Tōdō-kai 当道会
Tōdō no za 当道の座
Tōdō Ongaku-kai 当道音楽会
Tōdō Shokuyashiki 当道職屋敷
Tōdō Yūraku-kai 当道友楽会
Tōdō-za 当道座
tomekō 止甲
tomezuke 止付け
Tomi-suji 富筋
torii 鳥居
Tsugaru Ikuta-ryū 津軽郁田流
Tsuguyama-ryū 継山流
tsuki 突き
tsukiiro 突き色
Tsukushigoto 筑紫箏

Tsukushi-ryū 筑紫流
tsume 爪
tsumekawa 爪皮
tsumeobi 爪帯

U
uchi 内
uchiawase 打合せ
uchizume 打爪
uenejizuke 上ねじ付け
ue no ana 上の穴
umi 海
unkaku 雲角
uraana 裏穴
ura-gumi 裏組
uraita 裏板
uraren 裏連
urayurushi 裏許
urazuri 裏摺り
ushiroashi 後足
usuita 薄板
utagoto 歌箏
utamono 歌物
uwakō 上甲
uwazuno 上角
uwazunomaki 上角巻
uzukuri ウズクリ
uzuramoku 鶉杢

W
wa 輪
wagakki 和楽器
wagon 和琴
waren 輪連
warizume 割り爪

Y
Yamada gogō kinkuchi kōkimaki 山田五号金口紅木巻
Yamada gogō kōkimaki 山田五号紅木巻
Yamadagoto 山田箏
Yamada hachigō kurikō tamabuchi
kōkimaki 山田八号刳甲玉縁紅木巻
Yamada ichigō beta karinmaki 山田一号べた花林巻
Yamada jūgō kurikō fukutamabuchi kōkimaki
山田十号刳甲複玉縁紅木巻
Yamada jūichigō kurikō tamabuchi
zōgeiri kōkimaki 山田十一号刳甲玉縁象牙入紅木巻
Yamada jūichigō masagoto zōge
tamabuchimaki 山田十一号柾琴象牙玉縁巻
Yamada jūnigō kurikō zōge
tamabuchimaki 山田十二号刳甲象牙玉縁巻
Yamada jūsangō kurikō sōzōge
tamabuchimaki 山田十三号刳甲総象牙玉縁巻
Yamada Kengyō 山田検校
Yamada kyūgō kurikō tamabuchi kōkimaki
山田九号刳甲玉縁紅木巻

Yamada nanagō kurikō tamabuchi 山田七号刳甲玉縁

Yamada nanagō kurikō tamabuchi kōkimaki
山田七号刳甲玉縁紅木巻

Yamada nigō kuchizuno karinmaki 山田二号口角花林巻

Yamada nigō kuchizuno shitanmaki 山田二号口角紫檀巻

Yamada nigō shitanmaki 山田二号紫檀巻

Yamada rokugō nijūmaki honemaki

kinkuchi kōkimaki 山田六号二重巻骨巻金口紅木巻

Yamada-ryū 山田流

Yamada-ryū Sōkyoku Kyōkai 山田流箏曲協会

Yamada sangō han'uwazuno

shitanmaki/kōkimaki 山田三号半上角紫檀巻／紅木巻

Yamada sangō kōkimaki 山田三号紅木巻

Yamada sangō shitanmaki 山田三号紫檀巻

Yamada sangō shitanmaki kotobuki satsuki
山田三号紫檀巻寿皐月

Yamada yongō kōkimaki 山田四号紅木巻

Yamada yongō uwazuno kōkimaki 山田四号上角紅木巻

yamatogoto 大和琴・倭琴・日本琴

Yatsuhashi Kengyō 八橋検校

Yatsuhashi-ryū 八橋流

yōgakki 洋楽器

yōgaku 洋楽

yōgin 揺吟

yokogaki 横書き

yoko-shiki 横式

yokozume 横爪

yongō kōki uwazunomaki 四号紅木上角巻

yongō uwazuno 四号上角

yonshakugoto 四尺箏

yosegizaiku 寄木細工

yuriiro 揺色

Z

za 座

Zatō 座当

zōgan 象眼

zōgan-iri zōge tamabuchimaki 象眼入象牙玉縁巻

zōge 象牙

zōge-iri kōki tamabuchimaki 象牙入紅木玉縁巻

zōgemaki 象牙巻

zōge-sukashi tamabuchimaki 象牙すかし玉縁巻

zokugaku 俗楽

zokusō 俗箏

Bibliography

Abraham, Otto and Erich M. von Hornbostel. 1975. Studies on the Tonsystem and Music of the Japanese. Trans. Gertrud Kurath, with William Malm, consultant. In *Hornbostel opera omnia*, eds. Klaus P. Wachsmann, Dieter Christensen and Hans-Peter Reinecke, Vol. 1. The Hague: Martinus Nijhoff. First published in *Sammelbände der Internationalen Musikgesellschaft* 4 (1902-3): 302-60.

Ackermann, Peter. 1979. Towards an Understanding of the Dynamics at Work in *Koto* Music. In *European Studies on Japan*, eds. Ian Nish and Charles Dunn. Tenterden: Paul Norbury Publications.

_____. 1986. *Studien zur Koto-Musik von Edo*. Basel: Bärenreiter Kassel.

_____. 1990. *Kumiuta: Traditional Songs for Certificates; A Study of their Texts and Implications*. Bern: Peter Lang.

Adachi, Fumie, trans. [1913] 1972. *Japanese Design Motifs: 4260 Illustrations of Heraldic Crests*. Reprint, New York: Dover Publications.

Adriaansz, Willem. 1967. Research into the Chronology of Danmono. *Ethnomusicology* 11(1): 25-53.

_____. 1970. A Japanese Procrustean Bed: A Study of the Development of *Danmono*. *Journal of the American Musicological Society* 23(1): 26-60.

_____. 1971. The Yatsuhashi-ryu: A Seventeenth Century School of Koto Music. *Acta Musicologica* 43:55-93.

_____. 1973. *The Kumiuta and Danmono Traditions of Japanese Koto Music*. Berkeley: University of California Press.

_____. 1984. Koto. In *The New Grove Dictionary of Musical Instruments*, ed. Stanley Sadie, Vol. 2. London: Macmillan.

_____. 2001. Koto; Repertory and Social context; Tsukushi-goto; Yatsuhashi-ryū; Ikuta-ryū; Yamada-ryū. In *The New Grove Dictionary of Music and Musicians*. 2nd ed., s.v. Japan, Koto. Ed. Stanley Sadie, Vol. 12. London: Macmillan.

Anderson, Benedict. 1991. *Imagined Communities: Reflections on the Origin and Spread of Nationalism*. Revised edition. London: Verso.

Anderson, Jennifer L. 1987. Japanese Tea Ritual: Religion in Practice. *Man* 22:475-98.

Andō, Masateru. 1982. Koto to jūshichigen ni okeru hatsugen dōsa no jikan teki kaiseki (An Analysis of the Time Elements in the Plucking Movements of the *Koto* and *Jūshichigen*). *Tōkyō Geijutsu Daigaku Ongaku Gakubu Nenshi* 8:45-87.

_____. 1986. *Ikuta-ryū no Sōkyoku* (Ikuta-ryū *Koto* Music). Ed. Kikkawa Eishi. Tokyo: Kōdansha.

Asahi Shinbun. 2002. Traditional Music Stages a Comeback. 17 August. Available at www.asahi.com.

Asquith, Pamela J. and Arne Kalland, eds. 1997. *Japanese Images of Nature: Cultural Perspectives*. Richmond: Curzon.

Aston, W. G., trans. [1896] 1956. *Nihongi: Chronicles of Japan from the Earliest Times to A.D. 697*. Reprint, London: George Allen & Unwin.

Ayer, Christopher Andrew. 1997. Miyagi Michio and his Works for Koto and Shakuhachi. Ph.D. Diss., University of Cincinnati.

Baily, John. 1977. Movement Patterns in Playing the Herati *Dutār*. In *The Anthropology of the Body*, ed. John Blacking. London: Academic Press.

Beasley, W. G. 1990. *The Rise of Modern Japan*. Tokyo: Charles E. Tuttle Company.

Befu, Harumi. 1971. *Japan: An Anthropological Introduction*. San Francisco: Chandler Publishing.

_____. 1980. A Critique of the Group Model of Japanese Society. *Social Analysis* 5/6:29-43.

Ben-Ari, Eyal, Brian Moeran and James Valentine, eds. 1990. *Unwrapping Japan: Society and Culture in Anthropological Perspective*. Manchester: Manchester University Press.

Benedict, Ruth. 1946. *The Chrysanthemum and the Sword: Patterns of Japanese Culture*. Boston: Houghton Mifflin Company.

Bestor, Theodore C. 1989. *Neighborhood Tokyo*. Stanford: Stanford University Press.

Blakemore, Frances. 1978. *Japanese Designs Through Textile Patterns*. New York: Weatherhill.

Burnett, Henry. 1980. An Introduction to the History and Aesthetics of Japanese Jiuta-tegotomono. *Asian Music* 11(2): 11-40.

_____. 1989. Minezaki Kōtō's *Zangetsu*: An Analysis of a Traditional Japanese Chamber Music Composition. *Perspectives of New Music* 27(2): 78-117.

Busōgafu taiseishō. 1805. Ed. Takai Bankan.

Chiba, Junnosuke. 1989a. Hachijūgen. In *Nihon ongaku daijiten* (Japanese Music Dictionary), eds. Hirano Kenji, Kamisangō Yūkō and Gamō Satoaki. Tokyo: Heibonsha.

_____. 1989b. Tangoto. In *Nihon ongaku daijiten* (Japanese Music Dictionary), eds. Hirano Kenji, Kamisangō Yūkō and Gamō Satoaki. Tokyo: Heibonsha.

_____. 1993. Miyagi Michio ga hachijūgen de hiita kyoku (Miyagi Michio's Pieces for the *Hachijūgen*). *Miyagi-kai Kaihō* 156:35-38; 157:32-35; 158:37-42.

_____. 1995. Shō-jūshichigen no kōan to sono shūhen (The Invention of the *Shō-jūshichigen* and its Surroundings). *Tōhō Ongaku Daigaku Kenkyū Kiyō* 10:1-16.

Chiba, Junnosuke and Chiba Yūko, eds. 1993. *Miyagi Michio no sekai: Miyagi Michio seitan 100 nen kinen* (The World of Miyagi Michio: Celebrating One Hundred Years since his Birth). Tokyo: Miyagi Michio Kinenkan.

Chūjō, Nobuyuki and Hotta Toshiko. 1985. *Ikuta-ryū sōkyoku to jiuta sangen* (Ikuta-ryū *Koto* and *Shamisen* Music). Tokyo: Naka Shuppan Purodakushon.

Condit, Jonathan. 1976. Differing Transcriptions from the Twelfth-century Japanese Koto Manuscript *Jinchi Yōroku*. *Ethnomusicology* 20(1): 87-95.

Creighton, Millie. 1997. Consuming Rural Japan: The Marketing of Tradition and Nostalgia in the Japanese Travel Industry. *Ethnology* 36(3): 239-54.

Dale, Peter N. 1986. *The Myth of Japanese Uniqueness*. London: Croom Helm.

Davis, F. Hadland. [1913] 1992. *Myths and Legends of Japan*. Reprint, New York: Dover Publications.

de Ferranti, Hugh. 2000. *Japanese Musical Instruments*. New York: Oxford University Press.

Department of Performing Arts, National Theater of Japan, ed. 1994. *Reconstructed Music Instruments of Ancient East Asia*. Trans. Steven G. Nelson. Tokyo: Japan Art Council.

DeVale, Sue Carole. 1988. Musical Instruments and Ritual: A Systematic Approach. *Journal of the American Musical Instrument Society* 14:126-60.

Doi, Takeo. 1971. *Amae no kōzō* (Structure of Dependence). Tokyo: Kōbundō. Trans. as *The Anatomy of Dependence* by John Bester. Tokyo: Kodansha International, 1973.

Elkinton, Jane. 1990. Koto no ma: The High Context of the Japanese Koto. *Progress Reports in Ethnomusicology* 3(1): 1-22.

Ellingson, Ter. 1992. Notation. In *Ethnomusicology: An Introduction*, ed. Helen Myers. London: The Macmillan Press.

Eppstein, Ury. 1994. *The Beginnings of Western Music in Meiji Era Japan*. Lewiston: The Edwin Mellen Press.

Fairbank, John K., Edwin O. Reischauer and Albert M. Craig. 1973. *East Asia: Tradition and Transformation*. Boston: Houghton Mifflin.

Falconer, Elizabeth. 1990. A New Decade for Hōgaku. *Japan Quarterly* 37(4): 468-78.

_____. 1993. Sawai Kazue, Avant-garde Kotoist. *Japan Quarterly* 40(1): 86-91.

_____. 1995. Koto Lives: Continuity and Conflict in a Japanese Koto School. Ph.D. Diss., University of Iowa.

Fritsch, Ingrid. 1991. The Sociological Significance of Historically Unreliable Documents in the Case of Japanese Musical Guilds. In *Tradition and its Future in Music: Report of SIMS 1990 Ōsaka (The Fourth Symposium of the International Musicological Society)*, ed. Tokumaru Yosihiko et al. Tokyo: Mita Press.

_____. 1996. *Japans blinde Sänger im Schutz der Gottheit Myōon-Benzaiten* (Japan's Blind Singers under the Protection of the Goddess Myōon-Benzaiten). Munich: Iudicium-Verl.

Fujie, Linda. 1986. Matsuri-bayashi of Tokyo: The Role of Supporting Organizations in traditional Music. Ph.D. Diss., Columbia University.

Fujita, Shun'ichi. 1973. *Gendai sankyoku meikan: Sankyoku hyakunen-shi* (Present-day *Sankyoku* Directory: One Hundred Years of *Sankyoku*). Tokyo: Nihon Ongakusha.

Fukumori, Toshiko. 1986. "Rōritsu no Sato". Tokyo: Hōgakusha.

Fukushima, Kazuo and Steven G. Nelson. 1983. *Nihon no gakufu-ten: Tenpyō biwa-fu kara bakumatsu no koteki-fu made* (Music Notations of Japan: From Tenpyō-period *Biwa* Notation to Nineteenth-century Military Notation). Tokyo: Ueno Gakuen Nihon Ongaku Shiryō Shitsu.

Furukawa, Seiji, ed. 1911-12. *Sōkyoku bibō* (*Koto* Music Reminder). Tokyo: Tōkyōdō.

Galliano, Luciana. 2002. *Yōgaku: Japanese Music in the Twentieth Century*. London: The Scarecrow Press.

Garfias, Robert. 1974. Koto Ornamentation Technique in 11th Century Japanese Gagaku. In *Studia instrumentorum musicae popularis III*, ed. Gustaf Hilleström. Stockholm: Nordiska Musikförlaget.

_____. 1975. *Music of a Thousand Autumns: The Tōgaku Style of Japanese Court Music*. Berkeley: University of California Press.

Geertz, Clifford. 1973. *The Interpretation of Cultures*. London: Hutchinson of London.

Green, William. 1985. The Blind of Old Japan As Seen Through the Eyes of Ukiyo-e Artists. *Ukiyo-e Art* 85:1-11.

_____. 2001. Darkness and the Sounds of Music: Blind Musicians of Tokugawa Japan Seen in Ukiyo-e. *Andon* 68:5-23.

Groemer, Gerald. 2001. The Creation of the Edo Outcaste Order. *The Journal of Japanese Studies* 27(2): 263-93.

Gulik, R. H. van. [1940] 1969. *The Lore of the Chinese Lute: An Essay in the Ideology of the Ch'in*. New edition. Tokyo: Sophia University and Charles E. Tuttle.

Gunji, Sumi. 1986. Indication of Timbre in Orally Transmitted Music. In *The Oral and the Literate in Music*, eds. Tokumaru Yosihiko and Yamaguti Osamu. Tokyo: Academia Music.

Gutzwiller, Andreas. 1992. Polyphony in Japanese Music: Rokudan for Example. *CHIME: Journal of the European Foundation for Chinese Music Research* 5:50-57.

Haags Gemeentemuseum. 1975. *Japanese Woodcuts with Music*. Trans. Ruth Koenig. The Hague: Haags Gemeentemuseum.

Hall, John W. and Marius B. Jansen, eds. 1968. *Studies in the Institutional History of Early Modern Japan*. Introduction by Joseph R. Strayer. Princeton: Princeton University Press.

Halliwell, Patrick. 1994a. Learning the Koto. *Canadian University Music Review* 14:18-48.

_____. 1994b. The 'Rokudan Cadence' in Japanese *Koto* Music: A Semiotic Approach to Interpretation. *Music Analysis* 13(1): 73-98.

Harich-Schneider, Eta. 1953. The Present Condition of Japanese Court Music. *The Musical Quarterly* 39(1): 49-74.

_____. 1965. *Rōei: The Medieval Court Songs of Japan*. Tokyo: Sophia University Press.

_____. 1973. *A History of Japanese Music*. London: Oxford University Press.

Hayashi, Kenzō. 1964. *Shōsōin gakki no kenkyū* (A Study of the Musical Instruments of the Shōsōin). Tokyo: Kazama Shobō.

Hendry, Joy. 1987. *Understanding Japanese Society*. London: Croom Helm.

_____. 1993. *Wrapping Culture: Politeness, Presentation and Power in Japan and other Societies*. Oxford: Clarendon Press.

Hendry, Joy and Jonathan Webber, eds. 1986. *Interpreting Japanese Society: Anthropological Approaches*. Journal of the Anthropological Society of Oxford Occasional Papers No. 5. Oxford: Journal of the Anthropological Society of Oxford.

Hibi, Sadao and Niwa Motoji. 2001. *Snow, Wave, Pine: Traditional Patterns in Japanese Design*. Tokyo: Kodansha International.

Higa, Etsuko. 1992 Okinawa no gakki (Okinawa Musical Instruments). In *Ryūkyū geinō jiten* (Ryūkyū Arts Dictionary), ed. Naha Shuppansha Henshūbu. Naha: Naha Shuppansha.

Hikone-jō Hakubutsukan, ed. 1996. *Nihon no gakki: Orinasu oto, miyabi no sekai* (Japanese Musical Instruments: Woven Sound in an Elegant World). Hikone: Hikone-shi Kyōiku Iin-kai.

Hirano, Kenji, ed. 1978. *Rokudan: Nihon ongaku no miryoku o saguru – Sono 1* (Rokudan: Discover Japanese Classical Music – Series 1). Editorial assistance by Mabuchi Usaburō; commentary and transcriptions by Kubota Satoko. Tokyo: Toshiba EMI, TH-60054-55.

_____. 1989a. Concerning the Names of *Koto* Tunings. *Tōyō Ongaku Kenkyū* 54:20-27.

_____, ed. 1989b. Sōkyoku denshō keifu (Lineage of the Transmission of *Koto* Music). In *Nihon ongaku daijiten* (Japanese Music Dictionary), s.v. Keizu (Genealogical Tables). Eds. Hirano Kenji, Kamisangō Yūkō and Gamō Satoaki. Tokyo: Heibonsha.

Hirano, Kenji and Fukushima Kazuo, eds. 1978. *Sources of Early Japanese Music: Specimens of Early Notation in Facsimile*. Tokyo: Benseisha.

Hirano, Kenji, Kamisangō Yūkō and Gamō Satoaki, eds. 1989. *Nihon ongaku daijiten* (Japanese Music Dictionary). Tokyo: Heibonsha.

Hirano, Kenji and Kubota Satoko. 1989. Gendai no sōkyoku no ryūha (Present-day Traditions of *Koto* Music). In *Nihon ongaku daijiten* (Japanese Music Dictionary), s.v. Sōkyoku. Eds. Hirano Kenji, Kamisangō Yūkō and Gamō Satoaki. Tokyo: Heibonsha.

Hirano, Kenji and Tanigaitō Kazuko. 1980. Jiuta sōkyoku-ka no kengyō tōkan-nen: Mōjin sho-shorui, omotebikae, zakudaribikae ni mirareru mōjin ongaku-ka no keifu (Dates of Assignments of the Title Kengyō to *Jiuta Sōkyoku* Musicians: Genealogy of Blind Musicians Constructed on the Basis of Information from *Mōjin sho-shorui, Omotebikae, and Zakudaribikae*). *Tōyō Ongaku Kenkyū* 45:23-69.

Hirata, Tsutomu. 1994. Fukuyama koto no dekiru made (The Manufacturing Process of Fukuyama *Koto*). In *Nihon koto hajime: Fukuyama koto e no nagare* (The Beginnings of the Japanese *Koto*: The Transmission of Fukuyama *Koto*), ed. Hiroshima Kenritsu Rekishi Hakubutsukan. Fukuyama: Hiroshima Kenritsu Rekishi Hakubutsukan.

_____. 1996. Gakki zukuri no konjaku: Koto no seisaku ni miru zairyō, gijutsu, tsukurite no kokoro (Making Musical Instruments Past and Present: Materials, Techniques, and Makers' Ideas on *Koto* Manufacture). In *Oto no konjaku* (Past and Present Sounds), eds. Sakurai Tetsuo and Yamaguchi Osamu. Tokyo: Kōbundō.

Hirata, Tsutomu and Kaihara Shōzō. 1988. Koto no hibiki (The Sound of the *Koto*). Ed. Kitamura Toshirō. Fukuyama: Fukuyama Hōgakki Seizōgyō Kyōdō Kumiai.

Hiroshima Kenritsu Kōgei Shikenjō. 1987. *Fukuyama koto no seisaku gihō* (The Technique of Manufacturing Fukuyama *Koto*). Fukuyama: Hiroshima Kenritsu Kōgei Shikenjō.

Hobsbawm, Eric. 1983. Introduction: Inventing Traditions. In *The Invention of Tradition*, ed. Eric Hobsbawm and Terence Ranger. Cambridge: Cambridge University Press.

Hobsbawm, Eric and Terence Ranger, eds. 1983. *The Invention of Tradition*. Cambridge: Cambridge University Press.

Hōgaku Jānaru, ed. 2001. Shin wagakki daishūgō! (Selection of New Traditional Japanese Musical Instruments!). *Hōgaku Jānaru* 175:52-54.

Holvik, Leonard C. 1992. Echoes and Shadows: Integration and Purpose in the Words of the Koto Composition "Fuki." *The Journal of Japanese Studies* 18(2): 445-77.

Hornbostel, Erich M. von and Curt Sachs. [1914] 1961. Classification of Musical Instruments. Trans. Anthony Baines and Klaus P. Wachsmann. *The Galpin Society Journal* 14:3-29. First published in *Zeitschrift für Ethnologie* 46 (1914): 553-90.

Howe, Sondra Wieland. 1997. *Luther Whiting Mason: International Music Educator*. Warren, Michigan: Harmonie Park Press.

Hsu, Francis L. K. 1975. *Iemoto: The Heart of Japan*. New York: John Wiley & Sons.

Hughes, David W. 1985. The Heart's Home Town: Traditional Folk Song in Modern Japan. Ph.D. Diss., University of Michigan.

_____. 1988. Music Archaeology of Japan: Data and Interpretation. In *The Archaeology of Early Music Cultures*, ed. Ellen Hickmann and David W. Hughes. Bonn: Verlag für systematische Musikwissenschaft.

Hunter, Janet. 1989. *The Emergence of Modern Japan: An Introductory History Since 1853*. London: Longman.

Inoue, Kochō. 1911. *Ikuta-ryū sōkyoku shinpu* (New Notation for Ikuta-ryū *Koto* Music). 3rd ed. Fukuoka: Sōkyoku Tsūshin Kyōjusho.

_____. 1917. *Tsūshin kyōju sōkyoku kōgi roku: Yamada-ryū dai ichi hen* (Correspondence Course in *Koto* Music: First Book for the Yamada-ryū). Tokyo: Sōkyoku Tsūshin Kyōjusho.

Jansen, Marius B. 1992. *China in the Tokugawa World*. Cambridge: Harvard University Press.

Jinchi yōroku. 1192. Comp. Fujiwara no Moronaga.

Jinrinkinmōzui (Illustrations of Everyday Life). [1690] 1990. Reprint, with notes by Asakura Haruhiko. Tokyo Bunko 519. Tokyo: Heibonsha.

Johnson, Henry. 1993. The Symbolism of the *Koto*: An Ethnomusicology of the Form and Function of a Traditional Japanese Musical Instrument. 2 vols., Ph.D. Diss., University of Oxford.

_____. 1996a. A Survey of Present-day Japanese Concepts and Classifications of Musical Instruments. *Musicology Australia* 19:16-39.

_____. 1996b. *Koto* Manufacture: The Instrument, Construction Process, and Aesthetic Considerations. *The Galpin Society Journal* 49:38-64.

_____. 1996-97. A *Koto* by Any Other Name: Exploring Japanese Systems of Musical Instrument Classification. *Asian Music* 28(1): 43-59.

_____. 1997. The *Koto*: Musical Instrument, Material Culture, and Meaning. *Journal of the American Musical Instrument Society* 23:56-93.

_____. 1999. Japanese Collections of Traditional Japanese Musical Instruments: Presentation and Representation. *Musicology Australia* 22:46-62.

_____. 2002. Invented Traditions of *Koto* Notation from the Meiji Period. *Asian Musicology* 2:69-88.

_____. 2003. Traditions Old and New: Continuity, Change, and Innovation in Japanese *Koto*-related Zithers. *Journal of the American Musical Instrument Society* 29:181-229.

_____. 2004. The *Koto*, Traditional Music, and an Idealized Japan: Cultural Nationalism in Music Performance and Education. In *Japanese Cultural Nationalism: At Home and Abroad*, ed. Roy Starrs. Folkestone: Global Oriental.

Joly, Henri L. 1908. *Legend in Japanese Art: A Description of Historical Episodes Legendary Characters, Folk-lore Myths, Religious Symbolism Illustrated in the Arts of old Japan*. London: Kegan Paul, Trench, Trubner.

Kamisangō, Yūkō. 1979. Fukugen sareta "maboroshi no gakki" hachijūgen (Reconstruction of the Visionary *Hachijūgen*). *Kikan Hōgaku* 19:50-52.

_____. 1986. Oral and Literate Aspects of Tradition Transmission in Japanese Music: With Emphasis on *Syōga* [*Shōga*] and *Hakase*. In *The Oral and the Literate in Music*, ed. Tokumaru Yosihiko and Yamaguti Osamu. Tokyo: Academia Music.

Kartomi, Margaret J. 1990. *On Concepts and Classifications of Musical Instruments*. Chicago: University of Chicago Press.

Kasai, Harue, ed. 1999. *Tsugaru sōkyoku Ikuta-ryū no shiori* (A Guide to Tsugaru Ikuta-ryū *Koto* Music). Aomori: Kasai Harue.

Katō, Yasuaki. 1974. *Nihon mōjin shakai shi kenkyū* (The History of the Blind in Japanese Society). Tokyo: Miraisha.

Katō, Jō and Ueno Masaaki. 2002. Koto no gakufu ni tsuite (About *Koto* Notation). In *Hōgaku koto hajime: Kyō kara no jugyō no tame ni* (Introduction to the *Koto* and Traditional Japanese Music: For Today's Lesson), ed. Yamaguchi Osamu and Tanaka Kenji. Tokyo: Kawai.

Katsumura, Jinko. 1986. Some Innovations in Musical Instruments of Japan during the 1920's. *Yearbook for Traditional Music* 18:157-72.

Kawada, Junzō. 1986. Verbal and Non-verbal Sounds: Some Considerations of the Basis of Oral Transmission of Music. In *The Oral and the Literate in Music*, ed. Tokumaru Yosihiko and Yamaguti Osamu. Tokyo: Academia Music.

Kichimi, Shōsuke, ed. 1984. *Suzuki Koson: Sōkyoku Kyōgoku-ryū gendai hōgaku no senkusha* (Suzuki Koson: The Kyōgoku-ryū, A Forerunner of Modern Japanese Music). Tokyo: Hōgakusha.

Kikkawa, Eishi. 1961. Notes for *Sōkyoku to jiuta no rekishi* (The History of *Sōkyoku* and *Jiuta*). SLR-510-13. Tokyo: Victor.

_____. 1967. Yatsuhashi-ryū sōkyoku ni tsuite (About Yatsuhashi-ryū *Koto* Music). In *Sōkyoku to jiuta* (*Sōkyoku* and *Jiuta*), ed. Tōyō Ongaku Gaku-kai. Tokyo: Ongaku no Tomosha.

_____, ed. 1984a. *Hōgaku hyakka jiten: Gagaku kara min'yō made* (Encyclopedia of Traditional Japanese Music: From *Gagaku* to Folk Music). Tokyo: Ongaku no Tomosha.

_____. 1984b. *Vom Charakter der japanischen Musik* (*Nihon ongaku no seikaku*). Basel: Bärenreiter Kassel.

_____. 1986. The Musical Sense of the Japanese – The Wind in the Pines, the Sounds of Insects, *Ashirai*. *Aesthetics* 2:1-9.

_____, ed. 1992. *Zusetsu nihon no gakki* (Japanese Musical Instruments Illustrated). Ed. Kojima Tomiko, Fujii Tomoaki and Miyazaki Mayumi. Tokyo: Tōkyō Shoseki.

_____. 1997. *A History of Japanese Koto Music and Ziuta* [*Jiuta*]. Trans. and supplemented by Leonard C. Holvik; ed. Yamaguti Osamu. Tokyo: Mita Press.

Kikuhara, Hatsuko. 1987. Fuki. In *Nogawa-ryū, Ikuta-ryū, jiuta sōkyoku kumiuta gakufu zenshū* (The Complete *Koto* Works of Nogawa-ryū, Ikuta-ryū), ed. Kubota Satoko; commentary by Hirano Kenji. Tokyo: Hakusuisha.

Kikuyoshi, Shūchō. 1901. *Sōkyoku kyōkasho shin'an gakufu* (*Koto* Music Text Book with New Style Notation). n.p.

Kinden-ryū Taishōgoto Zenkoku Fukyū-kai, ed. 1995. *Daredemo hikeru: O-koto no tebiki* (Anybody Can Play: *Koto* Guidance). Nagano: Nihon Baiorin Kenkyūsho.

Kinkyoku shifu (Guide on *Koto* Music Notation). 1772. Ed. Gensui. Published in 1780.

Kinkyoku shō (Collection of *Koto* Pieces). 1695. Published by Umemura Yaemon, Ozaki Shichizaemon and Matsuba Seishirō.

Kishibe, Shigeo. 1967. Koto no tsukurikata (*Koto* Manufacture). In *Sōkyoku to jiuta* (*Sōkyoku* and *Jiuta*), ed. Tōyō Ongaku Gaku-kai. Tokyo: Ongaku no Tomosha.

_____. 1971. Means of Preservation and Diffusion of Traditional Music in Japan. *Asian Music* 2(1): 8-13.

_____, ed. 1973. *Yamada-ryū sōkyoku shi* (A History of the Yamada-ryū). Ed. Hirano Kenji. Tokyo: Yamada-ryū Sōkyoku Kyōkai.

_____, ed. 1975. *Tsugaru no ko sōkyoku: Ikuta-ryū* (Old *Koto* Music of Tsugaru: Ikuta-ryū). Commentary by Kishibe Shigeo and Sasamori Takefusa. Nihon Fonoguramu, PH-8506-7.

_____. 1982a. Seisaku (Manufacture). In *Ongaku daijiten* (Dictionary of Music), s.v. Sō. Ed. Shimonaka Kunihiko, Vol. 3. Tokyo: Heibonsha.

_____. 1982b. *The Traditional Music of Japan*. 2nd ed. Tokyo: The Japan Foundation.

_____. 1984. *Tenpyō no hibiki: Shōsōin no gakki* (Sounds of the Tenpyō Era: Musical Instruments of the Shōsōin). Tokyo: Ongaku no Tomosha.

Kishibe, Shigeo and Hirano Kenji. 1971. Tsukushigoto chōsa hōkoku (Research Report on the Tsukushigoto). *Tōyō Ongaku Kenkyū* 26-29:145-210.

Kishibe, Shigeo, Kondō Yukiko, and Kishibe Momoyo. 1971. Yamada Kengyō no shōgai to jiseki (The Life and Achievements of Yamada Kengyō). *Tōyō Ongaku Kenkyū* 26-29:1-64.

Kishibe, Shigeo and Sasamori Takefusa. 1976. *Tsugaru sōkyoku Ikuta-ryū no kenkyū: Rekishihen* (A Study of Tsugaru Ikuta-ryū *Koto* Music: Its History). Hirosaki: Tsugaru Shobō.

Koizumi, Fumio. 1977. Musical Scales in Japanese Music. In *Asian Musics in an Asian Perspective: Report of Asian Traditional Performing Arts 1976*, ed. Koizumi Fumio, Tokumaru Yoshihiko and Yamaguchi Osamu; assistant ed., Richard Emmert. Tokyo: Heibonsha.

Komiya, Toyotaka, ed. 1956. *Japanese Music and Drama in the Meiji Era*. Trans. and adapted by Edward G. Seidensticker and Donald Keene. Tokyo: Ōbunsha.

Koop, Albert J. and Inada Hogitarō. [1923] 1960. *Japanese Names and How to Read Them: A Manual for Art-collectors and Students*. Reprint, London: Routledge and Kegan Paul.

Kraus, Alexandre *fils*. 1878. *La musique au Japon*. Florence: Imprimerie de L'Arte della Stampa.

Kubota, Satoko. 1974. Mōjin ongaku-ka no keifu: Sandai seki no jiuta sōkyoku-ka o chūshin ni (Genealogies of Blind Musicians: With Emphasis on the *Jiuta Sōkyoku* Musicians who appear in *Sandai seki*). *Ryūkoku Daigaku Ronshū* 404:153-88.

_____. 1980. Sōkyoku ni okeru gagaku (The Influence of *Gagaku* on *Koto* Music). *Gagaku-kai* 55:90-102.

_____. 1983. A Guide to the Basic Literature and Records for Research in Jiuta and Sokyoku. *Hogaku* 1(1): 93-112.

_____. 1984. Koto. In *Hōgaku hyakka jiten: Gagaku kara min'yō made* (Encyclopedia of Traditional Japanese Music: From *Gagaku* to Folk Music), ed. Kikkawa Eishi. Tokyo: Ongaku no Tomosha.

_____. 1988. Sō shamisen ongaku no gakufu shuppan to kifu taikei (Systems of Notation and the Publication of *Koto* and *Shamisen* Music). In *Nihon no ongaku: Ajia no ongaku* (Japanese Music: Asian Music), ed. Gamō Satoaki et al., Vol. 4. Tokyo: Iwanami Shoten.

Kumakura, Isao. 1981. The *Iemoto* System in Japanese Society. *Japan Foundation Newsletter* 9(4): 1-7.

Kyrova, Magda et al. 2000. *The Ear Catches the Eye: Music in Japanese Prints*. Leiden: Hotei Publishing.

Lebra, Takie Sugiyama. 1976. *Japanese Patterns of Behavior*. Honolulu: University Press of Hawaii.

Lee, Sherman E. 1981. *The Genius of Japanese Design*. Tokyo: Kodansha International.

Lehmann, Jean-Pierre. 1982. *The Roots of Modern Japan*. London: The Macmillan Press.

Lieberman, Fredric. 1971. Music in *The Tale of Genji*. *Asian Music* 2(1): 39-42.

Loeb, David. 1976. An Analytic Study of Japanese Koto Music. *Music Forum* 4:335-93.

Mabuchi, Usaburō. 1991. Source Criticism and Interpretation in Historical Research on Japanese Music with Reference to the *Kajō-theory* of Tominaga Nakamoto. In *Tradition and its Future in Music: Report of SIMS 1990 Ōsaka (the Fourth Symposium of the International Musicological Society)*, ed. Tokumaru Yosihiko et al. Tōkyō: Mita Press.

Machida, Ōen. 1896. *Koto shamisen hitori geiko* (Self-Study in *Koto* and *Shamisen*). Tokyo: Tōundō.

_____. 1914. *Kinkyoku hitori manabi* (Self-Study in *Koto*). Tokyo: Seirindō.

Makimoto Gakki. 1977. *Makimoto shōhō* (Makimoto Bulletin). Brochure. Fukuyama: Makimoto Gakki.

_____. n.d. *Koto/sangen*. Unpaginated brochure (collected in 1994). Fukuyama: Makimoto Gakki.

Malm, William, P. 1971. The Modern Music of Meiji Japan. In *Tradition and Modernization in Japanese Culture*, ed. Donald H. Shively. Princeton: Princeton University Press.

_____. 2000. *Traditional Japanese Music and Musical Instruments*. New edition. Tokyo: Kodansha International. Originally published as *Japanese Music and Musical Instruments*, 1959.

Markham, Elizabeth J. 1983. *Saibara: Japanese Court Songs of the Heian Period*. 2 vols. Cambridge: Cambridge University Press.

Mathews, Gordon. 2000. *Global Culture/Individual Identity: Searching for Home in the Cultural Supermarket*. London: Routledge.

May, Elizabeth. 1963. *The Influence of the Meiji Period on Japanese Children's Music*. Berkeley: University of California Press.

McClain, Yoko Matsuoka. 1981. *Handbook of Modern Japanese Grammar: Including Lists of Words and Expressions with English Equivalents for Reading Aid*. Tokyo: The Hokuseido Press.

McCormack, Gavan. 2002. New Tunes for an Old Song: Nationalism and Identity in post-Cold War Japan. In *Nations Under Siege: Globalization and Nationalism in Asia*, ed. Roy Starrs. New York: Palgrave.

McCullough, Helen Craig, trans. 1988. *The Tale of the Heike*. Stanford: Stanford University Press.

Miki, Minoru. 1996. *Nihon gakkihō* (Techniques of Japanese Musical Instruments). Tokyo: Ongaku no Tomosha.

Mishima Gakki. n.d. *Koto/sangen*. Unpaginated brochure (collected in 1997). Fukuyama: Mishima Gakki.

Mitani, Yōko. 1980. *Higashi ajia kinsō no kenkyū* (A Study of East Asian Zithers). Tokyo: Zen'on Gakufu Shuppansha.

Miyagi, Michio. 1996. *Ikuta-ryū sōkyoku senshū: 1* (Selected Works of Ikuta-ryū *Koto* Music: 1). 47th ed. Tokyo: Hōgakusha.

Miyazaki, Mayumi. 1972. Tsukushigoto no seiritsu katei ni tsuite no kenkyū (A Study of the Formation of Tsukushigoto). *Ongakugaku* 17:169-85.

_____. 1979. Koto no jidaiteki hensen ni kan suru ikkōsatsu: Ii-ka denrai shiryō 35 ten no chōsa to bunseki (A Historical Study on the Style of *Koto*: Investigation and Analysis of the 35 *Koto* Handed Down by the Ii Family). In *Musashino Ongaku Daigaku Kenkyū Kiyō XII*, ed. Musashino Ongaku Daigaku Kiyō Iin-kai. Tokyo: Musashino Ongaku Daigaku.

_____. 1993. *Haniwa no gakki: Gakkishi kara mita kōko shiryō* (*Haniwa* Musical Instruments: Historical and Archaeological data). Tokyo: Sankōsha.

_____. 1995. Tsukushigoto no sōhō ni tsuite (Ways of Playing Tsukushigoto). *Miyazaki Daigaku Kyōiku Gakubu Kiyō* 78:55-72.

Mizuhara, Getsudō. 2000. Gakkō kyōzaiyō kogatagoto (Small-size *Koto* for Use in Primary Education). *Hōgaku Jānaru* 165:60.

Moeran, Brian. 1987. The Art World of Contemporary Japanese Ceramics. *The Journal of Japanese Studies* 13(1): 27-50.

Momotari, Noboru. 1894. *Kinkyoku no shiori* (*Koto* Music Guide Book). Tokyo: Hakubunkan.

Monbushō Ongaku Torishirabe Gakari, ed. 1881-84. *Shōgaku shōka shū* (Collection of Elementary School Songs). 3 vols. Tokyo: Tōkyō Ongaku Gakkō.

Morris, Ivan, trans. 1971. *The Tale of Genji Scroll*. Introduction by Tokugawa Yoshinobu. Tokyo: Kodansha International.

Mouer, Ross and Sugimoto Yoshio. 1986. *Images of Japanese Society: A Study in the Social Construction of Reality*. London: KPI.

Murasaki, Shikibu. 1976. *The Tale of Genji*. Trans. with Introduction by Edward G. Seidensticker. Harmondsworth: Penguin Books.

Musashino Ongaku Daigaku Gakki Hakubutsukan, ed. 1969. *Musashino ongaku daigaku gakki hakubutsukan mokuroku 1* (Musashino Academia Musicae, Museum of Musical Instruments, Catalogue 1). Catalogued by Kikuchi Shun'ichi and Yamaguchi Osamu. Tokyo: Musashino Ongaku Daigaku.

_____. 1974. *Musashino Ongaku Daigaku Gakki Hakubutsukan Mokuroku 2* (Musashino Academia Musicae, Museum of Musical Instruments, Catalogue 2). Catalogued by Kikuchi Shun'ichi and Yamaguchi Osamu. Tokyo: Musashino Ongaku Daigaku.

_____. 1979. *Musashino Ongaku Daigaku Gakki Hakubutsukan Mokuroku 3* (Musashino Academia Musicae, Museum of Musical Instruments, Catalogue 3). Tokyo: Musashino Ongaku Daigaku.

_____. 1985. *Musashino Ongaku Daigaku Gakki Hakubutsukan Mokuroku 4* (Musashino Academia Musicae, Museum of Musical Instruments, Catalogue 4). Tokyo: Musashino Ongaku Daigaku.

_____. 1989. *Musashino Ongaku Daigaku Gakki Hakubutsukan Mokuroku 5* (Musashino Academia Musicae, Museum of Musical Instruments, Catalogue 5). Tokyo: Musashino Ongaku Daigaku.

_____. 1995. *Musashino Ongaku Daigaku Gakki Hakubutsukan Mokuroku 6* (Musashino Academia Musicae, Museum of Musical Instruments, Catalogue 6). Tokyo: Musashino Ongaku Daigaku.

_____. 1996. *Kaleidoscope I*. Tokyo: Musashino Ongaku Daigaku.

Nakajima, Keiko and Kubota Satoko. 1984. *Nihon geinō seminā: Sō shamisen ongaku* (Japanese Entertainments Seminar: *Sō* and *Shamisen* Music). Ed. Hirano Kenji; revised by Suyama Chigyō. Tokyo: Hakusuisha.

Nakane, Chie. 1970. *Japanese Society*. London: Weidenfeld and Nicolson.

Nakanoshima, Kin'ichi. 1956. *Te hodoki kyōsoku hon* (Playing Techniques Guide Book). Tokyo: Hōgakusha.

_____. 1996. "Rokudan no Shirabe" ("Investigation in Six Sections"). Tokyo: Hōgakusha.

Nakao, Hidehiro. 2001. The Sun also Rises? What the New Governor of Tokyo Symbolizes. In *Asian Nationalism in an Age of Globalization*, ed. Roy Starrs. London: Curzon Press.

Nakashima, Utashito, ed. 1966. "Chidori no Kyoku" ("Song of Plovers"). Osaka: Maekawa Shuppansha.

Nelson, Andrew Nathaniel. 1974. *The Modern Reader's Japanese-English Character Dictionary*. Second rev. ed. Tokyo: Charles E. Tuttle.

Nelson, John K. 2000. *Enduring Identities: The Guise of Shinto in Contemporary Japan*. Honolulu: University of Hawai'i Press.

Nelson, Steven G. 1986. *Documentary Sources of Japanese Music*. Supervision by Fukushima Kazuo. Tokyo: Research Archives for Japanese Music, Ueno Gakuen College.

Nihon Gagaku-kai. 1979. *Sō fu* (*Sō* Notation). Fujisawa: Nihon Gagaku-kai.

Nippon Gakujutsu Shinkokai, ed. [1940] 1965. *The Manyōshū: The Nippon Gakujutsu Shinkōkai Translation of One Thousand Poems with the Texts in Romaji*. Foreword by Donald Keene. Reprint, New York: Columbia University Press.

Nishiyama, Matsunosuke. 1997. *Edo Culture: Daily Life and Diversions in Urban Japan, 1600-1868*. Trans. and ed. Gerald Groemer. Honolulu: University of Hawai'i Press.

Nogawa, Mihoko. 1994. Sō. In *Nyūgurōbu sekai ongaku daijiten* (The New Grove Dictionary of World Music). Supervised by Shibata Minao and Tōyama Kazuyuki, Vol. 12. Tokyo: Kōdansha.

Nosaka, Keiko. 1996. Ichion no hibiki o motomete (Seeking One Sound). *Hōgaku Jānaru* 119:18-19.

Obata, Jūichi and Sugita Eizi. 1931. Acoustical Investigations of Some Japanese Musical Instruments. Part IV. The *Koto*, A Thirteen-stringed Instrument. *Proceedings of the Physico-Mathematical Society of Japan*, 3rd Series, 13(5): 133-50.

Ogawa Gakki Seizō. 1990-93. *Ogawa no wagakki/sōgiri tansu sōgō katarogu* (Ogawa Japanese Musical Instruments/*Kiri* Drawers General Catalogue). Fukuyama: Ogawa Gakki Seizō.

_____. 1997-2004. *Ogawa no wagakki/sōgiri tansu sōgō katarogu* (Ogawa Japanese Musical Instruments/*Kiri* Drawers General Catalogue). Fukuyama: Ogawa Gakki Seizō.

Ohnuki-Tierney, Emiko. 1987. *The Monkey as Mirror: Symbolic Transformations in Japanese History and Ritual*. Princeton: Princeton University Press.

_____. 1993. *Rice as Self. Japanese Identities through Time*. Princeton: Princeton University Press.

Oka, Hideyuki. 1967. *How to Wrap Five Eggs*. Foreword: George Nelson. New York: Harper & Row.

_____. 1975. *How to Wrap Five More Eggs*. New York: Weatherhill.

_____. 1988. The Embodiment of Spirit: Reflections on Japan's Packaging Traditions. Unpaginated introduction to *The Art of Japanese Packages*, catalogue for Canadian tour of an exhibition of the same name. Québec: Musée de la Civilisation.

Okinawa Prefectural Board of Education, ed. 1998. *Cultural Properties of Okinawa. Part IV: Mukei/minzoku bunkazai*. Naha: Okinawa Prefectural Museum.

Okinawa Sōkyoku Hozon-kai, ed. 1995. *Kunkunshi*. Ginowan: Okinawa Sōkyoku Hozon-kai.

Olsen, Dale A. 1980. Japanese Music in Peru. *Asian Music* 11(2): 41-51.

_____. 1983. Japanese Music in Brazil. *Asian Music* 14(1): 111-31.

O'Neill, P. G. 1984. Organization and Authority in the Traditional Arts. *Modern Asian Studies* 18(4): 631-45.

Ortolani, Benito. 1969. *Iemoto*. *Japan Quarterly* 16(3): 297-306.

Ōsaka Ongaku Daigaku Fuzoku Gakki Hakubutsukan, ed. 1984. *Ōsaka ongaku daigaku fuzoku gakki hakubutsukan mokuroku* (Osaka College of Music Musical Instrument Museum Catalogue). Osaka: Gakkō Hōjin Ōsaka Ongaku Daigaku.

_____. 1998. *Ōsaka ongaku daigaku fuzoku gakki hakubutsukan mokuroku* (Osaka College of Music Musical Instrument Museum Catalogue). Osaka: Gakkō Hōjin Ōsaka Ongaku Daigaku.

Ōshima, Shizuko. 1929. *Sōkyoku shō* (Collection of *Koto* Pieces). Tokyo: Kinkōdō.

Parisi, Lynn, Sara Thompson and Anne Stevens. 1995. *Meiji Japan: The Dynamics of National Change*. Boulder: Social Science Education Consortium.

Pecore, Joanna T. 2000. Bridging Contexts, Transforming Music: The Case of Elementary School Teacher Chihara Yoshio. *Ethnomusicology* 44(1): 120-36.

Philippi, Donald L., trans. 1968. *Kojiki*. With an Introduction and Notes. Tokyo: University of Tokyo Press.

Picken, Laurence E. R. 2000. How the Tōgaku Repertory was Acquired by the Japanese; and the Processes of 'Acculturation' that Followed Its Acquisition. In *Music from the Tang Court 7: Some Ancient Connections Explored*, ed. Laurence E. R. Picken and Noël Nickson. Cambridge: Cambridge University Press.

Picken, Laurence E. R. and Mitani Yōko. 1979. Finger-techniques for the Zithers *Sō-no-koto* and *Kin* in Heian Times. In *Musica Asiatica* 2, ed. Laurence E. R. Picken. London: Oxford University Press.

Piggott, Francis. T. 1891. The Music of the Japanese. *Transactions of the Asiatic Society of Japan* 19(2): 271-367.

_____. 1892. The Music of Japan. *Proceedings of the Musical Association*. Eighteenth Session, 1891-92. London: Novello, Ewer and Co.

_____. [1909] 1971. *The Music and Musical Instruments of Japan*. 2nd edition. With Notes by T. L. Southgate. Reprint, New York: Da Capo Press. First published in 1893.

Prescott, Anne Elizabeth. 1997. Miyagi Michio - The Father of Modern Koto Music: His Life, Works and Innovations, and the Environment which Enabled his Reforms. Ph.D. Diss., Kent State University.

Read, Cathleen B. 1975. A Study of Yamada-ryū Sōkyoku and Its Repertoire. Ph.D. Diss., Wesleyan University.

Read, Cathleen B. and David L. Locke. 1983. An Analysis of the Yamada-ryu Sokyoku Iemoto System. *Hogaku* 1(1): 20-52.

Reese, Heinz-Dieter. 1987. Review of *Japanese Music: An Annotated Bibliography*, by Tsuge Gen'ichi. *The World of Music* 29(2): 75-77.

Sakamoto, Katoko. 1945. *Sōkyoku kōgiroku* (*Koto* Music Lectures). 60th ed. Fukuoka: Dai Nippon Katei Ongaku-kai.

Sanada, Shin. 1970. *Sōkyoku Yatsuhashi-ryū zenshū* (The *Koto* Works of Yatsuhashi-ryū). Commentary by Kikkawa Eishi. Tōshiba TH-7069-71.

Sanada, Yoshiko. 1980. *Koto no ie: Yatsuhashi-ryū sōkyoku no keifu* (The Home of *Koto*: Genealogy of Yatsuhashi-ryū). Nagano: Fūkeisha.

Seigle, Cecilia Segawa. 1993. *Yoshiwara: The Glittering World of the Japanese Courtesan*. Honolulu: University of Hawaii Press.

Sestili, Daniele. 2002. A Pioneer Work on Japanese Music: *La musique au Japon* (1878) and Its Author, Alessandro Kraus the Younger. *Asian Music* 33(2): 83-110.

Shadan Hōjin Nihon Sankyoku Kyōkai, Gakkō Ongaku Sankyoku Fukyū no Kai, ed. 1976. *Sankyoku no kihon to shidō* (Foundation and Guidance in *Sankyoku*). Ed. Hirano Kenji. Tokyo: Kōdansha.

Shichiku shoshinshū (Collection of Pieces for Beginners of String and Bamboo Instruments). 1664. Ed. Nakamura Sōsan.

Shōsōin, ed. 1967. *Shōsōin no gakki* (Music Instruments of the Shōsōin). Tokyo: Nihon Keizai Shinbunsha.

_____. 1989. *Shōsōin hōmotsu* (Treasures of the Shōsōin). Tokyo: Asahi Shinbunsha.

Siebold, Philipp Franz von. 1852. *Nippon. Archiv zur Beschreibung von Japan und dessen Neben- und Schutzländern*. Leyden: Verfasser.

Small, Christopher. 1987. Performance as Ritual: Sketch for an Enquiry into the True Nature of a Symphony Concert. In *Lost in Music: Culture, Style and the Musical Event*, ed. Avron Levine White. London: Routledge & Kegan Paul.

Sōkyoku taiishō (General Selection of *Koto* Music). [1779] 1903. Ed. Yamada Shōkoku. Nagoya: Eitō Shoten.

Starrs, Roy. 2001. Introduction. In *Asian Nationalism in an Age of Globalization*, ed. Roy Starrs. London: Japan Library.

Stockmann, Doris. 1991. Interdisciplinary Approaches to the Study of Musical Communication Structures. In *Comparative Musicology and Anthropology of Music: Essays on the History of Ethnomusicology*, ed. Bruno Nettl and Philip V. Bohlman. Chicago: University of Chicago Press.

Sugimoto, Yoshio. 1997. *An Introduction to Japanese Society*. Cambridge: Cambridge University Press.

Sugimoto, Yoshio and Ross E. Mouer, eds. 1989. *Constructs for Understanding Japan*. London: Kegan Paul International.

Sumita, Hiroshi, producer. 1986. *Shirīzu nihon no dentō kōgei dai 11-kan wagakki (gagaku, koto, sangen)* (Japanese Traditional Arts and Crafts Series, No. 11, Japanese Musical Instruments [*Gagaku* Musical Instruments, *Koto*, *Sangen*]). Tokyo: Riburio.

Suzuki, Koson. 1910. *Sōkyoku kōbai* (Red Blossom *Koto* Music). Tokyo: Kinkodō.

Takamatsu, Baisō, ed. 1907. *Sōkyoku shinpu: Shichidan Hachidan* (New Notation *Koto* Music: "Shichidan" ["Investigation in Seven Sections"], "Hachidan" ["Investigation in Eight Sections"]). Osaka: Sōkyoku Kyōfū-kai.

Tanabe, Hisao. 1919. *Nihon ongaku kōwa* (Lecture on Japanese Music). Tokyo: Iwanami Shoten.

_____. 1931. Music in Japan. In *Western Influences in Modern Japan: A Series of Papers on Cultural Relations*, ed. Nitobe Inazo et al. Chicago: University of Chicago Press.

_____. 1964. *Nihon no gakki* (Japanese Musical Instruments). Tokyo: Sōshisha.

_____. 1974. Miyagi Michio ni yoru gakki kairyō (Miyagi Michio's Improvements to Musical Instruments). *Kikan Hōgaku* 1:54-57.

Tanabe, Hisao and Hirano Kenji. 1982. Nihon no sō (The Japanese Sō). In *Ongaku daijiten* (Dictionary of Music), s.v. Sō. Ed. Shimonaka Kunihiko, Vol. 3. Tokyo: Heibonsha.

Tanigaitō, Kazuko. 1989. Jūgogen. In *Nihon ongaku daijiten* (Japanese Music Dictionary), ed. Hirano Kenji, Kamisangō Yūkō and Gamō Satoaki. Tokyo: Heibonsha.

_____, ed. 1994. *Jiuta sōkyoku no menjō mokuroku* (Catalogue of *Jiuta Sōkyoku* Licenses). Tokyo: Miyagi Michio Kinenkan.

Tanimura, Kō, ed. 1992. *Gakki no jiten (koto)* (Dictionary of Musical Instruments (*Koto*)). Ed. Matsuda Akira. Tokyo: Tokyo Ongakusha.

Tazaki, Enjirō. 1894. *Sōkyoku fushō* (*Koto* Music Notation). Tokyo: Tōyōdō.

Tenri-kyō Dōyūsha, ed. 1983. *Mikagura uta koto renshū fu* (*Koto* Notation for Practicing *Mikagura* Singing). Tenri: Tenri-kyō Dōyūsha.

Thompson, Robin. 2001. Koto Music in Ryūkyū. In *The New Grove Dictionary of Music and Musicians*. 2nd ed., s.v. Japan, Koto. Ed. Stanley Sadie, Vol. 12. London: Macmillan.

Thrasher, Alan R. 1995. The Melodic Model as a Structural Device: Chinese *Zheng* and Japanese *Koto* Repertories Compared. *Asian Music* 26(2): 97-118.

Tokumaru, Yoshihiko [Yoshihiko]. 1986. The Interaction of Orality and Literacy in Structuring *Syamisen [Shamisen]* Music. In *The Oral and the Literate in Music*, ed. Tokumaru Yoshihiko and Yamaguti Osamu. Tokyo: Academia Music.

_____. 1991. Preface. In *Tradition and its Future in Music: Report of SIMS 1990 Ōsaka (the Fourth Symposium of the International Musicological Society)*, ed. Tokumaru Yoshihiko et al. Tokyo: Mita Press.

_____. 1997. Putting on Traditional Japanese Music Concerts. *Acta Asiatica* 73:84-95.

Tōkyō Academy of Music, ed. 1888. *Collection of Japanese Koto Music*. Tokyo: Department of Education.

Tōkyō Geijutsu Daigaku Geijutsu Shiryōkan, ed. 1994. *Tōkyō geijutsu daigaku geijutsu shiryōkan. Zōhin mokuroku: Ongaku shiryō* (Tokyo University of Fine Arts and Music Archive. Catalogue of Collection: Music Archives). Tokyo: Daiichi Hōki Shuppan.

Tōyō Ongaku Gaku-kai, ed. 1967. *Sōkyoku to jiuta* (*Sōkyoku* and *Jiuta*). Tokyo: Ongaku no Tomosha.

Trends in Japan. 2001. The Japanese Instrument Revival: A New Wave in Music Education. Japan Information Network. Ed. Japan Echo. Available at www.jinjapan.org.

Tsuda, Michiko. 1983. *Sō no kiso chishiki* (Fundamental Knowledge on the *Sō*). Tokyo: Ongaku no Tomosha.

Tsuge, Gen'ichi. 1978. Bamboo, Silk, Dragon and Phoenix: Symbolism in the Musical Instruments of Asia. *The World of Music* 20(3): 10-19.

_____. 1981. Symbolic Techniques in Japanese Koto-kumiuta. *Asian Music* 12(2): 109-32.

_____, comp. and trans. 1983a. *Anthology of Sōkyoku and Jiuta Song Texts*. With Anthony H. Chambers, Carl Sesar, David A. Titus, and Richard K. Winslow Jr; Foreword by David P. McAllester. Tokyo: Academia Music.

_____. 1983b. Raiment of Traditional Japanese Musicians - Its Social and Musical Significance. *The World of Music* 25(1): 55-67.

_____. 1986a. Explicit and Implicit Aspects of *Koto Kumiuta* Notations. In *The Oral and the Literate in Music*, ed. Tokumaru Yoshihiko and Yamaguti Osamu. Tokyo: Academia Music.

_____. 1986b. *Japanese Music: An Annotated Bibliography*. New York: Garland Publishing.

Tsunoda, Ryusaku, Wm. Theodore de Bary and Donald Keene, comp. 1958. *Sources of Japanese Tradition*. New York: Columbia University Press.

Uraki, Ziro [Jiro], trans. 1984. *The Tale of the Cavern (Utsuho Monogatari)*. Tokyo: Shinozaki Shorin.

Visser, M. W. de. [1913] 1969. *The Dragon in China and Japan*. Reprint, Wiesbaden: Martin Sändig.

Vlastos, Stephen, ed. 1998. *Mirror of Modernity: Invented Traditions of Modern Japan*. Berkeley: University of California Press.

Wada, Katsuhisa. 1995. Sōkyoku Kyōgoku-ryū no chōsa hōkoku (Kyōgoku-ryū *Koto* Music). *Fukui Kōgyō Daigaku Kenkyū Kiyō* 25:41-50.

_____. 1996. Tsukushigoto no suwarikata ni tsuite: 'Dansō Shiki Jūnijō' no kaishaku o tsūjite (On the Sitting Style in Playing Tsukushigoto: Through the Explanation of 'The 12 Rules to Play Tsukushigoto'). *Tōyō Ongaku Kenkyū* 62:51-59.

Wade, Bonnie C. 1976. *Tegotomono: Music for the Japanese Koto*. Westport: Greenwood Press.

_____. 1994. Keiko Nosaka and the 20-stringed Koto: Tradition and Modernization in Japanese Music. In *Themes and Variations: Writings on Music in Honor of Rulan Chao Pian*, eds. Bell Yung and Joseph S. C. Lam. Harvard/Hong Kong: Department of Music, Harvard University/The Institute of Chinese Studies, The Chinese University of Hong Kong.

Webb, Herschel. 1983. Weights and Measures. In *Kodansha Encyclopedia of Japan*, ed. Itasaka Gen, Vol. 8. Tokyo: Kodansha.

Wittersheim, John. 2002. Interview with John Wittersheim. By Scott Robertson. Available at www.kotonokoto.org.

Yamada-ryū Sōkyoku Kyōju-kai, comp. 1975. "Rokudan no Shirabe" ("Investigation in Six Sections"). Tokyo: Hakushindō.

Yamaguchi, Iwao. [1913] 1918. "Rokudan no Shirabe" ("Investigation in Six Sections"). 30th ed. Fukuoka: Dai Nippon Katei Ongaku-kai.

_____. [1913] 1983. "Rokudan no Shirabe" ("Investigation in Six Sections"). Fukuoka: Dai Nippon Katei Ongaku-kai.

_____. [1913] 1986. "Chidori no Kyoku" ("Song of Plovers"). Fukuoka: Dai Nippon Katei Ongaku-kai.

Yamaguti [Yamaguchi], Osamu. 1986. Music and its Transformations in Direct and Indirect Contexts. In *The Oral and the Literate in Music*, eds. Tokumaru Yoshihiko and Yamaguti Osamu. Tokyo: Academia Music.

_____. 1991. Performance as a Historical Source in Music Research. In *Tradition and its Future in Music: Report of SIMS 1990 Ōsaka (the Fourth Symposium of the International Musicological Society)*, eds. Tokumaru Yoshihiko et al. Tokyo: Mita Press.

_____. 1994. Nihon koto hajime: Fukuyama koto e no nagare (The Beginnings of the Japanese *Koto*: The Transmission of Fukuyama *Koto*). In *Nihon koto hajime: Fukuyama koto e no nagare* (The Beginnings of the Japanese *koto*: The Transmission of Fukuyama *Koto*), eds. Hiroshima Kenritsu Rekishi Hakubutsukan. Fukuyama: Hiroshima Kenritsu Rekishi Hakubutsukan.

Yamaguchi, Osamu and Richard Emmert. 1977. Descriptions of Musical Instruments: ATPA 1976. In *Asian Musics in an Asian Perspective: Report of Asian Traditional Performing Arts 1976*, eds. Koizumi Fumio, Tokumaru Yoshihiko and Yamaguchi Osamu; assistant ed. Richard Emmert. Tokyo: Heibonsha.

Yamaguchi, Osamu and Tanaka Kenji, eds. 2002. *Hōgaku koto hajime: Kyō kara no jugyō no tame ni* (Introduction to the *Koto* and Traditional Japanese Music: For Today's Lesson). Tokyo: Kawai.

Yamakawa, Enshō, ed. 1980. "Rokudan no Shirabe" ("Investigation in Six Sections"). Fukuoka: Dai Nippon Katei Ongakusha.

Yamazaki, Michiko. 1995. Tsugaru sōkyoku Ikuta-ryū no gakkyoku to sono sōhō: Gendai no ensō denshō o chūshin shite (*Koto* Music of the Tsugaru Ikuta-ryū: Transmission of Performance Practice Today). M.A. Diss., Hirosaki University.

Yamazaki, Shinko. 1977. *Yatsuhashi-ryū koto kumiuta no kenkyū* (Study of Yatsuhashi-ryū *koto kumiuta*). Tokyo: Zen'on Gakufu.

Yano, Christine R. 1992. The *Iemoto* System: Convergence of Achievement and Ascription. *Transactions of the International Conference of Orientalists in Japan* 37:72-84.

Yonekawa, Hiroe, ed. 2002. Gakufu (Notation). In *Hōgaku koto hajime: Kyō kara no jugyō no tame ni* (Introduction to the *Koto* and Traditional Japanese Music: For Today's Lesson), eds. Yamaguchi Osamu and Tanaka Kenji. Tokyo: Kawai.

Yoshida, Tetsuro. 1955. *The Japanese House and Garden*. Trans. Marcus G. Sims. New York: Frederick A. Praeger.

Yoshino, Kosaku. 1992. *Cultural Nationalism in Contemporary Japan: A Sociological Enquiry*. London: Routledge.

_____. 2002. Globalisation as 'Internationalisation': Perspectives on Nationalism in Japan. In *Sights of Contestation: Localism, Globalism and Cultural production in Asia and the Pacific*, eds. Kwok-kan Tam, Wimal Dissanayake and Terry Siu-han Yip. Hong Kong: The Chinese University Press.

Yoshino, I. Roger and Sueo Murakoshi. 1977. *The Invisible Visible Minority: Japan's Burakumin*. Osaka: Buraku Kaiho Kenkyusho.

Zen'on Gakufu Shuppansha. 1996. Bunkagoto hagoromo (Culture
   Koto Hagoromo). Unpaginated brochure. Zen'on Gakufu
   Shuppansha.
Zomick, Elliott. 1986. Hagi no Tsuyu: An Analysis and Transcription.
   Hogaku 2(2): 35-80.

Index

Publishing	Hotei Publishing
	Imprint of KIT Publishers
	Mauritskade 63
	P.O. Box 95001
	1090 HA Amsterdam
	The Netherlands
	www.hotei-publishing.com
	www.kit.nl/publishers

ISBN 90-74822-63-0

NUR 646

| Editing | Amy Reigle Newland, |
| | New Plymouth, New Zealand |

| Design | Nel Punt, Amsterdam, The Netherlands |

| Production | Litholine, Zwolle, The Netherlands |